The Spiralling of the Securitisation of Migration in the European Union

This book investigates how migration has been transformed into a security threat in Europe. It argues that this process has taken place through a self-fulfilling spiralling process, which involves different actors and their specific narratives, practices and policies. The book examines how situations stemming from the so-called 'migration crisis' in the European Union (EU) have been dealt with by governments and non-governmental organisations. It also considers how actors treating migration as an ordinary phenomenon rather than a threat and sharing inclusive narratives can create the conditions for decelerating and eventually stopping securitisation processes. Some chapters examine the spiralling of the securitisation of migration in depth, by analysing increases in securitisation, as well as cases characterised by resistance. Others focus on examining the consequences of socially constructing migration as a crisis for the EU's relations with third countries. In sum, this book shows that there is a wide range of motives for which states and societies would benefit from a change in migration politics and move from the current management of a 'crisis' to a more positive governance of human mobility. It will be of interest to researchers and advanced students of sociology, politics, international relations, social and cultural anthropology, human geography, and social work. This book was originally published as a special issue of the *Journal of Ethnic and Migration Studies*.

Valeria Bello is Associate Professor of Sociology and Director of the Masters programme in Advanced Studies in International Affairs at the Blanquerna School of Communication and International Relations, University Ramón Llull, Barcelona, Spain.

Sarah Léonard is Professor of International Security at the University of the West of England, UK.

Research in Ethnic and Migration Studies

Series editor: **Paul Statham**, *Director, Sussex Centre for Migration Research (SCMR), University of Sussex, UK*

The *Research in Ethnic and Migration Studies* series publishes the results of high-quality, cutting-edge research that addresses key questions relating to ethnic relations, diversity and migration. The series is open to a range of disciplines and brings together research collaborations on specific defined topics on all aspects of migration and its consequences, including migration processes, migrants and their experiences, ethnic relations, discrimination, integration, racism, transnationalism, citizenship, identity and cultural diversity. Contributions are especially welcome when they are the result of comparative research, either across countries, cities or groups. All articles have previously been published in the *Journal of Ethnic and Migration Studies (JEMS)*, which has a rigorous peer review system. Collective volumes in this series are either the product of Special Issues published in the journal or published articles that the Editor has selected from individual submissions.

Migration and Marriage in Asian Contexts
Edited by Zheng Mu and Wei-Jun Jean Yeung

New Theoretical Dialogues on Migration in China
Edited by Hong Zhu and Junxi Qian

(Un)Settled Sojourners in Cities
Challenges of "Temporariness" among Migrants and Asylum Seekers
Edited by Elizabeth Chacko and Marie Price

Cross-Border Marriages
State Categories, Research Agendas and Family Practices
Edited by Apostolos Andrikopoulos, Joëlle Moret and Janine Dahinden

The Spiralling of the Securitisation of Migration in the European Union
Edited by Valeria Bello and Sarah Léonard

The Question of Skill in Cross-Border Labour Mobilities
Edited by Gracia Liu-Farrer, Brenda S.A. Yeoh and Michiel Baas

For more information about this series, please visit:
www.routledge.com/Research-in-Ethnic-and-Migration-Studies/book-series/REMS

The Spiralling of the Securitisation of Migration in the European Union

Edited by
Valeria Bello and Sarah Léonard

Routledge
Taylor & Francis Group

LONDON AND NEW YORK

First published 2023
by Routledge
4 Park Square, Milton Park, Abingdon, Oxon OX14 4RN

and by Routledge
605 Third Avenue, New York, NY 10158

Routledge is an imprint of the Taylor & Francis Group, an informa business

Chapters 1–9 © 2023 Taylor & Francis

British Library Cataloguing in Publication Data
A catalogue record for this book is available from the British Library

ISBN13: 978-1-032-43323-3 (hbk)
ISBN13: 978-1-032-43324-0 (pbk)
ISBN13: 978-1-003-36678-2 (ebk)

DOI: 10.4324/9781003366782

Typeset in Minion Pro
by Newgen Publishing UK

Publisher's Note
The publisher accepts responsibility for any inconsistencies that may have arisen during the conversion of this book from journal articles to book chapters, namely the inclusion of journal terminology.

Disclaimer
Every effort has been made to contact copyright holders for their permission to reprint material in this book. The publishers would be grateful to hear from any copyright holder who is not here acknowledged and will undertake to rectify any errors or omissions in future editions of this book.

Contents

Citation Information

The chapters in this book were originally published in the *Journal of Ethnic and Migration Studies*, volume 48, issue 6 (2022). When citing this material, please use the original page numbering for each article, as follows:

Chapter 1
The spiralling of the securitisation of migration in the EU: from the management of a 'crisis' to a governance of human mobility?
Valeria Bello
Journal of Ethnic and Migration Studies, volume 48, issue 6 (2022), pp. 1327–1344

Chapter 2
From Mobility Partnerships to Migration Compacts: security implications of EU-Jordan relations and the informalization of migration governance
Peter Seeberg and Federica Zardo
Journal of Ethnic and Migration Studies, volume 48, issue 6 (2022), pp. 1345–1362

Chapter 3
The 'refugee crisis' and its transformative impact on EU-Western Balkans relations
Jonathan Webb
Journal of Ethnic and Migration Studies, volume 48, issue 6 (2022), pp. 1363–1380

Chapter 4
People as security risks: the framing of migration in the UK security-development nexus
Eamonn McConnon
Journal of Ethnic and Migration Studies, volume 48, issue 6 (2022), pp. 1381–1397

Chapter 5
The EU and migration in the Mediterranean: EU borders' control by proxy
Stefania Panebianco
Journal of Ethnic and Migration Studies, volume 48, issue 6 (2022), pp. 1398–1416

Chapter 6

Chapter 7

Chapter 8

Chapter 9

For any permission-related enquiries please visit:
www.tandfonline.com/page/help/permissions

Notes on Contributors

Valeria Bello, Blanquerna School of Communication and International Relations, University Ramón Llull, Barcelona, Spain.

Katharina Crepaz, Institute for Minority Rights, Eurac Research, Bozen/Bolzano, Italy.

Maria Gabrielsen Jumbert, Peace Research Institute Oslo, Oslo, Norway.

Christian Kaunert, International Centre for Policing and Security, University of South Wales, Pontypridd, UK.

Sarah Léonard, Department of Social Sciences, University of the West of England (UWE Bristol), Bristol, UK.

Bruno Oliveira Martins, Peace Research Institute Oslo, Oslo, Norway; Malmö Institute for Studies of Migration, Diversity and Welfare, Malmö University, Malmö, Sweden.

Eamonn McConnon, Institute for International Conflict Resolution and Reconstruction, Dublin City University, Dublin, Ireland.

Stefania Panebianco, Department of Political and Social Sciences, University of Catania, Catania, Italy.

Peter Seeberg, Center for Contemporary Middle East Studies, University of Southern Denmark, Odense, Denmark.

Jonathan Webb, Wales Centre for Public Policy, Cardiff University, Cardiff, UK.

Federica Zardo, Department of Political Science (EIF), University of Vienna, Wien, Austria.

Introduction— The spiralling of the securitisation of migration in the EU: from the management of a 'crisis' to a governance of human mobility?

Valeria Bello

ABSTRACT
This special issue illustrates that the securitisation of migration is not a linear process but a spiralling phenomenon, which involves different actors, and their policies, practices and narratives, in a spiralling progression that both self-fulfils and reinforces migration-security nexus' dynamics. By proposing a cognitive ontology to understand the social construction of migration as a security threat, the introduction to this special issue proposes a categorisation of cognitions, mandates, constituencies and interests of state and non-state actors. Through a dichotomisation of these categories, it is possible to clarify how and why they either socially construct or deconstruct migration as a threat. In particular, the special issue identifies in prejudicial cognitions one of the main reasons for which a variety of actors enact practices and produce narratives that contribute to both securitising migration and reinforcing its nexus with crime, and the consequent social construction of 'migration crises'. The different contributions to this special issue prove the arguments here exposed with a different analysis of how migration has been dealt with at either governmental or non-governmental levels.

Introduction

The year 1995 marks the publication of a book, 'Global Migration Crisis: Challenge to States and to Human Rights' (Weiner 1995). Its title alone is emblematic of the reasons for which it has already been argued (Bello 2017a) that the current migration crisis is neither new nor isolated as a phenomenon. It is rather one among a series of scattered inflamed reactions to recurrent massive movements of people. Hence, we understand *global migration crises* as socially constructed scattered inflamed reactions that have been happening since the end of Cold War, as a consequence of forced movements of people that a variety of conflicts and instabilities have produced across the planet.

The first element that we intend to clarify is why we claim that these global migration crises are specific post-Cold War phenomena; a line of reasoning that situates this special issue among studies of the securitisation of migration (Buzan 1991; Bigo 1995). One could argue that heated reactions to migration have always happened within the international system of nation-states (Smith 1995; Koser 2007). We consider, however, that post-Cold War reactions to migration hold novel characteristics from those responses that existed during and before the Cold War. This diversity of features is, according to us, the consequence of the securitisation of migration. In addition, we contend that each of these global migration crises has entailed increasingly concerning outcomes but also manifestations of manyfold attempts to deconstruct migration as a security challenge. Our main argument is that several elements indicate that the securitisation of migration is not a linear process but a *spiralling* phenomenon (Bello 2017a; in this special issue see Léonard and Kaunert 2022).

This introduction lays out the ontological and epistemological reasons that have led us to reassess the process through which the securitisation happens. The contributions included in this special issue prove our argument with a collection of studies of the spiralling. This opening work thence proceeds to: firstly clarify the ontology and the epistemology informing the analysis of the research presented in this compendium; secondly, identify those characteristics of reactions to migration that are specific to the post-Cold War period; thirdly, explain those in terms of the spiralling of the securitisation of migration and the role that both state and non-state actors play in it.

In particular, we claim that human mobility has been socially constructed as a threat and a crisis to manage through the activity of both state and non-state actors, who hold a specific cognition of ethnicity and nation that informs a prejudicial narrative of migration. Our interpretation is that the spiralling progression of the securitisation of migration involves an array of actors, discourses, policies and practices embedded in a prejudiced narrative of migration. When prejudiced activities socially construct migration as a threat, their interplay speeds the securitisation process to an extent that human mobility will unlikely be regarded as different from a crisis to manage. Therefore, these pursuits act as driving forces of a spiralling progression that accelerates all those dynamics entailed in the creation of a migration-security nexus.

However, as it is true that some actors, by sharing and spreading a prejudicial narrative through their discourses, policies and practices, contribute to securitising the phenomenon, it is equally true that there are forces that push the process towards an opposite direction. It is indeed possible that alternative actors, who do not hold a discriminatory cognition, with their resistance to securitisation, enact discourses, techniques and practices, and induce policies, which are rather able to de-securitise this issue (in this special issue see Bello 2022; Crepaz 2022). As all socially constructed realities, migration can equally be socially constructed in diverse ways, and, as such, it can also be de-constructed as a threat (Weaver 1993; Balzacq 2015).

The compendium of this special issue examines how situations stemming from the so-called 'migration crisis' in the EU have been dealt with at governmental and non-governmental levels. Additionally, this introduction illustrates how it is possible to identify those circumstances, addressed only by a few studies (Bello 2017a; Della Porta 2018; Mitchell and Sparke 2018), that de-construct migration as a security threat. Actors both treating migration as an ordinary phenomenon rather than a threat and sharing inclusive narratives create the conditions for decelerating and eventually stopping the securitisation, thus pulling the spiralling in a downward direction (in this special issue see Bello 2022; Crepaz 2022). Several works in this special issue provide further insights of the spiralling of the securitisation of migration, by contemplating increases in terms of both securitisation (in this special issue see Léonard and Kaunert 2022; Martins and Jumbert 2022; McConnon 2022; Panebianco 2022) and those fortunate stances of resistance (in this special issue see Crepaz 2022), or elements able to discern both (in this special issue see Bello 2022). Other analyses highlight how socially constructing migration as a crisis is unprofitable for the EU, particularly in its relations with third countries (in this special issue see Seeberg and Zardo 2022; Webb 2022). The special issue thus proves that there exist plethora of motives for which states and societies would benefit from a change in politics and pass from the current management of a crisis to a more positive governance of human mobility.

We intend to position this special issue as a new window opened in a preexisting building of studies. Collectively, we provide a new angle from which to both interpret how human mobility has been 'managed' across the past three decades and consider the first emerging examples of attempts to more fairly both govern and socially construct migration as an ordinary phenomenon.

A cognitive constructivism for an episteme of the spiralling of the securitisation of migration

Our analysis of the research presented in this special issue is embedded in a constructivist perspective of the securitisation of migration but it actually departs from current analogous interpretations for reasons that have entailed an indispensable *distinguo* for both ontological and epistemological questions: why do there concurrently exist scattered manifestations of the securitisation of migration and resistances to this trend? How can we meaningfully depict this dotted reality in the wider frame of our world's global dynamics?

The starting point of our understanding is utterly adherent to Huysmans and Squire's one:

> Migration emerged as a security issue in a context marked both by the geopolitical dislocation associated with the end of the Cold War and also by wider social and political shifts associated with globalization. As such, current debates surrounding migration and security reflect changes both in the nature of migration, as well as in the nature of thinking about migration. (Huysmans and Squire 2010, 1)

Where our position instead departs from theirs is in the epistemology of how it is possible to disentangle the process that has constructed the migration-security nexus. This episteme is ultimately the consequence of a differently nuanced ontology, according to which the reality of our world is rooted in a cognitive framework that informs its social construction.

In our specific case of the securitisation of migration, it is a specific cognition of nation and ethnicity that, through a prejudicial narrative, informs discourses, policies and practices of both state and non-state actors, contributing to socially constructing migration as a security concern. The contemplation of diverse cognitions involves the possibility of appreciating an entire span of dynamics. This nuanced ontology opens the outlook of the spiralling process of the securitisation of migration. According to Huysmans and Squire: 'security is conceived of as a knowledge, discourse, technology or practice that mediates the relation between the social processes of human mobility and the search for governmental control and steering capacity over them' (Huysmans and Squire 2010, 2). However, theoretically, the security discourse can be conceived as one of international, regional, national or even human security. Therefore, we have wondered why is the national security discourse the one constituting this mediation between human mobility and political control? Why does this happen also in a post-national political entity, for instance, the EU, whose motto is 'united in diversity'? Is it *always* a national security framework that applies and why? Some scholars (Moreno-Lax 2018; Cusumano 2019) have stressed that the human security discourse has also sometimes been used to legitimise the tightening of borders in the name of migrants' own 'security'. In this special issue, Panebianco investigates the contradictions between the humanitarian dimension and the border controls in the name of the defense of states' frontiers (in this special issue see Panebianco 2022). We assume that the specific discourse of security that applies, when it comes to the governance of migration, depends on the particular cognition of nation hold by the actor promoting the discourse and/or undertaking certain practices. Some contributions to this special issue focus on this research question by looking: at policies (in this special issue see McConnon 2022; Panebianco 2022); at practices (in this special issue see Martins and Jumbert 2022; Seeberg and Zardo 2022; Webb 2022) or at the intersection of both narratives and practices (in this special issue, see Bello 2022; Léonard and Kaunert 2022; Crepaz 2022) of either state or non-state actors.

We share the starting point of most studies of the securitisation of migration and in particular that migration became one of the preferred fields where security has developed a new script after the end of the Cold War (Bigo 1995). Where we depart from other securitisation studies is in the reason that explains the non-linearity of the securitisation process.

After the end of the Cold war with the increasing globalisation of cultural, political, economic and virtual landscapes, people could choose among a wider span of cognitions through which comprehending their reality. The nation is no longer the only viewpoint from which to look at the world. At the very least, the nation is not the only outlook for those who are able to live and imagine their lives through cosmopolitan landscapes. A similar argumentation entails the opportunity of simultaneously factoring in alternative moves, including those attempts of de-constructing migration as a security threat (Weaver 1993; Balzacq 2015). Several extensive works on migration (Hirschman, Kasinitz, and DeWind 1999; Koser 2007), nations and nationalism (Delanty and Kumar 2006) and security (Buzan 1991; Bigo 1995) have noticed an important change after the end of the Cold War. We deem that, in the 'securitisation of migration' debate, Bigo's reply to the crisis of security studies and its ensuing extension of security concerns to new fields as a motive for the post-Cold War securitisation (Bigo 1995), only partly explains the phenomenon. Namely, it does not account for the desecuritising dynamics that also exist and the non-linearity of the process.

The key research question that opened our window and that this introduction replies to, is: how is it possible to explain the concurrent exponential, alternative reactions to migration? We have understood this possibility in the simultaneous existence of different, opposite, or even resistant cognitions of socio-cultural and political belonging to the nation. The ethnonation is no longer the sole socio-political imaginary. Many more persons than those few cosmopolitans who were living when Kant proposed the

'Eternal Peace Congress' or when Spinelli and Rossi wrote the Ventotene Manifesto, can imagine life outside a purely national landscape. Nevertheless, the prejudicial ultra-national logic still exists, and in between the two positions lie several nuances of political stances. One of the innovative aspects of our approach is that the language is not the one of security but the one of prejudice. Huysmans and Squire write:

> Rather than a value or a fact, security becomes a language and/or an interest, knowledge or professional skill linked to particular organizations, that are always shaped in a relation to other languages, actors and practices that contest it. (Huysmans and Squire 2010, 9)

We instead claim that, when the securitisation increases, it is the language not of security but of prejudice -of which security is a specific discourse- that renders migration, among other issues, a 'national' security concern. The phenomenon occurs not only through the governmental control but also through non-governmental activity.

Our approach is grounded in the idea that the nation is not an entity in the world but rather a perspective on the world (Brubaker, Loveman, and Stamatov 2004). One of the possible interpretations of the nation that would explain why migration is often depicted by elites and their dominant discourse as an external threat is the one formulated by Wimmer (2002). Wimmer has regarded the nation-building project as one of the strategies through which elites find allies in individuals of a range of social classes for the control over a territory. In his description, the concept of the nation has been proposed to tie together persons living in a broad territory but not sharing the same interests. In order to be successful, the nation-building project needs a common cause and interest. However, among classes that do not share the same interests, this can only be achieved by fighting together an external threat. This account of the nation as the precondition to any social construction of the outsider - and namely in our case the immigrant- as a threat, would explain why the modern state governs in the name of a people defined along ethnic and national lines (Wimmer 2002). For our approach, this interpretation is relevant because it also attests why the nation can actually be assumed as a *perspective* provided to certain people.

With an increasingly interconnected world, and imaginaries and cultural landscapes that transverse states, the development of universalistic and cosmopolitan awareness trigger more than a transnational egalitarian phenomenon such as the cosmopolitanism of Kantian memory. A larger category of persons has the possibility to challenge the particularistic national discourse framed around the construction of outer threats. For this and an array of other reasons,[1] migration has not always produced the same reactions everywhere and for everybody, and people have also expressed welcoming attitudes and solidarity movements (Bello 2017a; Della Porta 2018; Mitchell and Sparke 2018). Similar alternative movements constitute relevant efforts to deconstruct human mobility as a threat. Hence, it is worth investigating how the securitisation of migration is pushed and pulled through opposite dynamics, with upwarding and downwarding forces spiralling its process (see in this special issue McConnon 2022). In case the upwarding forces that construct migration as a security threat take the lead in the process, then the narratives of migration as an emergence and an exceptional challenge start to spin policies and practices that securitise the issue. The downwarding forces, instead, deconstruct it as a security concern. Therefore, the so-called 'migration crisis' has scattered manifestations and societies have diversely responded to it.

The reason for which a variety of actors either socially construct or help deconstruct the migration-security nexus depends on whether the upholding cognition of the nation is a prejudicial or an inclusive one. If nation is indeed only considered a perspective, and not an ethnical reification of a territory, there is indeed an opportunity 'for conceptualising ethnicity, race and nation as perspectives on the world rather than entities in the world, for treating ethnicity, race, and nationalism together rather than as separate subfields' (Brubaker, Loveman, and Stamatov 2004, 31). The imaginary, and consequent narrative, of a nation as an entity representing 'the pure soul of the state', instead, constitutes a frame of mind that, when accompanied by a prejudicial cognition, socially constructs migration as a threat (Bello 2017a). When and where this prejudicial mindset does not take place, several forces can enact a desecuritisation of migration.

Post-Cold War responses to migration: the spiralling as an epistemic that uphold a cognitive ontology

The other question to which this introduction aims to reply relates to an epistemic concern. As we understand the end of the Cold War as a turning point in reactions to migration, epistemically, in what ways can we comprehend a reality in which the continuity in responses to migration (the linear, normal variations in responses to migration) happens along with its novelty, namely the securitisation of migration?

The starting point in the literature is that after the end of the Cold War, global and more generally post-national dynamics have developed to a point that borders themselves have lost a fair part of importance in finance and economy, in cultural productions, and also in terms of political governance – and possibly within the European Union to a greater extent than in other regions, as national borders are less significant than in other geopolitical areas. In such a light, and in line with the literature on the securitisation of migration, we also grip the related reality by taking into account the latest changes in the international system and particularly the post-Cold War world (Buzan 1991; Heisbourg 1991; Bigo 1995; Huysmans and Squire 2010). In addition, we reckon from the debate both that nation-states have partly changed their constituencies, and the new meanings that these constituencies entail for the national (Portes, Guarnizo, and Landolt 1999; Nowicka 2007; Butcher 2009; Bello 2014). On the one hand, post-national citizens who experience beneficial effects of globalisation conceive their state no longer in terms of nations, races, and ethnicities. On the other hand, there are both those who live anchored to the idea of the nation, and those who suffer from globalisation and perceive and anticipate risks to a greater extent (Beck 1992). They become those persons whose frustrations can be exploited to request a revival of nationalism, and with it, its discriminatory politics, exclusionary dynamics and hard, untraversable borders (Bello 2017a).

The changes in reactions to migration have already been recorded in the 'Handbook of International Migration' through an historical perspective (Hirschman, Kasinitz, and DeWind 1999). Each chapter of that collection has compared the decade of the 1990s with previous ones. Perceptions of migration have altered not only in Europe but even in the American society recently, as the same national discourse has changed from 'a nation of immigrants' to 'a nation that becomes great again by fighting immigration', like one of the most popular slogan of the election campaign of the U.S. President

Donald Trump illustrates. We deem similar turns as additional proofs that nations and ethnicities are cognitions on the social world rather than fixed entities in the world. However, it is obvious that, if someone else (Smith 1995) has in mind a world in which nations and ethnicity are true and real entities that ethno-symbolically constitute our reality, then the peculiarity of the post-Cold War era when it comes to migration and, consequently, to nationalism, cannot be regarded as different from 'shallow or misleading' (Smith 1995, 1).

We hold a distinctive ontology. We wish to provide, as previously explained, an outlook 'for treating ethnicity, race, and nationalism together rather than as separate subfields' (Brubaker, Loveman, and Stamatov 2004, 31). Nevertheless, we take into account the criticisms of those colleagues who highlight that 'a cognitive approach underplays the social materiality of the securitising processes – security seems to exist primarily in the mind' (Huysmans and Squire 2010, 9). However, if the social construction would come before the prejudicial cognition and its consequent narrative, how could we explain the diversity of discourses? Only if prejudice comes before the social construction, we can epistemically explain the variety of stances that actually exist without falling into a theoretical loop. In fact, if the prejudicial comes as a consequence of the social construction of a securitised reality, then how can we say that a specific construction of reality creates prejudice without being prejudicial toward that particular social construction? If, instead, specific cognitions, conceptually fixed -such as the ones of prejudice and inclusivity- inform the social construction of alternative realities, then these phenomena (prejudice and inclusivity) can be taken into account and applied in the analysis both *before and after* the securitisation takes place, thus constituting self-reinforcing dynamics, engendering what we identify as a spiralling process of the securitisation of migration (for a case study of an epistemic of self-reinforcing dynamics see in this special issue Bello 2022). Therefore, we can grasp the object of study of the theory of the spiralling of securitisation. The latter happens through both narratives (Bello 2017a) and practices (Léonard 2007) that constitute this non-linear process and thus reflect the cognitions of the actors.

Our approach actually considers prejudice as a cognition that informs the social construction of migration as a threat. Prejudice is consequently the main qualifier of a perspective of the nation that ties a society through the discrimination of specific groups of individuals, whom are thus socially constructed as outer threats (Bello 2017a). The securitisation of migration first happens cognitively in actors' perspectives and then epistemically spirals through practices and narratives (see in this special issue Bello 2022), which are the concrete elements that can be analysed for research purpose. Discourses, policies, strategies and techniques ensue, enacted by both state and non-state actors, who systematise some self-reinforcing dynamics (see in this special issue Martins and Jumbert 2022).

The spiralling of the securitisation of migration

The theory of the spiralling of the securitisation of migration understands the non-linearity of the securitisation of migration as a consequence of both upwarding and downwarding forces that respectively construct or deconstruct migration as a security threat, and find their root causes in alternative cognitions of the nation (see in this special issue McConnon 2022).

As demonstrated in a multilevel analysis of prejudice in European countries, if the narratives that accompany the theme of migration are embedded in an exclusive and discriminatory cognition of the nation in a specific country, then the respective society would *in general* be more prejudiced towards migrants than societies of more inclusive states, and would regard their presence as a worsening factor for their country (Bello 2016). In support of this theory, another study has determined that, even in time of crises, only those individuals not holding intercultural values will negatively view migration (Bello 2017b). It is then not surprising that in Europe those countries presenting more concerning situations in terms of prejudice, Turkey, Greece, Russia, Czech Republic, Hungary, Ukraine, Italy, the United Kingdom and Austria (Bello 2017a), actually coincided with those that have more harshly reacted to the 'migration crisis'. Migration as a crisis to be managed emerges as the main narrative where there is a cognitive framework enabling a prejudicial language that informs discourses, policies, strategies and techniques.

An akin grip of the migration-security nexus provides us with those lenses to identify why disparate actors have diversely responded to migration: the role of a variety of EU institutions have not only had dissimilar but sometimes divergent roles in the securitisation of migration (Bello 2017a). Panebianco has considered this plurality of institutional voices and levels in the EU through an analysis of the border control. Namely, she has investigated how Italy, one of the most relevant countries in terms of arrivals and first reception, and the rest of Europe have coordinated these activities (see in this special issue Panebianco 2022). The need to 'manage the crisis' has also led to policy changes and shifted power dynamics. Seeberg and Zardo argue in this special issue that the EU-led securitisation of migration has contributed to the increasing informalisation of EU-third country agreements. As they have shown with their work, although the securitisation in EU-MENA relations dates back to the end of the Cold War, the crisis has had scattered manifestations also in the EU-Jordan relations. The condition has occurred particularly since 2011, when the pressures on the EU to adapt its policy toolbox in Jordan have substantially intensified (see in this special issue Seeberg and Zardo 2022). Both Webb, and Seeberg and Zardo, analysed the usage of a prejudicial cognition of migration. They both find that the EU has recognised the 'interest of limiting migrants' entry' as more valuable than its crucial consequence; namely, a decreasing power of influence in negotiating with neighbouring (see in this special issue Webb 2022) and third countries (see in this special issue Seeberg and Zardo 2022). Webb shows that the construction of the narratives of the 'migration crisis' and its ensuing securitisation of migration has been used by Macedonia and Serbia to reshape their roles within the EU borders' regime and reduce some conventional power asymmetry between them and the EU (see in this special issue Webb 2022). These analyses hence show how a prejudicial cognition of migration has led to an increase of the spiralling of the securitisation of migration to the extent of reducing EU's power in its external relations with neighbouring countries.[2] In the past, the ability to use migration to achieve power of influence upon other countries has also made some authors contend that there is a coercive use of migration and refugees as non-military weapons (Greenhill 2010). Although, in this case, Macedonia and Serbia have not purposefully created migration, they used the influxes of migrants and refugees to successfully socially construct and depict migration as a crisis at their borders so as to leverage with the EU (see in this special issue Webb

2022). Seeberg and Zardo arrive at a conclusion akin. The relations between the EU and a third country, Jordan, which used the 'migration crisis' to improve its negotiating power with the EU, rendered policies and practices between the two partners increasingly informal (see in this special issue Seeberg and Zardo 2022). These findings and conclusions are also supported by other works in the European studies' debate on 'reverse conditionality'; Tittel-Mosser, for instance, looking at the EU mobility partnership with Morocco, also found that Morocco in particular has used the considerable weight that the theme of migration has in the EU to demand increased funding (Tittel-Mosser 2018).

The necessity to manage what has been identified as 'the migration crisis' has therefore cost the EU an evident change in its bargaining power with third countries but it has also weakened internal relations. However, despite these attempts to manage the crisis, and despite the decreasing number of arrivals, the scattered inflamed reactions to migration have not stopped. They have instead increased in a number of places, and namely in those countries that already presented important prejudicial contexts. McConnon examines how, even in the sector of development policy, the discourse in the UK has shifted from the impact of migration on poorest countries to the risks for UK's national security (see in this special issue McConnon 2022).

The phenomenon of the securitisation of migration self-fulfils its own assumption: if migration is expertly described as a threat, then the arrival of migrants, no matter whether in increasing numbers or not, will always constitute a crisis to manage (Maguire 2015). The securitisation of border controls has been so blatant that the same EU agency Frontex presented a clearly securitised language in its own reports, in which the vocabulary used to depict migrants had become completely dehumanised (Bello 2017a). And yet, by making migration more difficult, governments have not managed to reduce either migration or prejudice. Instead, it is clear that, when migrants are treated as criminals, detained in immigration centres or deported, negative attitudes towards them also increase (Bello 2017a). As prejudice rises, the securitisation also spirals (see in this special issue Bello 2022). Such an origin explains our perspective of the exponential spiralling of the securitising forces. The post-Brexit situation in the UK, or the electoral results in the Czech Republic and in Italy, with a strong increase of far-right, xenophobic and nationalistic parties, are clear examples of these dynamics. Léonard and Kaunert have analysed how Frontex's practices clearly show a spiralling progression of the securitisation since 2015 (see in this special issue Léonard and Kaunert 2022). Martins and Jumbert instead investigate the way by which emerging technologies, like drones, and specific information and surveillance technologies installed on them, shape the security-migration management nexus at the EU borders and self-reinforce the logics of the securitisation (see in this special issue Martins and Jumbert 2022).

In the same Frontex report (FRONTEX 2016), it is evident that the hardening of border policies has not diminished the number of those arriving in Europe through irregular and perilous journeys but has instead increased the market opportunity for smugglers and human traffickers (FRONTEX 2016; Bello 2017a). Situations of this kind have multiplied the numbers of migrants in undocumented or irregular status in several parts of the world (Avdan 2012; Dunn 2009). It has been highlighted that the hardening of border policies and the securitisation of migration concurrently increase the numbers of migrants in detention centres, a fact that is prejudicial because travelling undocumented cannot be considered a crime in itself – eventually only a misdemeanour offense

(Lazaridis and Wadia 2015; Bello 2017a). However, until migrants' claims about their status, if refugees or not, are verified, it is impossible to say whether the act of travelling undocumented or with unproper documents, also constitutes an infringement of the law of the state. As a consequence, the detention of undocumented persons is unlawful and a prejudicial practice of great concern. The European Commission itself has lamented the existence of such a practice, when considering the case of migrants detained in Libya (European Commission 2016). The situation in Europe is not entirely divergent, with almost 130,000 migrants detained, along with 21,000 recorded detained asylum seekers in 2017 (Bello 2017a, 54). The practice of detaining those who have travelled undocumented is another way through which the securitisation of migration renders migrants into criminals and both self-fulfils and reinforces the security threat that it anticipates.

Because there also exist inclusive cognitions of the nation, and state and non-state actors who deconstruct migration as a threat, societies of states start to polarise around these topical debates. The polarisation of the debate is also performatively represented by the very 'ambivalent attempts of concurrently saving the vulnerable migrants and its hardening of both external and internal borders to a point that makes migrants' journeys almost impossible and their stay in Europe often unbearable, such as in the example of the 'Mare Nostrum' operation, at once a rescue mission and a border control operation' (Bello 2017a, 58; Cusumano 2019). A relevant part of the phenomenon that has remained unexplained in previous literature is the plethora of non-state actors that expedited the spiralling of the securitisation of migration, with exponential pulls and pushes of opposite forces.

The role of non-state actors in the securitisation of migration

The interpretation of what is actually a non-state actor could vary – and has varied – depending on the particular perspective employed in a range of disciplinary literatures (Armstrong et al. 2010). With this term, scholars could refer mainly to 'civil society', as, in Locke's terms, a force standing in opposition to oppressive state power, or, as in Held's conception, 'those areas of social life – the domestic world, the economic sphere, cultural activities and political interaction – which are organised by private or voluntary arrangements between individuals and groups outside the direct control of the state' (Held 1993, 6). With the increasing involvement of private corporations and violent non-state actors in the field of international relations, the concept of non-state actors has progressively separated from the one of civil society to become closer to the concept of 'private actors'. In particular, 'in security governance, private actors have become involved with policy surveillance, and even military tasks' (Jakobi and Wolf 2013, 7). Furthermore, defining non-state actors chiefly by their independence from states and state authority would be misleading (Josselin and Wallace 2001).

The role of non-state actors also depends on the particular field under scrutiny and what is the relation between that domain and its global governance (Armstrong et al. 2010). In the field of migration, some domestic actors, which are normally regarded as part of the state, end up assuming a distinct role from the one that states and governments play. Vice versa, some non-state actors can be under the direct control of the state (Josselin and Wallace 2001). In particular, courts of justice, cities' authorities, detention centres' officials and guards, and border guards can exercise a particular power through activities that are possibly not intended in their relevant state's or government's politics. Similar actors cannot be counted among private non-state actors. However, they cannot either be contemplated as *state* actors. Furthermore, IGOs have been considered non-state actors because they do not always represent States' interests but develop their own bodies that act autonomously from the states that constitute them. An akin interpretation of IGOs as non-state actors has been applied more generally in the field of global governance (Art 2000; Josselin and Wallace 2001).[3] To make justice to their function, this special issue will take these actors into account as public non-state actors.

For a further understanding of the diverse roles that public and private non-state actors play in the securitisation of migration, it has been suggested that it is worth examining the main interests they hold, if collective or individualist (Bello 2017a), as previously suggested for a distinctive field (Bello 2015). Non-state actors' interests can be counted as of *individualist* type if they are framed to only benefit their constituency. A non-state actor that instead views its main interests as beneficial also for individuals and collectivities beyond its actual constituency can be categorised as a non-state actor holding *collective interests*. The proposed non-state actors' characteristics are crucial to grasp the variety of roles they play in the securitisation, because only non-state actors with collective interests will need to publicly clarify their cognitions to perform successfully. They would not be able to effectively show their collective agency if they do not illustrate what the cognitions justifying their goals are. Instead, non-state actors with individualist interests do not need to always manifest their cognitions in order to correctly perform, as their agency is not addressed externally to their constituency (Bello 2017a). In this sense, the individualist non-state actor is much more independent from the audience than a collective non-state actor. For non-state actors holding individualist interests, a further element of differentiation is necessary in order to recognise their role in either securitising or desecuritising human mobility. In the light of the theoretical framework presented here, such an element could be found in the specific cognition that individualist non-state actors hold, in particular if prejudicial or inclusive.

Table 1 provides an overview of the diverse typologies of non-state actors and their nature, interests and cognitions. The dichotomy helps categorise non-state actors according to the elements discussed and whether or not it is possible to identify both those non-state actors that are prejudiced from those that are inclusive towards migrants, and their role in the spiralling of the securitisation of migration.

Through this threefold dichotomisation – and keeping in mind, on the one hand, the role of those agencies that translate narratives and practices into perceptions of threats and, on the other, those deconstructing this nexus – it becomes clear that public non-state actors holding mainly collective interests usually de-securitise migration. As it is evident from the case that Kaunert and Léonard (2012) illustrate, courts of justice, both at regional and national level, play an increasingly important role in improving the fair treatment of migrants. However, this process seems to be not only peculiar of the EU but is certainly more global. Gurowitz, for instance, analyses the impact of international human rights standards in Japan on policies towards migrant workers (Gurowitz 1999). Conversely, actors that here have been identified as public non-state actors with individualist interests, for example, the EU Council, have often been associated with the securitisation of migration (Huysmans 2006; Lazaridis and Wadia 2015; Squire 2015).

Table 1. Categorisation of non-state actors involved in the securitisation of migration and their performative roles.

Type of non-state actors / Type of interests	Public non-state actors	Private non-state actors
Collective interests	Predictable cognitions towards migrants: Mostly inclusive - IGOs (UN; IOM; World Bank IMF;). - National and regional courts of justice. - International agencies (European Union Agency for Fundamental Rights - EUFRA-; UN High Commissioner for Refugees; UN High Commissioner for Human Rights-OHCHR) ⌄ Desecuritizing role	Predictable cognitions towards migrants: Mostly inclusive - Civil society associations (Churches; Trade Unions; Social movements; Volunteers) - NGOs ⌄ Desecuritizing role Prejudiced towards migrants - Extremist groups - Xenophobic or racist movements. ⌄ Securitizing role
Individualist interests	Variable cognitions towards migrants - Regional Actors (EU/AU/ASEAN/OIC). ⌄ Variable roles	Variable cognitions towards migrants Newcomers Diasporas Established persons Employers Reception centres Detention centres' officials and guards Border guards ⌄ Variable roles

When private non-state actors are taken into account, it is evident that they abound in the securitisation of migration (Bloom 2014). For those with collective interests, their cognitions are mostly predictable and so is their specific contribution to the spiralling. Inclusive civil society associations, volunteers, social movements, all are able to mitigate those practices and narratives that are feeding the intensity of the securitisation process. Those immediately predictable as prejudiced non-state actors -for instance white supremacist groups and other xenophobic movements and associations, and more generally all extremist groups- they always securitise migration because they exacerbate the negative framing of the phenomenon. They reinforce the upwarding spiralling of the securitisation of migration, by engendering more prejudicial attitudes as in a domino effect (see in this special issue Bello 2022).

The cognitions of private non-state actors with individualist interests cannot be *a priori* determined as prejudiced or inclusive; in addition, some of them could change their cognitions and means from inclusive to prejudiced, and vice versa, at different steps in the process (see in this special issue Léonard and Kaunert 2022). Their role in either securitising or desecuritising migration needs further studies to be clarified. For private non-state actors are of difficult categorisation and it is not possible to establish *a priori* if there are prejudiced or inclusive towards migrants and migrations, it makes them a relevant case study to contemplate the role of cognitions in the securitisation of migration and whether these eventually lead to a spiralling process. In this collection of works, Bello has specifically focused on one of these ambivalent non-state actors, namely reception centres, which could either construct or deconstruct human mobility as a threat, depending on the cognitions and the narratives they reproduce (see in this special issue Bello 2022).

The de-construction of migration as a security threat

Several articles in this special issue have highlighted that there already exist ways in which state and non-state actors strive to socially deconstruct migration as a security threat. Civil society associations, NGOs and other spontaneous social movements, for instances, solidarity movements and volunteers, which are clearly inclusive towards migration, contribute to decelerating the spiralling of the securitisation of migration (see in this special issue Crepaz 2022). As anticipated, it is possible to consider that public non-state actors with collective interests usually help de-securitise the issue, as they do not normally hold prejudicial cognitions; examples of this category are the European Agency for Human Rights or the European Court of Justice. Instead, public non-state actors with individualistic interests, for instance the EU Council, if driven by a prejudicial narrative, as in the case of member states led by xenophobic parties, would act in the opposite direction. For an analysis of regional organisations, like the EU, which are not monoliths with a unitary policy approach towards the issue, a dichotomy of this kind is more than relevant. It is indispensable to distinguish its diverse bodies and their implications for an understanding of its participation in the spiral. The categorisation of institutions according to the mandate and the interests they represent allows to grasp the desecuritising role that the European Court of Justice and the European Union Agency for Fundamental Rights (EUFRA) play, in antithesis to the one of the Council of Europe. The Council of Europe, where decisions need to be taken unanimously, is disproportionately influenced by some of those EU destination and transit countries, whose societies are strongly prejudiced towards migrants, and in particular Cyprus, Czech Republic, Greece, Italy and Hungary (Bello 2016; Bello 2017a). As Huysmans (2006) has already highlighted, thanks to the socially constructed situation of emergency, its policymaking often avoids the balancing power of the Parliament, by leaving the decision-making process skewed towards the executive power.

The same effect applies with private non-state actors; when led with prejudicial cognitions, they are conducive to a securitisation of migration through practices and narratives. The role of FRONTEX in criminalising migrants, as well as refugees, is clear when one considers that it comprehended those fleeing war in Syria in the numbers of those called 'illegal border-crossers' (FRONTEX 2016, 18; Bello 2017a), as also pointed out in Martins and Jumbert's contribution (see in this special issue Martins and Jumbert 2022). It also occurs with other prejudicial non-state actors, holding either individualistic or collective interests, such as a variety of extremist groups including, among others, violent guards working in detention centres and violent border guards – as those who, at the border between Macedonia and Greece, were brutally beating women and children, as reported in news on 10 April 2016 (The Guardian 2016a). All actors akin to extremist or violent groups represent further gears in the chain that speeds the spiral of the securitisation of migration. The dehumanising situation of many detention centres is, unfortunately, not only the case in European countries. An article in The Guardian on 19 June 2016 reports the experience of the Australian psychologist (now also politician) Paul Stevenson in the two Australian detention centres of Manu Islands and Nauru, revealing a 'stream of despair and privation' (The Guardian 2016b).

In order to stop the securitising spiral, the intervention of public non-state actors with collective interests (Bello 2017a), and an effective control preventing prejudicial cognitions from intervening in the management of human mobility (see in this special issue Bello 2022) are crucial in order to pull down the forces spiralling the securitisation process. If measures are not taken to decelerate the securitisation, it is likely that private non-state actors holding mainly individualistic interests and prejudicial cognitions will participate in the securitisation of migration through narratives and practices that will spiral the process. In such a light, the inescapability of the migration–crime nexus becomes dependent on its routinised (Maguire 2015) or performative (Bello 2022) self-fulfilment. Martins' and Jumbert's work also provides elements so as to determine how self-reinforcing logics are created and how much they rely upon technological expertise (see in this special issue Martins and Jumbert 2022).

A partnership of inclusive private and public non-state actors could magnify their already critical voices in positively influencing the process. Associations, volunteers, spontaneous social movements, NGOs, along with border agencies and bodies, if holding a humanitarian and non-prejudicial approach, could all positively affect the situation and contribute to stopping the social construction of migration as a threat (see in this special issue Crepaz 2022). When it comes to the desecuritisation, Crepaz's case study explains how the Europeanisation of civil society activism intensifies 'the role of civil society as a desecuritising and humanitarian-focused force' (see in this special issue Crepaz 2022). Her case study of German, Italian, Austrian and Swiss activists networking and activity in a border zone, such as the one of the Brenner, a region at the border between Italy and Austria, exemplifies this fact.

Bello's contribution to this special issue, instead, analyses the effects of both prejudicial and inclusive cognitions in the management of receptions centres in Italy and what are the consequences in terms of both practices and narratives in socially constructing perceptions of migrants as security threats. In her analysis, the self-reinforcing role of prejudicial and stereotyped narratives confirms that there are elements of discourse that exert a diverse impact from the speech-acts upon which the literature of the securitisation of migration has until now focused. Narratives in fact do not need to be accepted by the audience to securitise an issue, as their perform-ance is automatically legitimised among spectators as 'true knowledge' (Lyotard 1979), if not resisted through alternative cognitions upholding opposite narratives (see in this special issue Bello 2022). The prejudicial cognition is found to be a crucial factor able to enact the spiralling of the securitisation and its self-reinforcing mechanisms through practices and narratives. Conversely, an inclusive cognition help deconstruct migrants as threats to security (see in this special issue Bello 2022). Hence, it also proves the argument that it is the cognition of an actor what effects its role in either constructing or deconstructing migration as a security threat, accelerating or decelerating forces of the spiralling of the securitisation process. More works and research are needed to enlarge the spectrum of this glance and further exploit the potential explanatory power of this approach. Addressing those blind spots that the literature still presents for a lack of a variety of empirical works looking for instance at this historical twist with longitudinal analyses of migration narratives would be a key contribution to the literature. Equally, both looking at ways migration narratives intersect with identity politics and their consequences on migration policies; and studying those positive examples of resistance to securitisation that exist both at governmental and non-gov-ernmental levels, would all deserve further attention among scholars. The usage of the dichotomisation of non-state actors proposed, which focuses on their mandates, con-stituencies, interests and cognitions, could help develop a clear discerning framework of their roles in the securitisation of the field of migration.

Notes

1. The variety of these reasons, which have been identified in different disciplinary fields, from social psychology to sociology and anthropology, and lately political science, cannot be sum-marised here. For a sociological account, you can read Bello (2017a).
2. For a discussion of the connections with the literature on the externalization of migration controls, please refer to Seeberg and Zardo's contribution in this special issue (2022).
3. For different interpretations, please consult Risse-Kappen.

Acknowledgements

This introduction has very much benefitted from the feedback received from both the reviewers and the contributors of this special issue, and, above all, from the exchanges that I have had over the years with the friend and colleague Sarah Léonard – who has also coedited this special issue – in occasion of the sections organised together within the European International Studies Association. Sarah and I would also like to thank all those colleagues, reviewers, contributors, and the editors of the journal, who, along the process, have engaged with us on such a complex comprehension of how our reality is socially constructed.

Disclosure statement

No potential conflict of interest was reported by the authors.

References

Armstrong, D., V. Bello, J. Gilson, and D. Spini. 2010. *Civil Society and International Governance: The Role of Non-State Actors in Global and Regional Regulatory Frameworks*. London: Routledge.

Art, B. 2000. "Regimes, Non-State Actors and the State System: A 'Structurational' Regime Model." *European Journal of International Relations* 6 (4): 513–542. doi:10.1177/1354066100006004003.

Avdan, Nazli. 2012. "Human Trafficking and Migration Control Policy: Vicious or Virtuous Cycle?" *Journal of Public Policy* 32 (3): 171–205. http://doi.org/10.1017/S0143814X12000128.

Balzacq, T. 2015. *Contesting Security: Strategies and Logics*. Oxon: Routledge.

Beck, U. 1992. *Risk Society. Towards a New Modernity*. London: Sage.

Bello, V. 2014. "Virtual Belongings, Dual Identities and Cultural Discomforts: The Role of Mediaspaces and Technospaces in the Integration of Migrants." *Crossings: Journal of Migration and Culture* 5 (2): 213–229. doi:10.1386/cjmc.5.2-3.213_1.

Bello, V. 2015. "One Concept for Different Roles? Private vs. Collective Interests in Nonstate Actors' Governance of Violence and Crime." *International Studies Review* 17 (2): 341–343. doi:10.1111/misr.12222.

Bello, V. 2016. "Inclusiveness as Construction of Open Identity: How Social Relationships Affect Attitudes Towards Immigrants in European Societies." *Social Indicators Research* 126 (1): 199–223. doi:10.1007/s11205-015-0881-1.

Bello, V. 2017a. *International Migration and International Security. Why Prejudice is a Global Security Threat*. New York: Routledge.

Bello, V. 2017b. "Interculturalism as a New Framework to Reduce Prejudice in Times of Crisis in European Countries." *International Migration* 55 (2): 23–38. doi:10.1111/imig.12262.

Bello, V. 2022. "The Role of Non-state actors' Cognitions in the Spiralling of the Securitisation of Migration: Prejudice, Narratives and Italian CAS Reception Centres." *Journal of Ethnic and Migration Studies* 48 (6): 1462–1478. https://doi.org/10.1080/1369183X.2020.1851472.

Bigo, D. 1995. "Grands Débats Dans Un Petit Monde." *Cultures & Conflits* automne-hiver 1995 (19-20): 1–29. https://doi.org/10.4000/conflits.54.

Bloom, Tendayi. 2015. "The Business of Migration Control: Delegating Migration Control Functions to Private Actors." *Global Policy* 6 (2): 151–157. http://doi.org/10.1111/1758-5899.12188.

Brubaker, R., M. Loveman, and P. Stamatov. 2004. "Ethnicity as Cognition." *Theory and Society* 33 (1): 31–64. doi:10.1023/B:RYSO.0000021405.18890.63.

Butcher, M. 2009. "Ties That Bind: The Strategic Use of Transnational Relationships in Demarcating Identity and Managing Difference." *Journal of Ethnic and Migration Studies* 35 (8): 1353–1371. doi:10.1080/13691830903123153.

Buzan, B. 1991. "People, States & Fear. An Agenda for International Security Studies." *In the Post-Cold War Era*. 2nd ed. London: Harvester Wheatsheaf.

Crepaz, K. 2022. "Overcoming Borders: The Europeanization of Civil Society Activism in the 'Refugee Crisis.'" *Journal of Ethnic and Migration Studies* 48 (6): 1448–1461. https://doi.org/10.1080/1369183X.2020.1851471.

Cusumano, E. 2019. "Migrant Rescue as Organized Hypocrisy: EU Maritime Missions Offshore Libya Between Humanitarianism and Border Control." *Cooperation and Conflict* 54 (1): 3–24. doi:10.1177/0010836718780175.

Delanty, G., and K. Kumar. 2006. *Handbook of Nations and Nationalism*. London: Sage.

Della Porta, D. 2018. *Solidarity Mobilizations in the 'Refugee Crisis': Contentious Moves*. Basingstoke and New York: Palgrave MacMillan.

Dunn, T. 2009. *Blockading the Border and Human Rights: The El Paso Operations that Remade Immigration Enforcement*. Austin: The University of Texas Press.

European Commission. 2016. "Communication from the Commission to the European Parliament, the European Council, the Council and the European Investment Bank on establishing a new Partnership Framework with third countries under the European Agenda on

Migration." Document COM(2016) 385 final. Accessed February 12, 2018. http://eur-lex. europa.eu/legal-content/EN/TXT/?uri=CELEX%3A52016DC0385.

FRONTEX. 2016. "Risk Analysis for 2016." Frontex Staff Working Document. Warsaw, Poland. Accessed February 15, 2018. http://frontex.europa.eu/assets/Publications/Risk_Analysis/ Annula_Risk_Analysis_2016.pdf.

Greenhill, K. M. 2010. *Weapons of Mass Migration: Forced Displacement, Coercion and Foreign Policy*. Ithaca, NY: Cornell University Press.

Gurowitz, Amy. 1999. "Mobilizing International Norms: Domestic Actors, Immigrants, and the Japanese State." *World Politics* 51 (3): 413–445. http://doi.org/10.1017/S0043887100009138.

Heisbourg, F. 1991. "Population Movements in Post-Cold War Europe." *Survival* 33 (1): 31–43. doi:10.1080/00396339108442572.

Held, D. 1993. *Political Theory and the Modern State*. London: Polity Press.

Hirschman, C., P. Kasinitz, and J. DeWind. 1999. *Handbook of International Migration. The American Experience*. New York: Russel Sage Foundation.

Huysmans, J. 2006. *The Politics of Insecurity. Fear, Migration and Asylum in the EU*. London: Routledge.

Huysmans, J., and V. Squire. 2010. "Migration and Security." In *The Routledge Handbook of Security Studies*, edited by M. Dunn Cavelty and V. Mauer, 169–179. Abingdon, Oxon: Routledge.

Jakobi, A. P., and K. D. Wolf. 2013. *The Transnational Governance of Violence and Crime: Non-State Actors in Security*. London: Palgrave Macmillan.

Josselin, D., and W. Wallace. 2001. *Non-State Actors in World Politics*. Basingstoke: Palgrave.

Kaunert, Christian, and Sarah Léonard. 2012. "The Development of the EU Asylum Policy: Venue-Shopping in Perspective." *Journal of European Public Policy* 19 (9): 1396–1413. http://doi.org/ 10.1080/13501763.2012.677191.

Koser, K. 2007. *International Migration. A Very Short Introduction*. Oxford: Oxford University Press.

Lazaridis, G., and K. Wadia. 2015. *The Securitisation of Migration in the EU: Debates Since 9/11*. Basingstoke: Palgrave Macmillan.

Léonard, S. 2007. *"The "Securitization" of Asylum and Migration in the European Union: Beyond the Copenhagen School's Framework."* SGIR Sixth Pan-European International Relations Conference, 12 September 2007.

Léonard, S., and C. Kaunert. 2022. "The Securitisation of Migration in the European Union: Frontex and its Evolving Security Practices." *Journal of Ethnic and Migration Studies* 48 (6): 1417–1429. https://doi.org/10.1080/1369183X.2020.1851469.

Lyotard, J. F. 1979. *La Condition Postmoderne: Rapport sur le Savior. English Translation* [The Postmodern Condition: A Report on Knowledge]. Manchester: Manchester University Press.

Maguire, M. 2015. "Migrants in the Realm of Experts: The Migration–Crime–Terrorist Nexus After 9/11." In *The Securitization of Migration in the EU. Debates Since 9/11*, edited by G. Lazaridis and K. Waadia, 62–87. Basingstoke: Palgrave Macmillan.

Martins, B. O., and M. G. Jumbert. 2022. "EU Border Technologies and the Co-Production of Security 'Problems' and 'Solutions'." *Journal of Ethnic and Migration Studies* 48 (6): 1430–1447. https://doi.org/10.1080/1369183X.2020.1851470.

McConnon, E. 2022. "People as Security Risks: The Framing of Migration in the UK Security-Development Nexus." *Journal of Ethnic and Migration Studies* 48 (6): 1381–1397. https://doi. org/10.1080/1369183X.2020.1851467.

Mitchell, K., and M. Sparke. 2018. "Hotspot Geopolitics Versus Geosocial Solidarity: Contending Constructions of Safe Space for Migrants in Europe." *Environment and Planning D: Society and Space* 0 (0): 1–21.

Moreno-Lax, V. 2018. "The EU Humanitarian Border and the Securitization of Human Rights: The 'Rescue-Through-Interdiction/Rescue-Without-Protection' Paradigm." *JCMS: Journal of Common Market Studies* 56 (1): 119–140. doi:10.1111/jcms.12651.

Nowicka, M. 2007. "Mobile Locations: Construction of Home in a Group of Mobile Transnational Professionals." *Global Networks* 7 (1): 69–86. doi:10.1111/j.1471-0374.2006.00157.x.

Panebianco, S. 2022. "The EU and Migration in the Mediterranean. EU Borders' Control by Proxy." *Journal of Ethnic and Migration Studies* 48 (6): 1398–1416. https://doi.org/10.1080/1369183X.2020.1851468.

Portes, A., L. Guarnizo, and P. Landolt. 1999. "The Study of Transnationalism: Pitfalls and Promise of an Emergent Research Field." *Ethnic and Racial Studies* 22 (2): 217–237. doi:10.1080/014198799329468.

Seeberg, P., and F. Zardo. 2022. "From Mobility Partnerships to Migration Compacts: Security implications of EU-Jordan Relations and the Informalization of Migration Governance." *Journal of Ethnic and Migration Studies* 48 (6): 1345–1362. https://doi.org/10.1080/1369183X.2020.1851465.

Smith, A. 1995. *Nations and Nationalism in a Global Era*. Cambridge: Polity Press.

Squire, V. 2015. "The Securitisation of Migration: An Absent Presence?" In *The Securitisation of Migration in the EU: Debates Since 9/11*, edited by G. Lazaridis and K. Wadia, 19–36. Basingstoke and New York: Palgrave Macmillan.

The Guardian 2016. *The worst I've seen - trauma expert lifts lid on 'atrocity' of Australia's detention regime*. The Guardian 19 June 2016. Available online at: www.theguardian.com/australia-news/2016/jun/20/the-worst-ive-seen-trauma-expert-lifts-lid-on-atrocity-of-australias-detention-regime.

The Guardian 2016a. *Hundreds hurt in police clashes at Greece-Macedonia border, The Guardian* 10 April 2016. Available online at: www.theguardian.com/world/2016/apr/10/clashes-between-migrants-and-police-at-border-between-greece-and-macedonia.

Tittel-Mosser, F. 2018. "Reversed Conditionality in EU External Migration Policy: The Case of Morocco." *Journal of Contemporary European Research* 14 (4): 349–363. doi:10.30950/jcer.v14i3.843.

Weaver, O. 1993. "Securitization and Desecuritization." In *On Security*, edited by R. D. Lipschutz, 46–86. New York: Columbia University Press.

Webb, J. 2022. "The 'Refugee Crisis' and its Transformative Impact on EU-Western Balkans Relations." *Journal of Ethnic and Migration Studies* 48 (6): 1363–1380. https://doi.org/10.1080/1369183X.2020.1851466.

Weiner, M. 1995. *Global Migration Crisis: Challenge to State and to Human Rights*. New York: Harper Collins.

Wimmer, A. 2002. *Nationalist Exclusion and Ethnic Conflict. Shadows of Modernity*. Cambridge: Cambridge University Press.

From Mobility Partnerships to Migration Compacts: security implications of EU-Jordan relations and the informalization of migration governance

Peter Seeberg ⓘ and Federica Zardo

ABSTRACT
Recent events in the Middle East and North Africa entailed a proliferation of policy tools for EU external migration governance. After the signature of Mobility Partnerships, the EU launched Migration Compacts, whose inner logic is to 'avoid the risk that concrete delivery is held up by technical negotiations for a fully-fledged formal agreement'. This paper examines the development of the EU's external migration governance and frames it into a formalization/informalization dichotomy. We argue that the EU-led securitisation of migration has contributed to the increasing informalization of EU-third countries agreements. The case of Jordan is relevant in understanding the EU's approach, as a strategy to muddle through in a region in turmoil.

Introduction

In May 2015 the Jordanian *General Population and Housing Census* counted the total population within the Jordanian borders as 9,531,712 persons, including 1,265,514 Syrians (Census 2015). Of the latter the UNHCR by December 2017 had registered a little less than 660,000 as Syrian refugees in Jordan (UNHCR 2017). A World Bank report presented in April 2016 emphasised that the impact of security spillovers on the stability of the Kingdom combined with the refugee crisis remained Jordan's utmost challenges. The report pointed at the so-called 'Jordan Compact' of 2016, a joint EU-Jordan initiative aiming at addressing challenges related to the presence of the Syrian refugees in Jordan. More specifically, the Compact seeks to compensate Jordan for its important intake of refugees and migrants and to support its efforts in avoiding secondary movements towards Europe by deepening cooperation on trade and strengthening its migration dimension. As Annex to the EU-Jordan Partnership Priorities 2016–2018, the Compact complements the existing EU-Jordan Association Agreement by engaging the counterparts in improving the bilateral trade regime to 'strengthen the resilience of the Jordanian economy' (European Commission 2017b) and integrate migrants in the Jordanian economic system. In this perspective, some of the activities mentioned in the Compact include creating 'jobs for up to 200,000 Syrian Refugees contingent on international support' (Hakim, Matta, and Hasna 2016, 11).

Underlining the political character of migration, this would seem to be a controversial policy, with which many Jordanians would disagree, arguing that even though the activities would also include unemployed Jordanians, it might lead to a situation where the Syrians are outcompeting the Jordanians – typically in unskilled, low-salary sections of the Jordanian labour market.[1] The Syrian refugees play an important role in internal Jordanian politics, but they also play a significant role in regional and international negotiations and/or agreements, where the different dimensions of the Jordanian migration profile function as reference points (Achilli 2015). Historically the Compact follows the agreement between the EU and Jordan on a Mobility Partnership (MP), conceived as 'a long-term framework based on political dialogue and operational cooperation' capable of addressing 'the broader political, economic, social and security context' and having a 'broad understanding of security' (European Commission 2011a). In the MENA region, MPs have been signed with Morocco (2013), Tunisia (2014) and Jordan (2014), and are gradually being implemented (Seeberg 2017).

Jordan has received large numbers of refugees for decades – and has apparently been able to live with playing a role as a safe haven for people in need from Syria, Iraq, etc. The UNHCR 2015 update on the refugee situation in Jordan stated that 'UNHCR's foremost priority remains to ensure that Jordan's largely favourable protection environment is maintained in 2015, despite new arrivals of Syrians potentially further straining already limited resources' (UNHCR 2016). The Jordanian approach to receiving Iraqi and Syrian refugees has been one of hospitality, despite substantial problems for a country with relatively scarce resources. The expectation of continued rapid growth in the number of refugees has not been met by the actual demographic development; rather the number, reaching 600.000 in the summer of 2014, showed a moderate growth until mid-2016. Since then Jordan has hosted a stagnating number of around 650.000 Syrian refugees. Against this background, this article sets out to analyse the relationship between the EU and Jordan on migration policies, with particular focus on those policies dealing with refugees.

As highlighted in the Introduction to this Special Issue, the framing of migration as a threat based on prejudiced narratives has contributed significantly to the crisis. And the spiralling of the securitisation of migration involves different actors, discourses, policies and practices, the interplay of which leads to further increased securitisation processes (Bello 2022). We contend that the more dynamic and, in many ways, unmanageable migration-security nexus, has heightened the EU's attempts to change the nature of its working relations with its partners from the Middle Eastern and North African (MENA) region towards increasing informal, local and pragmatic dimensions. Rather than looking for more legally binding and formal cooperation – and against increasing resistance by third countries to engage in such agreements – the EU has discursively linked informality with flexibility and with reactiveness to security threats. In this way, it has succeeded in securing cooperation with Neighbourhood countries. Arguing that the case of Jordan provides a relevant example to understand the EU's changing approaches, the article asks to what extent and in which ways the EU is resorting to more informal strategies to increase cooperation on migration with third countries.

The article draws on material from EU and Jordanian political institutions, including semi-structured interviews with staff from EU offices in Brussels, negotiators and EU experts from Jordanian Ministries, and international organisations in Brussels and Amman. Taking its point of departure in how the EU's foreign and security policy instruments related to migration and refugees have gradually changed from political dialogue framed in the ENP to Mobility Partnerships up to Migration Compacts, we first develop an analytical framework for the article; then we outline the challenging impact of the refugee crisis for the coherence of both Jordan and the EU. The last analytical section discusses how securitisation influences the interplay between formal and informal dimensions of the EU–Jordan migration governance framework.

From Mobility Partnerships to Migration Compacts: an analytical framework

The typology of EU instruments to cooperate with third countries on migration and mobility has significantly broadened over the last year and reflect both the vicissitudes of the integration process and the evolving dialogues on migration at the international level. The EU-instruments are briefly described below.

After a long phase of highly institutionalised but rather limited EU-Neighbourhood cooperation on migration and mobility through the Euro-Mediterranean Association Agreements and the Action Plans, the post-uprisings migration flows in 2011 made it necessary for the EU to rethink its approach towards its partners.

While the securitisation of migration in EU-MENA relations goes back to the end of the Cold War, as pointed to by Valeria Bello in the Introduction to this Special Issue (Bello 2022), pressures on the EU to adapt its policy toolbox to better deal with the crisis have substantially intensified since 2011. This seems to confirm that, particularly under circumstances when expectations of increased migration flows occur, we see scattered intensified manifestations of securitisation. These manifestations constitute an important element of the analytical framework for the article.

The Communication of the European Commission *A partnership for democracy and shared prosperity* called for setting up partnerships with non-EU countries to make cooperation on migration mutually beneficial through 'Dialogues for Migration, Mobility and Security' (European Commission 2011b). This approach was reinforced by the adoption of the EU's renewed Global Approach to Migration and Mobility (GAMM) in November 2011, which aims to initiate a more strategic phase of the original Global Approach of 2005 by means of MPs and Common Agendas on Migration and Mobility (Carrera, den Hertog, and Parkin 2012; Seeberg 2013).

The European Commission qualified these instruments as 'the most innovative and sophisticated tool to date of the Global Approach to Migration' (European Commission 2009) as well as a 'flexible instrument' developed under a 'tailor-made, country-by-country approach' (European Commission 2011a). They are non-legally binding joint declarations negotiated between the Commission on behalf of interested member states and a third country. Through the MPs, member states are supposed to offer several benefits, among which visa facilitation schemes and regular channels for temporary migration, in exchange for cooperation in the management of irregular migration, in particular readmission, return and border control/surveillance policies.

However, the Communication of the European Commission on *Establishing a new Partnership Framework with third countries under the European Agenda on Migration* states that 'experience in dialogues with partner countries has shown a gap between expectations and results on returns and readmission' (European Commission 2016b). Therefore, the EU prompted the launch of Migration Compacts to also be negotiated with countries such as Jordan, having recently signed an MP. The compacts are 'coherent and tailored engagements with third countries to better manage migration in full respect of our humanitarian and human rights obligations', with short- and long-term quantifiable objectives funded through 'flexible and rapid financial support' (European Commission 2016a).

Similarities among these policy instruments basically abound, yet their inner logics differ. While Association Agreements remain the only legally binding documents signed between the EU and third countries, MPs are conceived as flexible but institutionalised frameworks to conduct dialogues on migration and mobility (Lavenex and Stucky 2011). With the Migration Compacts the EU seems to be taking a further step towards informal governance. As explained in the first 2016 progress report on the Partnership Framework with Third Countries (European Commission 2016b), the main idea behind the compacts is that 'formal international agreements can flow ... but the Compact's approach avoids the risk that concrete delivery is held up by technical negotiations for a fully-fledged formal agreement.' The practice of going informal is not new in EU policy making and scholars have increasingly focused on this dimension, providing useful insights into the workings of the European Union (Christiansen and Piattoni 2003; Schneider and Tobin 2013; Kleine 2014).

Some authors have analysed informalization within the study of formal politics 'as a part of, rather than outside of, a formal institutional framework' (Reh et al. 2011), while some others have conceptualised informal governance as 'uncodified, non-institutional social relationships and webs of influence' (Harsh 2012). Whether broadly or narrowly conceiving informalization, scholars overall agree that formal provisions rarely provide the full story of EU politics and policies, since they are often bypassed to make the system work (Christiansen and Neuhold 2013). This is particularly true in contentious policy areas, where informal arrangements tend to become useful coping strategies (Gel'man 2004) or 'devices for minimizing the impediments to cooperation' (Lipson 1991). The clashes between highly formalised routines for decision making and continuous negotiation of policies that engender informal relations (Christiansen and Piattoni 2003) might occur at many levels, involving the EU, EU member states and the third country.

A closer look at EU–Jordan cooperation on migration shows how the pressure to manage the crisis created tensions at all levels and altered the interplay between formal and informal politics. In the process, it accounts for the role of both the EU and Jordan in framing cooperation as a security priority. A narrative on the need to react quickly, with flexibility and circumventing lengthy negotiations or bureaucratic procedures, gradually backed the design of more informal policies and instruments.

Adapting from Reh et al. (2011), informality is conceptualised in this paper as the presence of un-codified rules and decisions taken outside official bilateral channels, unofficially drawn boundaries of participation in the policy-making process and non-binding or intermediate (rather than final) outcomes.

The formalization/informalization trajectory can involve the framework within which decisions are taken (organisations, governments or networks), the policy-making process (politics, arrangements, activity) or the outcome (rules, agreements) of such process (Christiansen and Neuhold 2013). However, a caveat is needed. Besides being the result of specific negotiation processes at the three levels mentioned above, EU–MENA arrangements – such as the Association Agreement and Action Plans, the MPs and the Migration Compacts – are overarching engagements establishing arenas for further bargaining, decision-making processes and outcomes. In the actual practice the Migration Compacts form basis for 'day-to-day' decisions on EU 'rules of origin' for specific products, issuing of work permits, liberal investment procedures etc. (European Commission 2016c).

This study is primarily interested in understanding the nature of the migration governance system put in place by these agreements. Hence, it considers them once they have been brought on the bilateral negotiation table and only partially touches upon the intra-EU processes prior to this phase. In doing so, it also speaks the most recent governance and multi-level governance literature exploring how the crisis affects the interaction among the global, regional and local levels of cooperation (Panizzon and Riemsdijk 2018). In order to understand whether, to what extent and at which level EU–Jordan relations are 'going informal', the analysis first looks at EU–Jordan dialogues on pivotal agreements on migration and then examines the governance framework resulting from their implementation.

The impact of the refugee crisis and the migration-management of the EU and Jordan

Taking Jordan as the example, Laurie Brand shows how 'Jordan has been profoundly shaped by multiple episodes of immigration and emigration, voluntary and forced, economic and conflict-induced' (Brand 2010). It is precisely the question of migration, in particular the Iraqi refugees following the US-led invasion of Iraq in 2003, that gave rise to domestic criticism against the Jordanian state even before the start of the Arab uprisings, since the presence of the Iraqis was controversial among the Jordanians, as shown by several authors (Mokbel 2007; Sassoon 2008; Lacroix and Al-Qdah 2012).

Migration and asylum became impacting issues for the European Union in the 1970s and 1980s and the management of migration flows quickly got on top of what the President of the European Commission Jean-Claude Juncker called the current EU polycrisis (EPRS 2016). On the one hand, as noted by Köprülü, the Arab uprisings can be described as a legitimacy crisis, where the regimes lost support of their people (Köprülü 2014). This was also the case in Jordan, even though there was never the same intense pressure on the Hashemite regime as in Tunisia, Egypt and Syria. On the other hand, the refugee crisis affected both the internal and international legitimacy of the European Union, since it challenged the balance of power among supranational and national institutions, and among the member states (Falkner 2016) but it also questioned the soundness of its core values vis-à-vis its citizens and third countries (Carrera et al. 2015).

The situation regarding Syrian refugees fleeing to Jordan was interfering with the situation for the Iraqis, as mentioned in a UNHCR update: 'The continuing influx of Syrians is likely to affect UNHCR's activities to address the needs of Iraqi refugees in Jordan'

(UNHCR 2016). The rising regional tensions as a result of the active presence of IS in both Iraq and Syria and the continued fighting in both countries added a security dimension to the refugee issue (Köprülü 2014). This made it even more important for the regime in Jordan to ensure that its policies enjoyed the support of both its population and its regional and international allies.

Following the entrance of IS on the political scene in Iraq and Syria, the security dimension of the regional turmoil became emphasised since problematic radical organisations might hide members of their network among refugees while crossing the Jordanian borders.

This meant that the rise of IS became a security concern that was just as highly important as the ongoing Syrian civil war itself. The realities on the ground in the region became increasingly challenging, and a tragic incident, where a Jordanian Air Force pilot was burned alive by the IS, contributed to uniting the Jordanians behind the foreign policies of the regime (Shteiwi, Walsh, and Klassen 2015), thus providing the legitimacy for an increasing securitisation of migration. Jordan obviously has incurred (and is still doing so) huge expenses in connection with receiving the refugees from Iraq and Syria, but the refugees also provide Jordan with regional and international support. Furthermore, the political role Jordan is playing while dealing with the regional conflicts strengthens the Jordanian regime internally in Jordan.

The presence of the Syrian (and Iraqi) refugees in Jordan has contributed to securing economic support from regional state actors in the Gulf, from international donors like the IMF and the World Bank, and not least from the US and the EU. More than 80 per cent of the Syrian refugees have settled outside the camps and live in Jordan's major towns and cities. Being refugees, they are not legally allowed to work in Jordan, so they rely on food parcels, cash vouchers and charitable donations distributed by the UNHCR and other programmes (Martínez 2014). Added to that, they live on their own savings and to an increasing degree on poorly paid jobs in the informal Jordanian service sector, exposed to competition from Egyptians and migrants from Asia.[2] Due to the Jordanian open-door policy, the Syrian refugees have access to some Jordanian public services like health care and education and other programmes for poor Jordanians also shared by the refugees. The significant expenses related to the foreigners staying and the newcomers arriving in Jordan create an interest in exaggerating the costs and the Jordanian policies no doubt contribute to a positive attitude towards the Jordanian regime among international donors.

Unofficially the share of Syrians who are active on the Jordanian labour market is even relatively high – and perceived negatively by many Jordanians.[3] An ILO study shows that male Syrian refugees mainly work in the low-paid informal sector, primarily competing with Egyptian work migrants rather than Jordanians (Ajluni and Kawar 2014). A huge grey zone of informal work, for instance within restaurant businesses of different types, is a reality in particular in Amman, and frequent control visits take place resulting, from time to time, in the closing of businesses – for illegally hiring Syrians for the low-paid work. The Jordanian National Resilience Plan 2014–16 emphasised that the influx of refugees from Syria affected the Jordanian labour market. The overall assessment of the situation was, that 'the main impact of the increasing number of Syrian workers in the labour market has been to put significant downward pressure on wages, which has led to an enlarged informal economy' (MPIC 2014).

Hence, over the years, migration flows destabilised the Jordanian host communities from the social and economic point of view and put increasing pressure on the regime – and thereby indirectly the external donors – to compensate for the impact of Iraqis and Syrian refugees on both the local economy and the labour market. However, the crisis could challenge neither the institutions nor the domestic policy-making process, since the proximity of external threats provided the regime with a solid backing in the population as well as in regional and international partners. These Jordanian ambitions are also obvious in 'Jordan 2015. A National Vision and Strategy', an official Jordanian 'script' for the decade from 2015 to 2025, showcasing Jordanian economic and social aspirations (Jordan 2025).[4]

This was not the case for the European Union facing the 'polycrisis'. The combination and interaction of the euro-area instability, the global economic crisis, the UK referendum and the migration challenge have not only nurtured social tensions and raised citizen's criticisms vis-à-vis the EU. It also affected the internal balance of power (Carrera et al. 2015), and influenced the EU policy-making process (Falkner 2016).

Formal or unintended institutional reforms following periods of crisis have involved many policy areas. Yet, there are few doubts that the area of economic governance and that of justice and home affairs (JHA) have been historically affected the most by European and international turbulences. In the realm of JHA in particular, insecurities beyond the EU borders, in particular in the MENA countries, have substantially determined institutional developments. Since until the 1990s southern Mediterranean 'problems' 'were expected to arrive not on boats but via the diaspora' (Bilgin 2016), the management of third countries' nationals living in European member states and issues such as family reunification dominated the EU agenda rather than illegal migration and border control. Instead, reforms introduced after the Amsterdam Treaty speak of the need for the member states to coordinate their immigration and asylum policies in order to face the 'migration and refugee crisis'. The policies, resulting from securitisation of migration, appear in different scattered reactions depending on the level of crisis in the given context.

Whenever formal changes in the supranational architecture were not enough to deal with the crisis, the EU delivered new strategies and instruments to circumvent institutional struggles. Many agree that the gradual externalisation of security policies – among which concerning border functions – carried out through the ENP in 2003 and its revised versions was meant to make up for the limited integration of member states' internal security policies (Lavenex and Wichmann 2009; Monar 2010; Del Sarto and Steindler 2015; Del Sarto 2016).

The heightening of the refugee crisis in October 2013, when a boat carrying migrants sank and caused the death of about 400 people, increased the critical stances vis-à-vis the EU effectiveness in dealing with this challenge. First, Commissioner Malmström publicly reacted to the disaster by speeding up the negotiations of MPs with MENA countries, such as Tunisia and Jordan. In doing so, it made the most of the leeway granted to the European Commission by the GAMM (Zardo 2017).

Then, the new executive led by President Jean-Claude Juncker, one of whose vice-presidents, Federica Mogherini, is also the new High Representative leading the European External Action Service (EEAS), tried to re-legitimize the supranational level in the realm of migration. The architecture currently includes for the first time a first vice-president who is responsible for coordinating both Commissioners responsible for 'Justice' (DG JUST) and 'Home Affairs' (DG HOME), thus steering their work, including on migration policy (Carrera et al. 2015). The succession of deadly shipwrecks over 2015 and 2016 intensified the ever-louder chorus of EU leaders calling for more effort at the highest political level, more 'coordinated external action tools and an upgrade of the GAMM' (Italian Government 2015), until the launch of Migration Compacts. Again, EU policies and the balance of power between national and supranational institutions were questioned.

The ambitions of the Bratislava Summit of September 2016 were to restore control of the external borders, but also to ensure internal and external security and to fight terrorism. The roadmap from the summit stipulates that it was a main objective 'never to allow return to uncontrolled flows of last year and further bring down the number of irregular migrants' (EU Council 2016). In the context of Jordan, these ambitions were pursued in different specific ways, one of them aiming at creating economic development via a higher level of integration of Syrian refugees into the Jordanian labour market.

Hence, the London conference 'Supporting Syria and the Region' had a twofold significance for the EU. On the one hand, it was an opportunity to also pursue its agenda beyond traditional EU–third countries bilateral arenas. On the other, at times when Brexit seemed to represent an increasing legitimacy crisis, it was important that consensus among the member states was a stable reality. The Jordan Compact presented in that framework was not only supposed to condense the European and Jordan preferences, placing 'substantial responsibility on the donor community to turn the Syrian refugee crisis into a development opportunity' (European Commission 2016a, 12). The Compact furthermore made it possible to turn the EU-Jordan cooperation regarding the refugee crisis into pragmatic and asymmetric trade-offs, according to which Jordan accepted 'that the bulk of the refuges will remain in Jordan until the situation in Syria allows for their return, and the international community including the EU have [...] accepted to support Jordan accordingly' (European Commission 2016a, 12). Summing up the development reflected a progressive securitisation of migration from the EU side based on the perceived threats attached to the refugee crisis and to related threats stemming from the Syrian crisis in a broader sense, hereunder the role played by radical jihadist organisations in the war in Syria. Also in Jordan, not least due to the barbaric killing of a Jordanian pilot, the impact of the Syrian crisis constituted an important part of the background for the securitisation of migration.

EU–Jordan agreements and the formalization/informalization trajectory

EU–Jordan institutional relationship has always functioned relatively well. However, cooperation on migration was limited at least until 2011, when two projects were put in place with the aim of improving the working and living conditions of migrant workers (European Commission 2012). Regional initiatives such as those funded through the Aeneas programme also involved Jordan (European Commission 2004), but political dialogue developed extremely slowly within the formal ENP institutional framework formed by the Association Council and Committee, the sub-committees and the working groups, and so did targeted projects (EU Council 2005). It is unsurprising, then, that the first EU–Jordan Action Plan was highly asymmetrical towards the EU and did not touch upon refugees and migratory pressure on Jordan as the main concern for the country. In line with Article 77 of the Association Agreement, the improvement of statistical tools and the exchange of information on migration figured high on top of cooperation priorities, and the Ministry of Statistics could benefit a lot from EU funding.

The second Action Plan agreed in 2013, where 'Migrants in need of international protection'[5] eventually figured under the JHA chapter for the first time, reflected not only the centrality of migration in the agenda of both the EU and Jordan, but also the improved functioning of the ENP institutional architecture and the attempt to fit migration governance into the ENP framework. Technical dialogue progressed well within the Social and Migration Working Group and the sub-committees, and this led to more differentiated cooperation. Conversely, political dialogue in the high-level, formal arena, namely the Association Council and the Association Committee, remained stuck. Jordan resisted EU pressure to accept the readmission of both Jordanians and third-country nationals as an 'important step towards fighting illegal migration' (EU Council 2006). This resistance is in line with what many have argued when analysing EU-MENA relations in the realm of migration (Cassarino 2010; Wolff 2014; Zardo 2017).

The development of EU–Jordan relations on migration described so far accounts, in part, for the EU reaction to the Arab uprisings and the following Syrian crisis in this policy area. The proposal to establish 'dialogues for migration mobility and security' (European Commission 2011a) with Southern Mediterranean countries is conceived as a more flexible and informal layer within the existing framework of the renewed ENP. Since on the one hand high-level meetings did not deliver the expected results on readmission and, on the other, intergovernmental practices by some EU member states were blocking the accomplishment of common policy goals, the MP were expected to be discussed first at senior officials' level to circumvent political and institutional struggles. It is precisely during the EU–Jordan Social and Migration Working Group in June 2012 that Jordan expressed its interest in engaging in a Dialogue on Migration, Mobility and Security.

The MP agreement was then adopted in October 2014, Jordan being the third Arab country (after Morocco and Tunisia) to sign the political engagement (EU–Jordan 2014). The joint declaration has a broad scope, including legal and labour migration, migration and development, combating irregular migration, trafficking and smuggling of human beings, and capacity building in order to deal with refugees in line with international standards (EU–Jordan 2014, 3). In contrast to the situation for the countries in the Maghreb, the actual work migration of Jordanians to the EU is limited. Therefore, Jordan's efficiency in controlling transit migration as conceptualised in the EU–Jordan MP has more to do with the management of significant numbers of refugees and with phenomena like irregular migration, trafficking, and the 'prevention of the terrorist threat' (European Commission 2014). It is the securitisation of migration which turns the focus towards these differentiated phenomena – and from the EU side in particular towards limiting the number of migrants/refugees arriving in Europe. Jordan on its side can deliver on these dimensions by taking part via the international coalition in the fight against the IS, by working on avoiding radicalisation of youngsters in Jordan, and by taking care of the refugees in Jordan.[6]

The Jordanian policies are presented in plans for the required activities, for instance like the most recent Jordan Response Plan, which describes a three-year programme 'of high priority interventions to enable the Kingdom of Jordan to respond to the effects of the Syria crisis without jeopardising its development trajectory' (MPIC 2016). The plans are often developed in close cooperation with international organisations and/or donors, and over time the approach has shifted from the short-term humanitarian perspective to forms of practices that prioritise long-term developmental responses. With the scope of the refugee issue in Jordan as described above, financing the activities has become a significant challenge for the Jordanian state, so that attracting funding from international donors is a highly demanding aspect of Jordanian migration diplomacy.

The document furthermore mentions that the agreement 'is conceived as a long-term cooperation framework in line with the GAMM and with Jordanian migration policy' and that the EU agencies (Frontex, Europol, CEPOL, etc.) will be involved in the implementation of the partnership (EU–Jordan 2014, 8). The relatively limited weight of the MP in terms of funding[7] compared to other MENA countries and to allocations for crisis management from different donors is narrowing its potential as a 'cooperation framework'. Rather than a political declaration establishing a partnership, it tends to be considered as a stand-alone project, 'whose implementation is progressing well in rooted areas such as counter-trafficking, while being slow when more complex local institutional setup are required'.[8] However, the flexibility of the MP has left room for more informal coordination between local beneficiaries on the ground, European implementing actors and other international donors[9] but also among local, European and regional projects.

To the extent that political negotiations and the implementation of EU-funded programmes remain quite separated from each other,[10] strengthened informal relations at the operational level are not affecting decision making as described by Harsh in its conceptualisation of informal governance (2012). They are, though, contributing to bypassing long-lasting coordination struggles and the lack of coherence among donors' initiatives.

The 'Compact' maintains and reinforces the EU's attempt to add a less formal layer to its migration governance framework and more clearly embeds a crisis response approach. First, even if the Compact eventually fell under the document 'EU–Jordan Partnership Priorities', which is the substitute for the revised ENP Action Plan, and was finalised within the ENP Association Council, its development builds on a wider negotiation context at the global level. The international Migration Compacts strategy was presented in London on 4 February 2016 at the conference 'Supporting Syria and the Region', where the UN, 70 governments, the EU and major donors gathered to discuss the refugee crisis and raised almost $12 billion in funding and announced loans of $41 billion for the period 2016–20. During this event, Jordan migration diplomacy succeeded in mobilising international state actors and also the World Bank behind the Jordanian interests. The EU–Jordan Compact was then framed into the structure provided by the Communication of the European Commission on *Establishing a new Partnership Framework with third countries under the European Agenda on Migration* (European Commission 2016a) and was officially annexed to the '2016–2018 Partnership Priorities'. This process shows how, rather than being designed and discussed primarily within the official bilateral ENP channels, the Jordan Compact was shaped by negotiations taking place at the global level where the unofficially drawn boundaries of participation allowed both Jordan and the EU to increase international support.

Then, the commitment includes many references to support programmes from international donors such as the IMF and the World Bank. While this is not new in EU–Jordan relations, the lack of prescriptive planning suggests the attempt to rely on more flexible and less codified coordination mechanisms. Compared to the deterministic structure of the previous ENP Single Support Framework, where political objectives were linked to specific goals, actions, indicators and milestones in a project-like fashion, the annex to the Partnership Priorities is a patchwork of institutional relations, agreements and expressed intentions, and represent changing practices. The point is shown by one of the members of the Jordanian delegation to the nego-tiations related to the Compact, Thabet ElWir, a well-known Jordanian businessman and chairman of Jordan's Investment Commission (ElWir 2016), but also demon-strated at a EU–Jordan meeting in Brussels 3 May 2017, where, among others EU Commissioner Malmström and Colin Scicluna from the EEAS, underlined the additional flexibilities built into the Compact (European Commission 2017a). More-over, the fact that implementation largely relies on the EU regional Trust Fund in Response to the Syrian Crisis (Madad) also supports the argument of an informaliza-tion trajectory. The Trust Funds are instruments established in December 2014 'merging various EU financial tools and contributions from EU Member States and other donors into one single flexible and responsive mechanism' (European Commis-sion 2017b). While they have been formally set up by the Council to deal with the migration crisis (EU–Council 2015), their extension of scope beyond emergency activi-ties and the fact that they fall outside the EU budget have been criticised as a way to circumvent formal procedures of traditional EU development aid schemes. In this regards, the European Parliament raised some concerns on this practice (European Parliament 2016), not only in relation to the limited parliamentary control but also to the likelihood of the trust fund being implemented 'to the detriment of other devel-opment objectives' (European Parliament 2016).

The EU–Jordan Compact contains eight different objectives. The implementation of the measures will be a work in progress, since 'to support the delivery of the EU–Jordan Compact, regular review of the Compact will take place in the context of the bilat-eral cooperation between the EU and Jordan as well as other relevant dialogues and meet-ings' (European Commission 2016a, 10). It is hoped that the World Bank will provide Jordan with sufficient financing in addition to the funding received from the GCC, the EU, and the US (Final 2016).

International donors are not the only actors that the Compact Framework seemingly aims to involve. The EU commitment to ease customs regulations for specific goods pro-duced in industrial zones in Jordan, where both Jordanians and Syrian refugees work, in exchange for work permits for up to 200,000 refugees is, among others, a nod at businesses and private investors to contribute to the governance of migration.[11] The gradual 'normalization' of the Syrians present in Jordan is changing the practices of the country in the direction of a *de facto* non-encampment system. So far, the choice of bringing trade on the migration table slightly improved participation and informal coordination at the governmental level when dealing with the EU, since more ministries, such as the Ministry of Industry and Trade, took part in the negotiations.

Even if detailed planning of Compact interventions is progressing, only few results have materialised. Yet, as claimed by the responsible ministerial staff, it is now easier to detect weaknesses and, over time, reforming the work moves the attention from emergencies to more long-term planning. The funding has increased as the framework has become more transparent, not least for the involved partners in Jordan. The Compact has raised the awareness among international donors and this is deemed relevant by the Jordanian management.[12] Time pressure is also affecting early implementation. While improving informal coordination among donors and beneficiaries, the imperative of spending a large amount of money quickly and ensuring effectiveness is more likely to be met by experienced beneficiaries on the ground such as the International Organisation for Migration, UNCHR or the German cooperation (GIZ).

Compared to the MP, where the attempt to go informal did not question the formal architecture of EU–Jordan relations, the compact approach means thoroughly revising the ENP institutional structure. As mentioned in the agreement, 'a rethinking of the dialogues and sub-committees will be important. Grouping the sub-committees into a few thematic dialogues according to the partnership priorities and complementing the political dialogues will allow advancing cooperation in the agreed main strands of work' (European Commission 2016d).

Jordanian perceptions of the EU's changing approach are varied. On the one hand, as claimed by the ministerial staff from the Jordan Compact Unit,

> it is important to continue this focus on moving from quick fixes to long-term results. The Compact has been up and running for one and a half years and the process has been evaluated over the last six months with good results. People here and in the EU are impressed. It will probably continue after 2020, the perspectives are promising.[13]

A more sceptical view can be heard among employees in Jordanian Ministries working with trade, international cooperation etc, who emphasise that the Jordanian negotiators experience themselves as being pressured by the EU: 'You will need a full period to judge, but so far the Compact has not been successful.'[14] Trade rules in connection with export to the EU are by these Jordanians seen as an important obstacle for Jordan, who claim, that only very few Jordanian companies have taken advantage of the liberalisation of the rules.[15] Assessment should be seen against the background of a reality where, according to the Jordanian negotiators, 'the EU put pressure on Jordan, who negotiated from a weak position' and the kingdom is spending significant resources on security aspects that are highly important for the EU and international donors.[16]

Overall, the development of the EU's external migration policy toolbox point in the direction of more informal and pragmatic relations between the EU and Jordan. Increasing informalization has not prevented dialogue on the EU–Jordan Compact from being highly politicised, though. As claimed by one of the Jordanian negotiators: 'There is a lack of trust from the European side. In the short term, Jordan admittedly is lagging behind. We need more development, but the EU also needs to show much more flexibility.'[17] The Jordanian state in the first place considered the Compact as a flexible and beneficial answer to the challenges related to the refugees in Jordan. Later on, however, when the different elements of the Compact were implemented in the Jordanian reality, a scepticism occurred among the Jordanian partners as they realised that the conditionality inherent in Compact was too harsh in the sense, that they did not receive much additional funding for the projects after all (Mencütek 2019).

Conclusions and perspectives

This article was primarily interested in understanding the nature of EU–Jordan relations in the realm of migration as set out by the bilateral agreements that have succeeded over time, namely the ENP action plans, the declaration on a MP and the Migration Compact. Our hypothesis was that the security-led pressure to solve the migration crisis contributed to changing the nature of EU-Jordan relations towards higher levels of informality and pragmatism. We conceptualised informality as the presence of un-codified rules and decisions taken outside official channels, unofficially drawn boundaries of participation in the policy-making process and non-binding or intermediate (rather than final) outcomes.

The case of Jordan confirmed that, seising on the need for more reactivity, flexibility and efficiency prompted by the securitisation of migration, the EU is trying to advance cooperation on migration by adding less formal layers to the governance framework. With respect to informal arenas of decision making, it is shown how, after the Arab uprisings, dialogue has been increasingly carried out also beyond ENP-institutionalised channels. The 'migration threat' not only became a central topic of discussion during the growing number of formal diplomatic talks between the EU and Jordan. It started being on top of the agenda of meetings within many different international and regional arenas, strengthening linkages with other sectoral areas of cooperation such as trade or transport. However, contrary to our expectations, while informal channels for dialogue are growing in number, policy-making rules remain codified.

The informalization hypothesis is mostly confirmed also when looking at participation in the policy-making process. Urgency and crisis-related narratives facilitated the coordination of local and European beneficiaries of funding within the Mobility Partnership and the Jordan Compact, and fostered informal dialogue on the ground. Moreover, securitisation justified the usage of flexible mechanisms such as the Trust Funds, where the boundaries of participation are less determined than those of traditional EU funding schemes. This does not mean, though, that new actors are taking part in the decision-making process, since political dialogue and actual implementation remain separated from each other.

When it comes to the nature of the policy outcomes, the 'living' and non-binding nature of the agreements shows the preference for intermediate, rather than final, commitments, to prevent actors from getting stuck in formal international agreements and respond to the security threat.

While our findings overall confirm our hypothesis, a strict definition of informal governance, where decision making is led by actors other than the official ones (Harsh 2012), cannot be applied, since informalization is still to be found within the formal institutional framework.

Developments are taking place in a much securitised environment. On the one hand the MP and the Compact are controversial tools for Jordan, since the latter in particular deals with the issue of refugees, which is 'an open wound' in Jordanian public discourse. On the other, the EU is facing an internal and external legitimacy crisis, whose causes go far beyond the migration challenge. We consider that securitisation accounts for this interplay between formal and informal governance and that intra-European struggle played an even stronger role in the EU choice for more informal EU-Neighbourhood cooperation. The soft framework of the MP was meant to circumvent intergovernmental practices by some EU member states that were blocking the accomplishment of common policy goals. Similarly, the Compact approach should provide an answer to the call of the member states and the EU institutions for faster and better use of funding sources.

Dialogue beyond the formal bilateral arena contributed to reaching the agreements, and the flexibility of the financing schemes facilitated the launch of the activities. Yet, political divergences still exist and they are affecting implementation. To the extent that the Compact is a precondition for both European and Jordanian security, it is unsurprising that flexibility and more funding remain an open issue for Jordan, as it is the case for other MENA countries involved in the management of the EU's external migration policy.

The securitised realities of EU-Jordan cooperation on migration lead to a higher level of informalization of the policies and practices of the two partners. The Jordan Compact is in other words a flexible tool that responds to a security threat and is in this sense a product of securitisation. Its medium-long term development, however, deserves future analysis. To the extent that it indirectly brings into the governance of migration a broad spectrum of actors not traditionally involved in it – such as, for instance, Jordanian private businesses interested in exporting to Europe thanks to the relaxation of the rules of origin – this approach could contribute to deconstructing or re-constructing human mobility as a security concern, thus affecting the securitisation spiral.

Notes

1. This was confirmed in an interview (August 2017) by the authors with Chief Editor Mohammad Khazal, Jordan Times, Amman.
2. Still, as indicated by Khalaf in an interview by the authors, a majority of refugees prefer to work unregistered in this sector, because they are afraid to lose their public subsidies, Amman August 2017.
3. Interview by the authors with senior staff, Ministry of Industry, Trade and Supply, Amman August 2017.
4. Based on the National Vision posters have been produced and distributed to Jordanian Ministries: Interview by the authors with senior staff, Ministry of Planning and International Cooperation, Amman, August 2017.
5. EU–Jordan Action Plan 2013.
6. Khalaf, Jordan Times, interview by the authors, August 2017. Also underlined by Senior Advisor, EU Programmes Administration Office, Ministry of Planning & International Cooperation, Amman, interview by the authors, August 2017.
7. 2.5 million Euros.
8. Interview with a member of the staff from the International Centre for Migration Policy Development, Amman, July 2017.
9. Interview with EEAS-staff, Brussels, July 2017. Also mentioned by EEAS-staff, Politics, Press and Information Section, Delegation to the European Union to the Hashimite Kingdom of Jordan, August 2017.
10. Interview with member of the staff from the International Centre for Migration Policy Development Amman, July 2017. Interview with EEAS-staff, Brussels, July 2017.
11. Interview with EEAS-staff, Brussels, July 2017.
12. Interview with staff from the Jordan Compact Project Management Unit, Ministry of Planning and International Cooperation, Amman, August 2017.
13. Interview with staff from the Jordan Compact Project Management Unit, Ministry of Planning and International Cooperation, Amman August 2017.

14. Interview with senior staff, Ministry of Industry, Trade and Supply, Amman August 2017. This assessment was agreed upon by a Senior Advisor, EU Programmes Administration Office, Ministry of Planning & International Cooperation, Amman, August 2017.
15. See note 14. This is also argued by Khalaf, Amman, August 2017: 'The Jordan Compact does not work – the only examples of companies which have benefited from the EU relaxed rules of origin agreement are two companies in reality owned by Syrians.'
16. Interview with Senior Advisor, EU Programmes Administration Office, Ministry of Planning & International Cooperation, Amman, August 2017.
17. Interview with Senior Advisor, EU Programmes Administration Office, Ministry of Planning & International Cooperation, Amman, August 2017.

Disclosure statement

No potential conflict of interest was reported by the author(s).

ORCID

Peter Seeberg ⓘ http://orcid.org/0000-0002-8950-7507

References

Achilli, L. 2015. Syrian Refugees in Jordan: A Reality Check. EUI Policy Brief 2015/02.

Ajluni, S., and M. Kawar. 2014. *The Impact of the Syrian Refugee Crisis on the Labour Market in Jordan: A Preliminary Analysis*. Beirut: International Labour Organization. Regional Office for the Arab States.

Bello, V. 2022. "The Spiralling of the Securitisation of Migration in the EU: From the Management of a 'Crisis' to a Governance of Human Mobility?" *Journal of Ethnic and Migration Studies* 48 (6): 1327–1344. https://doi.org/10.1080/1369183X.2020.1851464.

Bilgin, P. 2016, January. *How not to think about the Mediterranean 'refugee crisis', Center for Mellemøststudier, Debate Analysis*, 1–7. https://www.sdu.dk/-/media/files/om_sdu/centre/c_mellemoest/videncenter/artikler/2016/bilgin+article+jan+16.pdf.

Brand, L. A. 2010. "National Narratives and Migration: Discursive Strategies of Inclusion and Exclusion in Jordan and Lebanon." *International Migration Review* 44 (1): 78–110.

Carrera, S., S. Blockmans, D. Gros, and E. Guild. 2015. "The EU's Response to the Refugee Crisis: Taking Stock and Setting Policy Priorities." *Centre for European Policy Studies Essay*, 20:27.

Carrera, S., L. den Hertog, and J. Parkin. 2012. EU Migration Policy in the wake of the Arab Spring – What Prospects for EU–Southern Mediterranean Relations? MEDPRO Technical Report No. 15/August 2012.

Cassarino, J. P. 2010. *Unbalanced Reciprocities: Cooperation on Readmission in the Euro-Mediterranean Area*. Washington: Middle East Institute.

Census. 2015. *General Population and Housing Census*. Amman, Jordan: DOS and UNICEF.

Christiansen, T., and C. Neuhold. 2013. "Informal Politics in the EU." *Journal of Common Market Studies* 51 (6): 1196–1206.

Christiansen, T., and S. Piattoni. 2003. *Informal Governance in the European Union*. Cheltenham (UK) and Northampton (US): Edward Elgar Publishing.

Del Sarto, R. A.. 2016. "Normative Empire Europe: The European Union, its Borderlands, and the 'Arab Spring'." *Journal of Common Market Studies* 54 (2): 215–232.

Del Sarto, R. A., and C. Steindler. 2015. "Uncertainties at the European Union's Southern Borders: Actors, Policies, and Legal Frameworks." *European Security* 24 (3): 369–380.

ElWir, T. 2016. Holistic Approach for Syrian Refugees Crisis (Jordan Compact) and the Main Challenges facing the Kingdom, PowerPoint Slides, Jordan Investment Commission, Amman.

EPRS. 2016. European Parliamentary Research Service, Briefing, Key Policy Challenges for the EU in 2017. PE 583.827.

EU Council. 2005. Fourth Meeting of the EU–Jordan Association Council (Brussels, 21 November 2005). Statement by the European Union. 14740/05 (Presse 310).

EU Council. 2006. Fifth Meeting of the EU–Jordan Association Council (Brussels, 14 November 2006). Statement by the European Union. 15138/06 (Presse 321).

EU Council. 2015. Council Conclusions on the EU Regional Strategy for Syria and Iraq as well as the ISIL/Da'esh threat, 16.03.2015, Doc 7267/15.

EU Council. 2016. *The Bratislava Declaration: The Bratislava Roadmap.* Brussels: European Council.

EU–Jordan. 2014. Joint Declaration Establishing a Mobility Partnership between the Hashemite Kingdom of Jordan and the European Union and ITS PARTICIPATING Member States. Accessed September 10, 2017. https://ec.europa.eu/home-affairs/sites/homeaffairs/files/what-is-new/news/news/docs/20141009_joint_declaration_establishing_the_eu-jordan_mobility_partnership_en.pdf..

European Commission. 2004. Aeneas Programme for Financial and Technical Assistance to Third Countries in the Area of Migration and Asylum. Overview of Projects Funded 2004–2006. Accessed September 10, 2017. https://ec.europa.eu/europeaid/sites/devco/files/publication-aeneas-programme-projects-funded-2004-2006_en_7.pdf.

European Commission. 2009. Staff Working Document, SEC(2009) 1240. 4.

European Commission. 2011a. A Dialogue For Migration, Mobility and Security with the Southern Mediterranean Countries. COM(2011) 0292final.

European Commission. 2011b. A Partnership for Democracy and Shared Prosperity with the Southern Mediterranean. COM(2011) 200 final 2011.

European Commission. 2012. Joint Staff Working Document. Implementation of the European Neighbourhood Policy in Jordan. Progress in 2011 and Recommendations for Action. SWD (2012) 116 final.

European Commission. 2014. EU–Jordan: A New Partnership to Better Manage Mobility and Migration. Edited by Press Release EU Commission, October 9.

European Commission. 2016a. Establishing a New Partnership Framework with Third Countries Under the European Agenda on Migration. COM(2016) 385final.

European Commission. 2016b. First Progress Report on the Partnership Framework with Third Countries Under the European Agenda on Migration. COM(2016)700final.

European Commission. 2016c. ANNEX to the Joint Proposal for a COUNCIL DECISION on the Union Position within the Association Council Set Up by the Euro–Mediterranean Agreement Establishing an Association Between the European Communities and their Member States, of the One Part, and the Hashemite Kingdom of Jordan, of the Other Part, with Regard to the Adoption of EU–Jordan Partnership Priorities and Annexed Compact. Brussels: European Commission.

European Commission. 2016d. Decision No 01/2016 of the 12th EU–Jordan Association Council Agreeing on EU–Jordan Partnership Priorities. JOIN(2016) 41 Final.

European Commission. 2017a. Launch Event on Trade and Business Opportunities in Jordan. Implementing the EU–Jordan Agreement on the relaxation of the EU Rules of Origin. Brussels, 03/05/2017.

European Commission. 2017b. Factsheet: EU Regional Trust Fund in Response to the Syrian Crisis. Accessed October 23, 2017. https://ec.europa.eu/neighbourhood-enlargement/neighbourhood/countries/syria/madad_en.

European Parliament. 2016. Motion for a European Parliament Resolution on the EU Trust Fund for Africa: the Implications for Development and Humanitarian Aid (2015/2341(INI)).

Falkner, G. 2016. "The EU's Current Crisis and Its Policy Effects: Research Design and Comparative Findings." *Journal of European Integration* 38 (3): 219–235.

Final. 2016. The Jordan Compact: A New Holistic Approach between the Hashemite Kingdom of Jordan and the International Community to deal with the Syrian Refugee Crisis. London: Conference: Supporting Syria & the Region, London, February 4.

Gel'man, V. 2004. "The Unrule of Law in the Making: The Politics of Informal Institution Building in Russia." *Europe-Asia Studies* 56 (7): 1021–1040.

Hakim, L., S. Matta, and Z. Hasna. 2016. Jordan Economic Monitor. The Challenge Ahead, Global Practice for Macroeconomics & Fiscal Management. World Bank, Jordan.

Harsh, M. 2012. "Informal Governance of Emerging Technologies in Africa." In *International Handbook on Informal Governance*, edited by T. Christiansen and C. Neuhold, 481–500. Cheltenham (UK) and Northampton (US): Edward Elgar Publishing.

Italian government non-paper, migration compact. 2015. Contribution to an EU strategy for external action on migration. April. Accessed July 23, 2017. http://www.governo.it/sites/governo.it/files/immigrazione_0.pdf.

Jordan. 2025. A National Vision and Strategy, Prime Ministry of Jordan, Amman, Jordan.

Kleine, M. 2014. "Informal Governance in the European Union." *Journal of European Public Policy* 21 (2): 303–314.

Köprülü, N. 2014. "Jordan Since the Uprisings: Between Change and Stability." *Middle East Policy* 21 (2): 111–126.

Lacroix, M., and T. Al-Qdah. 2012. "Iraqi Refugees in Jordan: Lessons for Practice with Refugees Internationally." *European Journal of Social Work* 15 (2): 223–239.

Lavenex, S., and R. Stucky. 2011. "'Partnering' for Migration in EU External Relations." In *Multilayered Migration Governance: The Promise of Partnership*, edited by R. Kunz, S. Lavenex, and M. Panizzon, 116–142. New York: Taylor & Francis.

Lavenex, S., and N. Wichmann. 2009. "The External Governance of EU Internal Security." *Journal of European Integration* 31 (1): 83–102.

Lipson, C. 1991. "Why are Some International Agreements Informal?" *International Organization* 45 (4): 495–538.

Martínez, J. C. 2014. "Bread Is Life. The Intersection of Welfare and Emergency Aid in Jordan." *Middle East Report* 272: 30–35.

Mencütek, Z. 2019. *Refugee Governance, State and Politics in the Middle East.* New York: Routledge.

Mokbel, M. 2007. "Refugees in Limbo: The Plight of Iraqis in Bordering States." *Middle East Report* 244: 10–17.

Monar, J. 2010. "The EU's Externalisation of Internal Security Objectives: Perspectives after Lisbon and Stockholm." *The International Spectator* 45 (2): 23–39.

MPIC. 2014. *National Resilience Plan. Proposed Priority Responses to Mitigate the Impact of the Syrian Crisis on Jordan and Jordanian Host Communities.* Amman: The Hashemite King of Jordan. Ministry of Planning and International Cooperation.

MPIC. 2016. *Jordan Response Plan 2016–2018.* Amman: Hashemite Kingdom of Jordan. Ministry of Planning and International Cooperation.

Panizzon, M., and M. van Riemsdijk. 2018. "Introduction to Special Issue: 'Migration Governance in an Era of Large Movements: A Multi-Level Approach'." *Journal of Ethnic and Migration Studies* 0 (0): 1–17.

Reh, C., A. Héritier, E. Bressanelli, and C. Koop. 2011. "The Informal Politics of Legislation: Explaining Secluded Decision Making in the European Union." *Comparative Political Studies* 46 (9): 1112–1142.

Sassoon, J. 2008. *The Iraqi Refugees: The New Crisis in the Middle East.* London and New York: I. B. Tauris.

Schneider, C. J., and J. L. Tobin. 2013. "Interest Coalitions and Multilateral Aid Allocation in the European Union." *International Studies Quarterly* 57: 103–114.

Seeberg, P. 2013. "The Arab Uprisings and the EU's Migration Policies—The Cases of Egypt, Libya, and Syria." *Democracy and Security* 9 (1–2): 157–176.

Seeberg, P. 2017. "Mobility Partnerships and Security Subcomplexes in the Mediterranean: The Strategic Role of Migration and the EU's Foreign and Security Policies Towards the MENA Region." *European Foreign Affairs Review* 22 (1): 91–110.

Shteiwi, M., J. Walsh, and C. Klassen. 2015. "Coping with the Crisis: A Review of the Response to Syrian Refugees in Jordan." In *Center for Strategic Studies 2014.* Amman: Centre for Strategic Studies, University of Jordan.

UNHCR. 2016. *UNHCR Global Appeal 2016–17*. New York: UNHCR.

UNHCR. 2017. *Syria Regional Refugee Response: Inter-Agency Information Sharing Portal*. Jordan; New York: UNHCR.

Wolff, S. 2014. "The Politics of Negotiating EU Readmission Agreements: Insights from Morocco and Turkey." *European Journal of Migration and Law* 16 (1): 69–95. doi:10.1163/15718166-00002046.

Zardo, F. 2017. "Migration, Mobility and the Challenge of Co-Ownership Exploring European Union–Tunisia Post-Revolutionary Agenda." *European Foreign Affairs Review* 22 (1): 75–89.

The 'refugee crisis' and its transformative impact on EU-Western Balkans relations

Jonathan Webb

ABSTRACT

The EU's relations with the countries of the Western Balkans are traditionally characterised by a set of stable relations and power dynamics. While the impact of the 'migration crisis' on EU migration policy has been examined, comparatively little attention has been placed on the social construction of the crisis and its impact on EU external relations. Specifically, there remains a lack of scholarship ascertaining the relationship between the framing of the crisis as a security threat, and EU policy change towards non-EU countries in Southeast Europe. To address these gaps, this article explores to what extent the securitisation of the crisis led to policy changes and the consequence of these changes on EU relations with the countries of Macedonia and Serbia. It demonstrates how in exchange for their cooperation with the EU to address the crisis, the Western Balkans governments extracted significant political concessions from the EU. Changes in policy and practice by the EU further enabled Macedonia and Serbia to justify concessions from the EU. This is argued to represent a continued shift in the relationship between the EU and Western Balkans countries, all be it one driven by the spiralling securitisation of the crisis.

Introduction

As the other articles in this special issue have suggested, securitisation and migration politics are closely intertwined. The escalation or de-escalation of securitisation can move migration policy and politics in different directions. This article explores this dynamic, while also focussing on the relationship between policy change and relations between states. A central question is posed: How did the securitisation of the refugee crisis affect EU external relations with the transit countries of Macedonia and Serbia?

The securitisation literature suggests that as an issue becomes securitised, the way in which actors understand an issue and formulate their interests in relation to an issue changes (Buzan and Waever 2003; Stritzel 2007). From this perspective, as the securitisation of migration accelerates, different actors will contribute to the securitisation or de-securitisation of the issue, readjust their interests and change the way they interact with one another (Ceyhan and Tsoukala 2002; McDonald 2008). This article intuitively builds on the distinct theory of spiralling securitisation outlined in the introduction to this special issue (Bello 2022) and applies it to the refugee crisis that developed from 2015 in Southeast Europe.

From 2015 to 2016, the Western Balkan countries saw large numbers of refugees crossing their borders. In total, Serbia received the second highest number after Greece with 596,000 arrivals, followed by Macedonia with 413,000 (Lilyanova 2016, 3). Yet, despite this, there is a shortage of scholarship examining the impact and implications of the crisis on relations between the EU and these EU Candidate States. Addressing this gap is important, given both the lack of scholarship on the crisis in the region and because our understanding of these events and the policy decisions made during the crisis are likely to be influenced by how the crisis was framed (Geddes and Hadj-Abdou 2018).

The analysis in this article addresses this gap and demonstrates that as the issue of migration was increasingly securitised within the EU, an external response was formulated to limit migration and reinforce the EU's external border. Methodologically, this article uses process tracing methods to ascertain how the construction of a securitisation narrative within the EU resulted in policy changes towards the countries of Macedonia and Serbia. These Western Balkan countries are selected as cases because they were the two main non-EU Member States in the Western Balkans that were tasked with securing the EU's external borders. A range of EU policy documents dated from 2014 to 2017 were analysed to understand how the framing of the crisis changed. In addition, news articles from both EU news sources and the Western Balkans countries, as well as other reports and policy statements documenting the crisis by international organisations, were examined. In total, over 60 documents were analysed. 14 semi-structured interviews are cited in this article, among a total number of 20 conducted with key policy actors. These interviews were used to further elaborate how the securitisation narrative developed, how it informed and framed policy, and ultimately how this securitisation resulted in changing relations between the EU and these countries. This ultimately resulted in a more political relationship emerging between the EU and the Western Balkans countries that was focused largely on resolving the crisis and less on fundamental reforms associated with the EU accession process.

The construction of a 'refugee crisis', migration governance and EU external relations

The wide ranging political consequences of Europe's so-called 'migration crisis' have led to a series of proactive migration policy changes within the European Union (EU) (Slominski and Trauner 2018; Trauner 2016). One area where there remains a relative absence of analysis is the 'refugee crisis'[1] in Southeast Europe and its impact on EU-Western Balkans relations. Traditionally, relations between the EU and the countries in this region have been defined by their asymmetry and the leverage the EU can exert over its regional partners (Schimmelfennig 2005; Vachudova 2005). However, recent scholarship has suggested that this relationship is far more political and that countries in the region have in fact been capable of shaping the process in a way that allows them to avoid undertaking fundamental reforms, if they cooperate to resolve key problems in the region as perceived by the EU (Zweers 2019).

While the impact of the crisis on the Western Balkans and its relations with the EU remains underexamined in the literature, existing scholarship supports a view that the crisis could have further transformed the relationship between the EU and Candidate States in the region. Existing scholarship suggests that the wider impact of the refugee crisis on the EU adversely affected EU solidarity, resulting in its actions being defined by its interest in resolving this crisis (Bello 2017). This change would reflect an even broader process of migration policy interacting with and shaping economic and security agreements between the EU and neighbouring countries (Geddes 2005; Ferrero-Waldner 2006). This includes countries in the Southern Mediterranean (Carrera, Den Hertog, and Parkin 2012) the Middle East and North Africa (Seeberg 2013), as well as Southeast Europe.

An analysis of EU Commission press statements on the crisis from 2014 to 2017 demonstrates how the crisis became increasingly constructed as a security threat to the EU. Statements towards the end 2015 show a continued focus on providing EU countries with financial assistance to accommodate and integrate refugees (European Commission 2015d). However, from 2016, this narrative changed. The crisis first became an event that needed to be managed, primarily through agreements with partner countries external to the EU (European Commission 2015f). However, alongside this, a narrative emerged that portrayed the refugee crisis as an external threat to the EU, and one that needed to be decisively dealt with beyond the EU's borders (European Commission 2015e). The impetus on migration management slowly shifted from the EU towards partner countries, who the EU believed were best positioned to tackle the 'root causes' of the crisis that threated the security and stability of the EU (European Commission 2015e, 2016a, 2016e).

Where there is literature on the crisis, scholars have been concerned with examining the crisis in terms of its impact on individual migrants and refugees (Arsenijević et al. 2017), the implications of the crisis for further European integration (Scipioni 2018), and the political as well as media rhetoric surrounding the crisis (Collyer and King 2016). However, there is a notable absence of scholarship examining the narratives of the crisis and how it affected EU-Western Balkan relations. Examining this region is important given there is a well-established body of literature demonstrating how the EU has structured its neighbourhood relations around the issue of migration (Boswell 2003; Lavenex 2006). Scholarship has shown how the construction of imaginaries and the creation of the EU's neighbourhood, have resulted in the externalisation of the EU's borders. In effect, this moves the responsibility of managing the EU's borders beyond its geographical limits and on to countries beyond its border (Bialasiewicz 2012; Scott, Celata, and Coletti 2019). However, often these accounts have not included the Western Balkans region in its analysis.

The transit countries of the Western Balkans have a protracted relationship with the EU. The EU's role in encouraging these countries to confront post-conflict legacies means that the promotion of human rights and transitional justice have been a key feature of EU-Western Balkans relations (Elbasani 2008; Bieber 2011). This has manifested in a policy framework that has focused on offering the countries of the region a credible prospect of EU membership, in exchange for transposing the EU *acquis* (Vachudova 2014). Similarly, when it comes to migration policy, it has traditionally been the transposition of the EU *acquis* that has determined Candidate State policy, given their exclusion from more reactive policy-making forums on migration policy (Byrne, Noll, and Vedsted-Hansen 2004).

As a consequence of substantive engagement between the EU and regional actors, the external relations of the countries in the region are orientated towards the EU and the prospect of EU membership (Elbasani 2013; Noutcheva and Aydin-Düzgit 2012). Consequently, all countries in the region hold EU membership aspirations and many have begun accession negotiations (European Commission 2015b).

Despite a strong body of literature demonstrating the EU's capacity to use various incentives to achieve policy outcomes in EU Candidate States (Bechev 2006; Schimmelfennig and Sedelmeier 2004), the literature on reverse conditionality suggests that initial cooperation that appears to favour the EU can be 'reversed' once a partner country in the EU's neighbourhood acquires a strategic position and is capable of leveraging its own policy interests (Cassarino 2007, 192). There remains however limited analysis of how the refugee crisis fits into the broader pattern of EU-Western Balkans relations and if the crisis did in fact allow for this reverse conditionality to occur. This analysis is important given scholars have noted a new form of political conditionally at play towards the Candidate States in the Western Balkans.

This new conditionality shares many of the same features of conditionality proposed by earlier scholars, but instead of being rewarded for transposing the *EU acquis*, political incumbents are offered political legitimacy in exchange for cooperating with the EU to resolve contemporary crises inflicting the EU (Zweers 2019;Kmezić 2020). Indeed, recent accounts have suggested that the refugee crisis in the region has resulted in the disintegration of the region from the European project as it once again becomes imagined as a frontier zone (Cocco 2017). There remains a need however for further scholarship to example how this might have evolved in practice and the precise impact this crisis has had on regional relations.

The increasingly politicised and security driven nature of EU-Western Balkans relations can be located in a broader shift towards strategic non-compliance with transposing the *EU acquis*, which is typically overlooked in the Europeanization literature. Where EU rules and norms are more clearly articulated and consistently promoted, non-compliance has been less likely (Noutcheva 2009; Noutcheva and Aydin-Düzgit 2012). In cases of ambiguity however, existing scholarship demonstrates the Western Balkan Candidates States have resisted the EU's transformative power (Bieber 2011; Rajkovic 2012). As such, Candidate States have used ambiguity to make the process more interest driven and avoid fundamental reforms that may be costly to incumbents (Bieber 2011).

The ambiguity in the EU's narrative of the crisis – first as a humanitarian crisis and then as a security threat – may have provided Western Balkan leaders with the opportunity to frame themselves as credible gatekeepers protecting EU security. It may also facilitate non-compliance with the EU's rule of law agenda in exchange for alignment with the EU's border security agenda, because the EU's regional priorities appear less clear and consistent. It is also reasonable to expect that due to the nature of accession negotiations and the need for Candidate States to transpose the EU *acquis*, that any change in EU migration governance will need to be transposed by Candidate States (Huysmans 2000; Lavenex 2001). In sum, the Western Balkans is important not only because it rests at the epicentre of new migratory routes to Europe, but because the region and its actors have a unique and protracted relationship with the EU beyond the context of the crisis.

In sum, the EU has historically been effective at ensuring partner countries work to reduce migration and act as 'gatekeepers', in exchange for different forms of assistance (Adepoju, Van Noorloos, and Zoomers 2010; Carrera, Den Hertog, and Parkin 2012, 5; Düvell 2012, 417–418; Paoletti 2010, 21). However, recent studies suggest that reverse conditionality can operate and provide non-EU countries with an opportunity to leverage desirable outcomes from the EU in exchange for policing their perceived frontiers (Cassarino 2007; Cocco 2017). Coupled with narrative ambiguity, this could provide an opportunity for Candidate States in the region to use new framing to achieve their interests and avoid implementing fundamental rule of law reforms.

The following section examines the theory of securitisation outlined elsewhere in this Special Issue and proposes how this securitisation might in practice reverse the conditionality between the EU and Macedonia and Serbia. This addresses a significant gap in the literature by providing more detailed analysis of the crisis in the Western Balkans and how the construction of events as a security crisis affected relations between the EU and countries in the region. At the same time, it complements developments in the literature that note a shift from the EU as the main leveraging actor to show how smaller countries can exert leverage over the EU.

Towards a theory of escalating securitisation and relation change

Having established a pre-existing relationship between the EU and Western Balkans countries and having identified the refugee crisis as a key event, it is possible to anticipate how EU-Western Balkans relations changed in the context of the crisis. First the emergence of a salient discourse of the crisis as a threat to the stability and security of the EU shaped the position of EU actors. Securitisation theory outlines the importance of discourse in shaping the way actors understand and respond to an issue (Buzan and Waever 2003; Stritzel 2007). When migration is increasingly talked about as a threat, it reinforces a hostile narrative and it becomes increasingly difficult for alternative narratives to be constructed (Ceyhan and Tsoukala 2002; McDonald 2008). The framing of the refugee crisis as a threat to EU security and stability intersected with facts, policies, practices, other narratives and techniques, to intensify the securitisation of the refugee crisis (Bello 2017, 62). The securitisation of the crisis undermined solidarity within the EU. For example, the hostility shown by many Central and Eastern European Member States to a proposed quota system has corresponded with the emergence of an increasingly hostile discourse towards refugees and migrants, and the representation of the crisis as a threat to Member State interests (Falkner 2016; Geddes and Scholten 2016, 85–86; Trauner 2016). Securitisation can lead to prejudice and negatively impact the formation of solidarity processes that are indispensable to EU integration (Bello 2017). This securitisation process is proposed to explain the emergence of a new border regime, which was designed to address the threat through external border enforcement. To assess the relationship between securitisation and action, analytical focus is placed primarily on the EU's collective response. However, the role that individual Member States have played in framing the crisis is referenced where appropriate.

Building on a theory of securitisation, it is anticipated that to reduce internal contestation and resolve the crisis, the EU tried to restrict entry into the EU through the Western Balkans route. In this case, the strategic approach of state actors in the Western Balkans was to reinforce the securitisation of the crisis. Recognising an opportunity to gain from the crisis and extract financial and political rewards from the EU, Western Balkans actors actively contributed to the construction of the crisis as a threat to EU stability and security. This was done by perpetuating a discourse of the crisis as a threat. Having perpetuated the crisis narrative, regional leaders presented their cooperation as an appropriate solution to stem the crisis. This cooperation was contingent on a relaxing of accession conditions relating to rule of law reform, and greater political support and inclusion of regional leaders in EU decision-making forums. From this perspective, it is also proposed that the narrative of the crisis as a threat changed the dispositions of EU actors, making them more susceptible to engaging with Serbia and Macedonia to help stem the crisis, allowing these countries to further reverse conditionality towards the EU.

The EU's reliance on the Western Balkans countries to help resolve the crisis allowed Macedonia and Serbia to use the narrative as a form of leverage by enforcing a new border regime, in exchange for rewards. State actors in the Macedonia and Serbia recognised that the crisis allowed them to exert leverage over the EU. This is because the EU's response to the crisis was contingent on effective cooperation with them to enforce a new border regime. In this regard, it is speculated that the EU was prepared to tolerate poor compliance or non-compliance in other areas of reform expected from Candidate States, in exchange for them acting as gatekeepers. Whether this occurred is ascertained through interviews with key informants who provided insight into how EU actors viewed these changes and the extent to which the EU was prepared to tolerate non-compliance with key rule of law criteria in exchange for these countries acting as gatekeepers.

The following sections demonstrate that in exchange for securing the EU's external borders, the Western Balkans countries were offered a range of rewards. Crucially, the provision of these rewards stem from the securitisation of the crisis and the impact this had on EU solidarity.

The refugee crisis and the EU's response

The first signs of EU action occurred in April 2015 at the height of the crisis. An extraordinary European Council meeting was originally called to address the deteriorating situation in the Mediterranean. Consequently, EU action to limit and supress the movement of people was devised and a raft of reforms launched to enhance the operational capacity of FRONTEX, rapidly transpose the Common European Asylum System in Member States and enhance Common Security and Defence Policy (CSDP) (European Commission 2015c). These policy actions reflected an increased concern within the EU about the crisis, its securitisation and the subsequent need enhance and enforce a securitised border regime (Neal 2009). These actions, which occurred in response to the emergence of a discourse that framed the crisis as a threat to EU stability (Heisbourg 2015), resulted in new forms of engagement between the EU and Western Balkans countries. This changing dynamic fits a broader pattern of EU reliance on non-EU countries to enforce its border regime (Geddes 2015; Bialasiewicz 2012). Increasingly, the Western Balkans countries were relied on to enforce the EU's border regime where previously, this had not been the case.

Despite the focus of the EU initially being centred on the Mediterranean, large numbers of people making their way across land routes through the Western Balkans further exacerbated existing political tensions and anti-migration sentiment within the EU. This necessitated the construction of a new external policy. On 8 October 2015, an Eastern Mediterranean-Western Balkans Route Conference was held (Council of the European Union 2015a). This was the first direct engagement between the countries of the Western Balkans and the EU to address the crisis. It made several recommendations that impacted the migration governance systems of the transit countries. This included recommendations to enhance humanitarian assistance, improve reception and accommodation facilities, and improve coordination between regional actors by enhancing information flows (Council of the European Union 2015b, 5–6). However, these policy changes accelerated in tandem with the emergence of a narrative of the crisis as a threat. Consequently, political contestation grew in EU Member States towards the crisis and the perceived influx of refugees (Allen et al. 2017, 12–13).

Initially, the EU sought to maintain a balanced response to the crisis that ensured humanitarian standards were upheld and that EU external borders were successfully controlled. However, events that transpired on the ground between 2015 and 2016 were considered by key interlocutors to poorly uphold humanitarian standards. In contrast, EU actors believed that policy actions helped manage the flow of refugees and limited the crisis' impact on EU security and stability.[2] During this period, there was an increased focus on border securitisation and a redistribution of resources designed to aid transit countries in reducing migration. Key political actors, particularly in Germany, sought to sure up their domestic power by responding to the crisis (Bulmer and Joseph 2016, 731). While at first policy responses were more open, they eventually focussed on supressing movement (Geddes and Scholten 2016, 96). Limiting migration required engaging with the Western Balkans countries. High-level discussions between EU Member State officials and leaders in the Western Balkans resulted in a joint statement on migration following the Western Balkans summit between regional leaders and the EU (France Diplomatie 2016).[3] This narrative was subsequently internalised and filtered down to border officials and actors on the ground who subsequently changed their practice.[4]

Considering the EU's response, two types of change are considered to have occurred in the context of the crisis: formal change and decisions made through informal venues. As the crisis progressed, decisions made informally through bilateral relations, helped the EU and partner countries to circumvent legal 'grey zones' (Baubӧck 2018; Niemann and Zaun 2018). New border practices were replicated inside and outside the EU and were subsequently legitimised, even when they were not formally mandated. These practices were informal because they were not legitimised by EU rules and norms. However, it is important to note that often formal EU rules and norms on migration management have been inconsistently implemented (Léonard 2010). In this case however, this change is notable as this disassociation between formal rules and norms and practices was not previously widespread in the Western Balkans before the construction of the crisis as a threat to stability. The perpetuation of new practices that included illegal pushbacks, abuse of refugees and forcibly preventing people from crossing borders, was not previously a feature of the region's border regime. This informal change led to a change in relations because it made it acceptable to deviate from EU rules and norms that were previously used to structure EU relations with Macedonia and Serbia through the EU accession process.

In terms of a change in practice, reports on the border between Bulgaria and Serbia documented a long-running and persistent pattern of abuse towards refugees including exhortation, abuse and forced deportation in violation of international law (Belgrade Centre for Human Rights 2016; Human Rights Watch 2015, 2016a). Increasingly, illegal pushbacks or forcibly restricting entry across borders became widespread (European Parliament 2016). None of these practices were consistently documented prior to the crisis. Despite the sustained documentation of such abuse, EU action to prevent abuse, condemn perpetrators and adhere to its humanitarian values, did not occur. This suggests that as the crisis grew, there was a further prioritisation of border control over adherence international human rights norms.

Further analysis demonstrates that the normative framework guiding EU border practices substantially changed with the onset of the crisis. Border abuses were documented on the Hungarian border (Human Rights Watch 2016b) and the Croatian border (Human Rights Watch 2017; Oxfam 2017). One interviewee argued that the EU's continued divergence away from humanitarian principles and representation of the crisis as a security issue was being noted in Serbia where small-scale cases of abuse had occurred. More problematically however, this interviewee believed that the deteriorating human rights focus of the EU had excused the Western Balkans countries from making human rights an essential part of their migration governance systems.[5] These changes transformed the way the Western Balkans actors understood migration management and responded to the crisis. Ultimately, Member State deviation from established norms legitimised the deviation of Western Balkans actors from those same norms. This legitimisation further emboldened Western Balkans actors to forcibly exert their agency and deter entry across their borders. Intentional pushbacks on the Macedonia-Greek border provides a strong example of this action and the lack of EU response further legitimised this forceful approach (Amnesty 2015).

This reinforced the strategic component of EU-Western Balkans relations. Regional actors were increasingly able to dismiss any focus the EU placed on human rights over political realities during their interactions as a claim of double standards.[6] In this regard, the EU was not seen as a 'normative power' driven by a desire to promote fundamental human rights norms (Manners 2002). Instead, it was perceived as an actor driven by political interests and security concerns. Cooperation between the EU and Western Balkans countries was increasingly framed around addressing the crisis and the threat it posed to EU stability. The relationship between the two sets of actors was thus increasingly reinforced by interests deriving from the belief that there was a pragmatic need to prevent further movement across the EU's border. A commitment to humanitarian norms and values increasingly played a diminished role.

This securitisation turn was further legitimised in practice through the rushed planning of a new asylum processing system. In November 2015, the EU provided additional support to the United Nations High Commissioner for Refugees (UNHCR) in the Western Balkans region to support up to 200,000 refugees (European Commission 2016d). While the UNHCR welcome the additional resources, they also pointed to some of the more problematic outcomes of the EU's strategy. For example, one interviewee argued that the EU's focus on preventing the movement of people and ensuring the efficient processing of asylum applications could not be implemented in line with international standards. The interviewee argued it was unfeasible in the current context as the Western Balkans countries did not have the capacity to accommodate large number of refugees or process asylum applications. They argued that if the EU insisted on these changes, they would sacrifice the construction of robust asylum procedures, in exchange for ensuring regional governments helped enforce their new border regime.[7]

Another interviewee pointed to the actions of neighbouring EU Member States, including Bulgaria and Croatia and emphasised how their treatment of refugees set a precedent for circumventing establish human rights norms in the region.[8] An examination of the events and interview responses from key actors in the region demonstrates a clear shift by the EU and its Member States away from principles of human rights, to enforcing stricter border controls and supressing migration. This was communicated to the countries of the Western Balkans. The ability of Macedonia and Serbia to prevent further entry of refugees into the EU was perceived as important for diffusing domestic discontent that was placing pressure on EU governments.[9] The permissibility of regional actors to abandon a migration governance framework that was focussed on human rights reflects not only an erosion of the EU's normative legitimacy, but also an increased reliance on external countries to enforce its border regime.

Over the course of the crisis, the EU sought to ensure that the countries of the Western Balkans would align with its deterrence policy. Before the EU formulated a coherent policy response to the crisis, the Western Balkans countries had typically pursued a laissez-faire approach to migration. However, as the crisis generated pressure within the EU, the EU sought to construct a policy response in cooperation with these countries that would limit movement into the EU and diffuse domestic contestation. Because Serbia and Macedonia are not EU Member States and lack robust asylum systems, their general strategy was to move refugees onwards to countries that had the capacity to accommodate larger numbers of refugees (Kogovšek Šalamon 2016). As the crisis developed however, the EU explicitly encouraged refugees to seek asylum in Serbia and Macedonia to relieve the flow of people seeking entry into the EU (Peshkopia 2015, 175–176). To ensure these countries would comply with this policy and that they had the capacity to accommodate refugees, increased financial incentives were provided (European Commission 2016d). Furthermore, two interviewees believed that leaders in Macedonia and Serbia helped co-construct a narrative of the crisis as a threat to EU stability in the hope of extracting further material and political rewards from the EU.[10] This is also reflected in the statements of key politicians, with the Serbian Prime Minister for example speaking of Serbia's desire to 'protect Serbia and Europe from another migration wave.' In adopting the language of the crisis and perpetuating a public discourse of refugee inflows as a threat to stability, the notion of crisis was reinforced (B92 2016d):

> It is clear that the EU functions excellently in times of peace and prosperity, but not in an emergency situation … The times when European security could be defended at its external frontiers with the Middle East and north Africa are long gone. Now, European security has to be defended within Europe itself- Gjorge Ivanov, then president of Macedonia (National Post 2016).

The political salience of the crisis and the paramount concern to stop the movement of people into the EU also afforded the Western Balkan countries with a powerful 'bargaining chip' in their current accession negotiations with the EU. Regional elites strategically emphasised their compliance with the EU to enhance their power within Serbia and Macedonia and improve their regional standing. Interviews conducted with public officials in the region suggested that in exchange for assisting with the crisis, leverage was exerted to gain political concessions from the EU. This included a reduced focus on the transposition of key EU rule of law *acquis,* as well as an agreement to increasingly include the leadership of Macedonia and Serbia in the European Agenda on Migration.[11] Several high-profile visits by EU leaders to the Western Balkans countries and public praise for the leadership of these countries in tackling the crisis also improved the domestic legitimacy of PM Gruevski in Macedonia and PM Vucić in Serbia.[12] One interviewee referred to how refugees had been treated in Bulgaria, Croatia and Hungary. They argued that the actions of these EU Member States explicitly violated the humanitarian principles preached by EU negotiators during accession negotiations. An interviewee from the UNHCR argued that this had been seized upon by politicians as an opportunity to exert rare leverage over the EU in exchange for addressing the crisis.[13] This leverage was exerted most profoundly in Macedonia, where the government's compliance with the EU's agenda was actively used to divert attention away from its on-going democratic crisis (Spasov 2016). More generally however, a position emerged from regional actors that their adequate treatment of refugees should be held as an example of their readiness to assume EU membership. This position was adopted to help them bargain for a relaxation of accession conditions. In the words of one interviewee: 'if we aren't allowed in the EU [for how we treat refugees], look at Hungary!'[14]

Political considerations that occurred in response to the crisis reflect the interests of key actors and the way in which they evaluated their positions in the context of the crisis. The rhetoric of the Western Balkans leaders communicated their belief that they were acting in defence of the EU and securing its external borders (B92 2016b; Gruevski 2015). These statements also reflect that regional actors recognised the crisis provided them with the opportunity to restructure their relations with the EU. From the EU side, there was a need to find a response that halted growing discontent within the EU surrounding the issue of refugee migration (Vertovec 2017, 1577). From the Serbian and Macedonian perspective, the crisis was an opportunity to gain important material rewards and political concessions from the EU. This included both financial support to supress migration and reduced scrutiny from the EU regarding rule of law violations in Macedonia and Serbia.[15] Crucially, this process began with the framing of the crisis as a threat and escalated to the point where actions on the ground and policy decisions changed. These changes required a change in EU relations with Macedonia and Serbia and the deepening of cooperation between the two sets of actors.

At the beginning of 2016, the consequences of the EU's response to the crisis were beginning to emerge. It became apparent that the EU's policy response had a broader impact beyond the way in which migration is managed in the region. It had also begun to transform regional relations between the EU and the Western Balkan countries. It did so by fostering the increased inclusion of Macedonia and Serbia in EU decision-making. It also changed the focus of the EU's accession negotiations with these countries. In terms of their increased inclusion, the Western Balkan countries were included in EU intergovernmental discussions on migration (EEAS 2015). One interviewee was keen to state how increased concerns about migration and refugee flows could be reflected onto the accession process.[16]

In this sense, the countries accession negotiations were used as an ad-hoc instrument for channelling funds to address the emerging crisis. This change is also reflected in the focus of accession progress reports. Enlargement strategy reports from 2015 to 2016 clearly reflect an increased focus on border management and control. For example, the 2016 enlargement strategy outlined how the EU's 'comprehensive and rights-sensitive' approach to the crisis had effectively closed the Western Balkans route. However, con-tinuous action would be needed to monitor the route and prevent further entry into the EU (European Commission 2016c, 4–5). This contrasts sharply with previous enlar-gement strategy papers. For example, prior to the crisis in 2014, the sole issue structuring EU-Western Balkans relations was the 'strict but fair conditionality, established criteria and the principle of own merit' (European Commission, 2014, 1). In terms of mentions alone, the reports from 2016 mention migration 16 times (European Commission 2016c), the report from 2015 mentioned migration nine times (European Commission 2015a) and the report from 2014 seven times (European Commission 2014). These references reflect the EU's evolving concern for border control and migration management, as well as an acknowledgement of the role played by the Western Balkans countries in its increasingly securitised border regime. Restricting movement through the Western Balkans route thus became a key factor influencing the EU's approach to the region and its regional relations.

The representation of the crisis as a threat reinforced a belief that it could destabilise the EU. Policy changes were thus consequential of the way EU publics and politicians reacted to the refugee crisis. Member State governments responded to social discord and constructed a border regime with the Western Balkans countries to reinforce the EU's border and reduce domestic contestation (Laffan 2016, 922–924). This was outlined in discussions with one interlocutor, who believed that the crisis required reassessing EU-Western Balkans relations and re-engaging with regional leaders to construct a common solution. Prior to this, the EU's regional policy had been orientated around accession negotiations. The prospect of accession was perceived to be distant and for many Euro-pean diplomats, the Western Balkans was 'not on their radar'.[17] However, because the crisis was construed as a salient security issue, the EU increasingly consulted regional state actors and relied on them to enforce its new border regime.

The commitment of the EU to end the refugee crisis through the enforcement of a new border regime is also visible when the material concessions provided to the Western Balkans countries are examined. Material incentives emboldened regional actors by sup-porting their belief that power relations were being reconfigured. The type of material support given to the countries was indicative of the new highly securitised border regime which was to be enforced. The crisis led to additional aid disbursements and the relaxation of political scrutiny on key EU accession issues, primarily rule of law reform (Wunsch, Dimitrov, and Cvijic 2016). In terms of material support, Serbia received €7 million to assist government actors and NGOs in responding to the crisis. The European Investment Bank contributed a further €5 million to the Migrants and Refugee Fund (MRF), which sought to improve the living conditions of refugees and migrants in reception centres (European Western Balkans 2016). Similarly, Macedonia received €4.4 million from the EU to provide assistance at transit points and immediate humanitarian aid (European Commission 2016b). This support was provided despite evidence the Macedonian authorities were seeking to deter, disperse and pushback refugees entering its borders (Nenov 2016). By 2017, both countries received over €21.74 million in assistance to respond to the crisis (European Commission 2016b). Furthermore, the government of Serbia has also used the crisis to rhetorically press the EU for further funding (B92 2015). EU assistance has not been purely humanitarian and both countries have been in receipt of equipment to control their borders and supress the movement of peoples. This equipment included SUV vehicles, quad bikes and security equipment to help prevent border crossings from neighbouring countries (B92 2016c; EURACTIV 2016; European Western Balkans 2017).

While these material resources are a fraction of the EU's outlay in external aid, they are significant in the context of the Western Balkans. New sources of funding increased the political legitimacy of regional actors. The fact they have gained materially from the EU is presented as a domestic victory and a sign of their countries increased accession prospects (B92 2016a; de la Baume and Surk 2016). In sum, the cumulative effects of the crisis have had a consequential effect in the Western Balkans. In response to the representation of the crisis as a threat to EU stability, EU-Western Balkans relations place less emphasis on the promotion of humanitarian norms. This is reflected in border practiced designed to secure the EU's external border. Increased inclusion in EU-decision-making processes and financial assistance have been important for implementing this changed approach.

Conclusion

This article has demonstrated that the social construction of the crisis had a profound impact on relations between the EU and Western Balkans countries. First, the emergence of a discourse, which framed the crisis as a threat to EU security and stability, sowed discontent within the EU. This threatened EU solidarity and initiated a policy response whereby the EU sought to reinforce its external border with the Western Balkans. Western Balkans actors cooperated with the EU to instigate a new border regime, in exchange for enhanced cooperation and rewards. This allowed the Western Balkan countries to exert leverage over the EU. This represents a further transformation in the relationship between the EU and these countries noted elsewhere from one traditionally defined by the EU's ability to expert power over these countries, to one where these countries are capable of leveraging power of the EU and resisting fundamental rule of law reforms (Zweers 2019; Kmezić 2020).

As the other contributions in this special issue have set out, the securitisation of migration can have a range of political consequences. This article highlighted the relationship between securitisation as a driver of migration politics and international relations. It demonstrated how the escalation of securitisation accelerated a change in policy and ultimately, EU-Western Balkans relations. While this contribution has focussed on the escalation of securitisation, it is important to acknowledge the possibility for de-escalation that was not exhibited in this case. De-escalation would initiative a change in policy and practice that reasserts a more humanitarian approach to migration. Based on the relationship established here, we can also predict that it would readjust relations between the EU and Western Balkans countries. The primary contribution of this article has been to demonstrate the interconnectedness of securitisation, migration politics and international relations. In doing so, it has demonstrated the explanatory value of research which is situated at the intersection between security studies, migration studies and international relations.

Notes

1. In respect to terminology, while the more general crisis inflicting the EU has been termed the migration crisis, the empirical focus of this paper is on a facet of this crisis, the refugee crisis that occurred in the Western Balkans. A clear majority of people moving through the Western Balkans between 2015 and 2016 were refugees, primarily from Syria.
2. Interviewee A, DG NEAR, Brussels. Interview conducted 6 June 2016.
3. The Western Balkans Summit were initially formulated as a forum for discussing UE Enlargement. With the onset of the crisis, establishing cooperation from the Western Balkans countries to tackle migration became a main priority of the forum. Source: Interview with former policy lead, DG NEAR, Brussels. Interview conducted 3 June 2016.
4. Interview with senior staff from the UNHCR, Belgrade. Interview conducted 28 February 2016.
5. Interviewee with staff, Centre for European Policy, Belgrade. Interview conducted 28 February 2016.
6. Interview with minister, Ministry of Justice, Belgrade. Interview conducted 20 April 2016.
7. Interview with former member of staff, IOM, Belgrade. Interview conducted 30 March 2016.
8. Interviewee with staff, Centre for European Policy, Belgrade. Interview conducted February 2016.
9. Interviewee with MEP, EU-Serbia Stabilisation and Association Parliamentary Committee (SAPC), Brussels. Interview conducted 15 June 2016.
10. Interview with two members of staff, Norwegian embassy, Belgrade (embassy also covers activity in Macedonia). Interview conducted 22 April 2016.
11. A series of meetings between leaders from the region and EU officials at the beginning of 2016 resulted in the prioritisation of migration. Although this technically occurred in parallel to a continued focus on rule of law reform, there was a perception amongst EU officials that migration had become the main priority of regional collaboration. Source: Interviewee A, DG NEAR, Brussels. Interview conducted 6 June 2016.
12. Two interviewees, one from the Serbian Ministry of Justice and the other from the Ministry of Interior communicated the expectation that cooperation with the EU on the issue would result in either a loosening of certain accession criteria. Interviews conducted in April and May 2016.
13. Interview with senior staff from the UNHCR, Belgrade. Interview conducted 28 February 2016.
14. Interview with minister for Serbian border police, Belgrade. Interview conducted 8 May 2016.
15. These violations included poor performance in the fight against corruption and pressure placed on judicial processes. Interview with former policy lead, DG NEAR, Brussels. Interview conducted 3 June 2016.
16. Interviewee A and Interviewee B, DG NEAR, Brussels. Interviews conducted 6 June 2016.
17. Interview with staff, Swiss Development Agency, Belgrade. Interview conducted April 2016.

Disclosure statement

No potential conflict of interest was reported by the author(s).

References

Adepoju, A., F. Van Noorloos, and A. Zoomers. 2010. "Europe's Migration Agreements with Migrant-Sending Countries in the Global South: A Critical Review." *International Migration* 48 (3): 42–75.

Allen, W., B. Anderson, N. V. Hear, M. Sumption, F. Düvell, J. Hough, L. Rose, R. Humphris, and S. Walker. 2017. "Who Counts in Crises? The New Geopolitics of International Migration and Refugee Governance." *Geopolitics* 0 (0): 1–27.

Amnesty. 2015. Lockdown at the Macedonian Border – Illegal Pushbacks of Refugees to Greece. Accessed 4 March 2016. https://www.amnesty.org/en/latest/news/2015/12/lockdown-at-the-macedonian-border/.

Arsenijević, J., E. Schillberg, A. Ponthieu, L. Malvisi, W. A. E. Ahmed, S. Argenziano, F. Zamatto, et al. 2017. "A Crisis of Protection and Safe Passage: Violence Experienced by Migrants/Refugees Travelling Along the Western Balkan Corridor to Northern Europe." *Conflict and Health* 11 (1): 6.

B92. 2015. State Budget Cannot Sustain Further Inflow of Migrants, July 16. Accessed 11 August 2017. http://www.b92.net/eng/news/politics.php?yyyy=2015&mm=07&dd=16&nav_id=94780.

B92. 2016a. Vucic Backs Merkel's Migrant Policy, Takes on Her Critics, January 28. Accessed 11 August 2017. http://www.b92.net/eng/news/politics.php?yyyy=2016&mm=01&dd=28&nav_id=96846.

B92. 2016b. Serbia 'To Protect Itself and Europe' from New Migrant Wave - - on B92.net, August 12. Accessed 1 August 2017. http://www.b92.net/eng/news/politics.php?yyyy=2016&mm=08&dd=12&nav_id=98893.

B92. 2016c. Border Patrols Prevent 2,275 Migrants from Entering Serbia - - on B92.net, August 16. Accessed 28 July 2017. http://www.b92.net/eng/news/politics.php?yyyy=2016&mm=08&dd=16&nav_id=98912.

B92. 2016d. Serbia to Protect Itself and Europe from New Migration Wave. Accessed 4 March 2018. https://www.b92.net/eng/news/politics.php?yyyy=2016&mm=08&dd=12&nav_id=98893.

Bauböck, R. 2018. "Refugee Protection and Burden-Sharing in the European Union." *JCMS: Journal of Common Market Studies* 56 (1): 141–156.

Bechev, D. 2006. "Carrots, Sticks and Norms: The EU and Regional Cooperation in Southeast Europe." *Journal of Southern Europe and the Balkans* 8 (1): 27–43.

Belgrade Centre for Human Rights. 2016. Safe Passage: Testimony of People Arriving in Dimitrovgrad, Serbia from Bulgaria. Accessed 1 August 2017. http://www.bgcentar.org.rs/bgcentar/eng-lat/wp-content/uploads/2015/12/Safe-Passage1.pdf.

Bello, V. 2017. *International Migration and International Security: Why Prejudice Is a Global Security Threat.* New York: Routledge.

Bello, V. 2022. "The Spiralling of the Securitisation of Migration in the EU: From the Management of a 'Crisis' to a Governance of Human Mobility?" *Journal of Ethnic and Migration Studies* 48 (6): 1327–1344. https://doi.org/10.1080/1369183X.2020.1851464.

Bialasiewicz, L. 2012. "Off-shoring and Out-Sourcing the Borders of Europe: Libya and EU Border Work in the Mediterranean." *Geopolitics* 17 (4): 843–866.

Bieber, F. 2011. "Building Impossible States? State-Building Strategies and EU Membership in the Western Balkans." *Europe-Asia Studies* 63 (10): 1783–1802.

Boswell, C. 2003. "The 'External Dimension' of EU Immigration and Asylum Policy." *International Affairs* 79 (3): 619–638.

Bulmer, S., and J. Joseph. 2016. "European Integration in Crisis? Of Supranational Integration, Hegemonic Projects and Domestic Politics." *European Journal of International Relations* 22 (4): 725–748.

Buzan, B., and O. Waever. 2003. *Regions and Powers: the Structure of International Security.* Cambridge: Cambridge University Press.

Byrne, R., G. Noll, and J. Vedsted-Hansen. 2004. "Understanding Refugee law in an Enlarged European Union." *European Journal of International Law* 15 (2): 355–379.

Carrera, S., L. Den Hertog, and J. Parkin. 2012. *EU Migration Policy in the Wake of the Arab Spring: What Prospects for EU-Southern Mediterranean Relations?* (SSRN Scholarly Paper No. ID 2135477). Rochester, NY: Social Science Research Network. Accessed 6 August 2017. https://papers-ssrn-com.sheffield.idm.oclc.org/abstract=2135477.

Cassarino, J. P. 2007. "Informalising Readmission Agreements in the EU Neighbourhood." *The International Spectator* 42 (2): 179–196. Accessed 10 August 2020. https://halshs.archives-ouvertes.fr/hal-01232695/document.

Ceyhan, A., and A. Tsoukala. 2002. "The Securitization of Migration in Western Societies: Ambivalent Discourses and Policies." *Alternatives: Global, Local, Political* 27 (1 suppl): 21–39.

Cocco, E. 2017. "Where is the European Frontier? The Balkan Migration Crisis and its Impact on Relations Between the EU and the Western Balkans." *European View* 16 (2): 293–302.

Collyer, M., and R. King. 2016. "Narrating Europe's Migration and Refugee 'Crisis'." *Human Geography: A New Radical Journal* 9 (2): 1–12.

Council of the European Union. 2015a. Eastern Mediterranean – Western Balkans route conference, 08/10/2015 – Consilium, October 8. Accessed 1 August 2017. http://www.consilium.europa.eu/en/meetings/jha/2015/10/08/.

Council of the European Union. 2015b. Declaration of the High-level Conference on the Eastern Mediterranean – Western Balkans Route, October 9. Accessed 14 July 2017. http://data.consilium.europa.eu/doc/document/ST-12876-2015-INIT/en/pdf.

de la Baume, M., and B. Surk. 2016. Macedonia Seeks Date for EU Membership Talks, March 17. Accessed 11 August 2017. http://www.politico.eu/article/macedonias-eu-membership-nightmare-refugees-migrants-border-nato/.

Düvell, F. 2012. "Transit Migration: A Blurred and Politicised Concept." *Population, Space and Place* 18 (4): 415–427.

EEAS. 2015. Western Balkans Leaders Agree on 17-point Plan on Migration –, October 26. Accessed 1 August 2017. https://eeas.europa.eu/headquarters/headquarters-homepage_en/2609/EU&WesternBalkansLeadersagreeon17-pointplanonmigration.

Elbasani, A. 2008. "EU Enlargement in the Western Balkans: Strategies of Borrowing and Inventing." *Journal of Southern Europe and the Balkans* 10 (3): 293–307.

Elbasani, A. 2013. *Europeanization Travels to the Western Balkans: Enlargement Strategy, Domestic Obstacles and Diverging Reforms.* (SSRN Scholarly Paper No. ID 2553282). Rochester, NY: Social Science Research Network. https://papers-ssrn-com.sheffield.idm.oclc.org/abstract=2553282.

EURACTIV. 2016. EU Gives Equipment to Help Serbia Control Migration, September 21. Accessed 28 July 2017. https://www.euractiv.com/section/enlargement/news/eu-gives-equipment-to-help-serbia-control-migration/.

European Commission. 2014. Enlargement Strategy 2014, October 8. Accessed 5 October 2017. https://ec.europa.eu/neighbourhood-enlargement/sites/near/files/pdf/key_documents/2014/20141008-strategy-paper_en.pdf

European Commission. 2015a. Enlargement Strategy 2015. Accessed 11 June 2016. http://ec.europa.eu/enlargement/pdf/key_documents/2015/20151110_strategy_paper_en.pdf

European Commission. 2015b. European Neighbourhood Policy and Enlargement Negotiations – Conditions for membership – European Commission. Accessed 6 November 2015. http://ec.europa.eu/enlargement/policy/conditions-membership/index_en.htm.

European Commission. 2015c. Press release: Special Meeting of the European Council, 23 April 2015 – statement – Consilium, April 23. Accessed 14 July 2017. http://www.consilium.europa.eu/en/press/press-releases/2015/04/23-special-euco-statement/.

European Commission. 2015d. Daily News 23/12/2015. Accessed 1 March 2019. http://europa.eu/rapid/press-release_MEX-15-6393_en.htm.

European Commission. 2015e. European Council – Keeping Up Momentum on the Management of Migration. Accessed 1 March 2019. http://europa.eu/rapid/press-release_AC-16-2026_en.htm.

European Commission. 2015f. Refugee Crisis: Commission Reviews 2015 Actions and Sets 2016 Priorities. Accessed 1 March 2019. http://europa.eu/rapid/press-release_AC-16-2026_en.htm.

European Commission. 2016a. European Commission – PRESS RELEASES – Press release – Implementing the European Agenda on Migration: Commission reports on progress in Greece, Italy and the Western Balkans, February 10. Accessed 7 July 2017. http://europa.eu/rapid/press-release_IP-16-269_en.htm.

European Commission. 2016b. The Former Yugoslav Republic of Macedonia: ECHO Factsheet, August. Accessed 28 July 2017. http://ec.europa.eu/echo/files/aid/countries/factsheets/fyrom_en.pdf.

European Commission. 2016c. Enlargement Strategy 2016, November 9. Accessed 14 November 2016.   http://ec.europa.eu/enlargement/pdf/key_documents/2016/20161109_strategy_paper_en.pdf.

European Commission. 2016d. Western Balkans Migration Route: European Commission supports UNHCR with resources for 200,000 refugees [Text], December 6. Accessed 21 July 2017. https://ec.europa.eu/home-affairs/what-is-new/news/news/2015/20151103_2_en.

European Commission. 2016e. Refugee Crisis: Commission Reviews 2015 Actions and Sets 2016 Priorities. Accessed 1 March 2018. http://europa.eu/rapid/press-release_IP-16-65_en.htm.

European Parliament. 2016. The Western Balkans: Frontline of the Migrant Crisis. Accessed 4 March 2017. http://www.europarl.europa.eu/RegData/etudes/BRIE/2016/573949/EPRS_BRI (2016)573949_EN.pdf.

European Western Balkans. 2016. Factsheet: EU Assistance for Migrants and Refugees in Serbia, March 17. Accessed 28 July 2017. https://europeanwesternbalkans.com/2016/03/17/factsheet-eu-assistance-for-migrants-and-refugees-in-serbia/.

European Western Balkans. 2017. EU's Assistance to Macedonia for the Refugee Crisis Amounts to EUR 19 Million, January 13. Accessed 28 July 2017. https://europeanwesternbalkans.com/2017/01/13/eus-assistance-to-macedonia-for-the-refugee-crisis-amounts-to-eur-19-million/.

Falkner, G. 2016. "The EU's Current Crisis and its Policy Effects: Research Design and Comparative Findings." *Journal of European Integration* 38 (3): 219–235.

Ferrero-Waldner, B. 2006. "Guest Editorial: The European Neighbourhood Policy: The Eu's Newest Foreign Policy Instrument." *European Foreign Affairs Review* 11 (2): 139–142.

France Diplomatie. 2016. Final Declaration by the Chair of the Paris Western Balkans Summit (4 July 2016). Accessed 4 March 2019. https://www.diplomatie.gouv.fr/en/country-files/balkans/events/article/final-declaration-by-the-chair-of-the-paris-western-balkans-summit-04-06-16.

Geddes, A. 2005. "Europe's Border Relationships and International Migration Relations." *JCMS: Journal of Common Market Studies* 43 (4): 787–806.

Geddes, A. 2015. "Temporary and Circular Migration in the Construction of European Migration Governance." *Cambridge Review of International Affairs* 28 (4): 571–588.

Geddes, A., and L. Hadj-Abdou. 2018. "Changing the Path? EU Migration Governance After the 'Arab Spring'." *Mediterranean Politics* 23 (1): 142–160.

Geddes, A., and P. Scholten. 2016. *The Politics of Migration and Immigration in Europe*. London: SAGE.

Gruevski, N. 2015. We Must Work Together to Help the Migrants, December 23. Accessed 1 August 2017. http://www.newsweek.com/we-must-work-together-help-migrants-408654.

Heisbourg, F. 2015. "The Strategic Implications of the Syrian Refugee Crisis." *Survival* 57 (6): 7–20.

Human Rights Watch. 2015. Dispatches: Asylum Seekers Stuck on the Serbia-Bulgaria Border, December 7. Accessed 1 August 2017. https://www.hrw.org/news/2015/12/07/dispatches-asylum-seekers-stuck-serbia-bulgaria-border.

Human Rights Watch. 2016a. Bulgaria: Pushbacks, Abuse at Borders, January 20. Accessed 1 August 2017. https://www.hrw.org/news/2016/01/20/bulgaria-pushbacks-abuse-borders.

Human Rights Watch. 2016b. Hungary: Migrants Abused at the Border, July 13. Accessed 1 August 2017. https://www.hrw.org/news/2016/07/13/hungary-migrants-abused-border.

Human Rights Watch. 2017. Croatia: Asylum Seekers Forced Back to Serbia, January 20. Accessed 1 August 2017. https://www.hrw.org/news/2017/01/20/croatia-asylum-seekers-forced-back-serbia.

Huysmans, J. 2000. "The European Union and the Securitization of Migration." *JCMS: Journal of Common Market Studies* 38 (5): 751–777.

Kmezić, M. 2020. "Recalibrating the EU's Approach to the Western Balkans." *European View* 19 (1): 54–61.

Kogovšek Šalamon, N. 2016. "Asylum Systems in the Western Balkan Countries: Current Issues." *International Migration* 54 (6): 151–163.

Laffan, B. 2016. "Europe's Union in Crisis: Tested and Contested." *West European Politics* 39 (5): 915–932.

Lavenex, S. 2001. "The Europeanization of Refugee Policies: Normative Challenges and Institutional Legacies." *JCMS: Journal of Common Market Studies* 39 (5): 851–874.

Lavenex, S. 2006. "Shifting Up and Out: The Foreign Policy of European Immigration Control." *West European Politics* 29 (2): 329–350.

Léonard, S. 2010. "EU Border Security and Migration Into the European Union: FRONTEX and Securitisation Through Practices." *European Security* 19 (2): 231–254.

Lilyanova, V. 2016. The Western Balkans: Frontline of the migrant crisis. European Parliamentary Research Service. Accessed June 2016. http://www.europarl.europa.eu/RegData/etudes/BRIE/2016/573949/EPRS_BRI(2016)573949_EN.pdf.

Manners, I. 2002. "Normative Power Europe: A Contradiction in Terms?" *JCMS: Journal of Common Market Studies* 40 (2): 235–258.

McDonald, M. 2008. "Securitization and the Construction of Security." *European Journal of International Relations* 14 (4): 563–587.

Neal, A. W. 2009. "Securitization and Risk at the EU Border: The Origins of FRONTEX." *JCMS: Journal of Common Market Studies* 47 (2): 333–356.

Nenov, S. 2016. Greece Condemns Macedonia Tear Gas and Rubber Bullets Against Migrants. *Reuters*. Accessed April 10 2016. https://www.reuters.com/article/us-europe-migrants-greece-teargas/macedonian-police-use-teargas-on-migrants-at-greek-border-idUSKCN0X70CD.

Niemann, A., and N. Zaun. 2018. "EU Refugee Policies and Politics in Times of Crisis: Theoretical and Empirical Perspectives." *JCMS: Journal of Common Market Studies* 56 (1): 3–22.

Noutcheva, G. 2009. "Fake, Partial and Imposed Compliance: The Limits of the EU's Normative Power in the Western Balkans." *Journal of European Public Policy* 16 (7): 1065–1084.

Noutcheva, G., and S. Aydin-Düzgit. 2012. "Lost in Europeanisation: The Western Balkans and Turkey." *West European Politics* 35 (1): 59–78.

Oxfam, G. B. 2017. Exposed: Abuse of Migrants by State Officials on Europe's Borders, April 6. Accessed 1 August 2017. http://www.oxfam.org.uk/media-centre/press-releases/2017/04/exposed-abuse-of-migrants-by-state-officials-on-europe-borders-balkans.

Paoletti, E. 2010. *The Migration of Power and North-South Inequalities: The Case of Italy and Libya.* London: Palgrave Macmillan.

Peshkopia, R. 2015. *Conditioning Democratization: Institutional Reforms and EU Membership Conditionality in Albania and Macedonia.* London: Anthem Press.

Post, National. 2016, March 8. *Gjorge Ivanov: Europe's Deepening Migrant Crisis.* Accessed 12 March 2019. https://nationalpost.com/opinion/gjorge-ivanov-europes-deepening-migrant-crisis.

Rajkovic, N. M. 2012. *The Politics of International law and Compliance: Serbia, Croatia and the Hague Tribunal.* London: Routledge.

Schimmelfennig, F. 2005. "Strategic Calculation and International Socialization: Membership Incentives, Party Constellations, and Sustained Compliance in Central and Eastern Europe." *International Organization*, 59 (4) 827–860.

Schimmelfennig, F., and U. Sedelmeier. 2004. "Governance by Conditionality: EU Rule Transfer to the Candidate Countries of Central and Eastern Europe." *Journal of European Public Policy* 11 (4): 661–679.

Scipioni, M. 2018. "Failing Forward in EU Migration Policy? EU Integration After the 2015 Asylum and Migration Crisis." *Journal of European Public Policy*, 25 (9) 1357–1375.

Scott, J. W., F. Celata, and R. Coletti. 2019. "Bordering Imaginaries and the Everyday Construction of the Mediterranean Neighbourhood: Introduction to the Special Issue." *European Urban and Regional Studies* 26 (1): 3–8.

Seeberg, P. 2013. "The Arab Uprisings and the EU's Migration Policies—The Cases of Egypt, Libya, and Syria." *Democracy and Security* 9 (1-2): 157–176.

Slominski, P., and F. Trauner. 2018. "How do Member States Return Unwanted Migrants? The Strategic (non-)use of 'Europe' During the Migration Crisis." *JCMS: Journal of Common Market Studies* 56 (1): 101–118.

Spasov, A. 2016. A Macedonian Perspective on the Migration Crisis. Accessed 28 July 2017. https://www.clingendael.nl/publication/macedonian-perspective-migration-crisis.

Stritzel, H. 2007. "Towards a Theory of Securitization: Copenhagen and Beyond." *European Journal of International Relations* 13 (3): 357–383.

Trauner, F. 2016. "Asylum Policy: The EU's 'Crises' and the Looming Policy Regime Failure." *Journal of European Integration* 38 (3): 311–325.

Vachudova, M. A. 2005. *Europe Undivided: Democracy, Leverage, and Integration After Communism*. Oxford: OUP.

Vachudova, M. A. 2014. "EU Leverage and National Interests in the Balkans: The Puzzles of Enlargement Ten Years On." *JCMS: Journal of Common Market Studies* 52 (1): 122–138.

Vertovec, S. 2017. "Mooring, Migration Milieus and Complex Explanations." *Ethnic and Racial Studies* 40 (9): 1574–1581.

Wunsch, N., N. Dimitrov, and S. Cvijic. 2016. The Migrant Crisis: A Catalyst for EU Enlargement? Balkans in Europe Policy Advisory Group. Accessed 5 October 2018. http://www.bosch-stiftung.de/content/language1/downloads/The_migrant_crisis_a_catalyst_for_EU_enlargement.pdf.

Zweers, W. 2019. Between Effective Engagement and Damaging Politicisation: Prospects for Credible EU Enlargement Policy to the Western Balkans. *Clingendael*. Accessed 18 August 2020. https://www.clingendael.org/sites/default/files/2019-05/PB_Western_Balkans_May19.pdf.

People as security risks: the framing of migration in the UK security-development nexus

Eamonn McConnon

ABSTRACT

The migration of people across international borders has long been an area of concern for the UK and was a key issue in the public debate surrounding Brexit. This paper examines this preoccupation with the movement of people in the context of the coordination of security and development in UK government policy. The UK responded to the migration crisis of 2015 by announcing the diversion of significant development funding to prevent the movement of people. This paper examines the UK development policy discourse of the past 2 decades through an analysis of key policy documents from the UK's Department for International Development (DfID) and traces the changing ways in which the issue of migration has been framed in DfID's policy. It argues that in UK development policy, whereas migration used to be discussed in terms of how it impacts on poorer countries, migration is now framed as a risk to UK national security. Development aid is now framed as a solution to the problem of migration. This paper argues that this is consistent with a broader shift in the merging of security and development in UK policy where development aid is expected to address potential risks to UK national security.

Introduction

The extent to which the movement of people across international borders has become a security issue is evident in the way the issue of migration is prevalent in public debate in the UK and was a crucial factor in the vote to leave the EU in June 2016. There was a strong anti-immigration strand to the pro-Brexit campaign with little nuance on distinguishing who was migrating from where. While the act of leaving the EU would only restrict migration from within the EU and not international migration there was occasionally a conflation of the two issues in public discourse (Glencross 2016, 3; Hobolt 2016, 1260; Evans 2017, 218). This public concern over migration is indicative of what Bello (2017) describes as the spiralling securitisation of migration, where multiple actors contribute to framing the movement of people as a security threat. The UK has responded to the on-going migration crisis in the Mediterranean by announcing the diversion of significant development funding to prevent the movement of people. In the coordination of security and development policy, migration is a crucial issue as it has direct links to development problems and is also framed as a threat to UK national security (DfID, MoD, FCO 2011, 8). These connections are summed up in the UK's 2015 *National Security and Defence Review*:

> The UK's development assistance also makes a significant contribution to our long-term national security and prosperity. Tackling poverty and instability overseas means tackling the root causes of many of the global challenges that we face including disease, migration and terrorism. (HMG 2015, 48)

Here the role of development aid is to tackle migration, which is framed as a national security problem for the UK on a par with terrorism and disease.

From the establishment of the Department for International Development (DfID) in 1997–2019, there has been a shift in how 'security' is defined in UK development policy discourse. As detailed by McConnon (2019, 125–132) in the late 1990s, DfID set clear limits on how development actors should get involved in security issues. 'Security' referred to the wellbeing of people in the developing world and it was stated that DfID should not get involved in any situation where development goals would be subverted by military concerns (DfID 1999, 6–7). Post-9/11, during the early and mid-2000s the definition of 'security' was broadened to also include issues such as terrorism and radicalisation, but DfID reiterated its commitment to prioritising the poorest and most vulnerable rather than security concerns (DfID 2005a, 5,6,13). From the late 2000s into the 2010s, there was another shift in DfID's policy to arguing that UK national security is a development issue (McConnon 2014, 1139–1141; 2019, 129–132; Wild and Elhaawary 2016, 44–45). Given the relevance of migration to the security-development nexus, a key question to ask is how has migration now come to be framed as a risk to UK national security? This question allows an investigation into the extent to which DfID as a state actor contributes to the spiralling securitisation of migration through an emphasis on security rather than a desecuritisation through an emphasis on human rights and the mutual benefits of migration. To explore this connection, this article examines UK development policy discourse of the past two decades through an analysis of key UK development policy documents and collaborative development, security and foreign policy documents.

Overall while there is a volume of literature dealing with the linkages between two of these three aspects there is a dearth of research on the intersection of all three of security-development-migration. For example, there are significant bodies of research on the issues of how security relates to development, how migration is connected to security and on how development intersects with migration. However, far less attention is given to how migration has become both a development *and* a security issue.

The case of the UK differs to that of other donors in a number of ways. One of which is that it engaged with the linkages between migration and development in the 1990s, earlier than many donors who only engaged with it during the 2000s, for example, Sweden, Denmark and Germany (Sørensen 2012, 65). The US has not framed migration in a positive way in development policy and has used its development aid to reinforce border capabilities and restrict migration in neighbouring countries such as Mexico and Colombia (Koff 2017, 11–13). As a collective donor, the EU brought migration into development policy in the 2000s, at a much later stage than the UK (Koff 2017, 16–18). Sørensen (2012, 66) argues that this is because of concern with increased migration from Sub Saharan Africa to the EU.

The EU has a number of mobility partnerships with third countries. These are non-binding agreements but they intend to externalise the management of migration to the EU and can make development aid conditional on cooperation on migration control measures (Brocza and Paulhart 2015, 6; Carrera et al. 2016, 13; Carrera, Hertog, and Parkin 2012, 6). This approach is problematic and the idea that capacity building through development aid can be an effective means of preventing migration has been strongly contested. de Haas, Miller and Castles (2020) argue that social transformation and development often increases the intensity of migration. As education and access to technology increases so does curiosity about the rest of the world (Collyer 2019, 171). Denmark also introduced migration into development policy later than DfID initially through the concept of 'poverty refugees' and poverty as a recognised reason to flee (Sørensen 2016, 67). The UK is an interesting case in that DfID's poverty focused approach to development may have more in common with Denmark or Sweden, its national security concerns are closer to that of the US- its ally in the War on Terror.

This article contributes to this special issue by exploring in-depth the case of the UK and how it has framed migration as a development and a security issue over an extended period of time. The key theoretical core of this special issue is the spiralling securitisation of migration and the investigation of 'the securitisation of migration is pushed and pulled through opposite dynamics, with upwarding and downwarding forces spiralling its process' (Bello 2022, 9). This article offers a contextual insight into this process through a detailed analysis of how the UK's framing of migration in development policy has shifted away from a 'upwarding' understanding of the development benefits of migration towards to a 'downwarding' framing of migration as a risk to UK national security.

This article begins with a discussion of the literature on migration, security and development. Second, is an outline of the sample of policy documents used in this analysis. Third is a discussion of three different frames through which UK policy presents the movement of people over this time: movement as opportunity, movement as disruption and movement as danger. Fourth is a discussion of how the movement of people is now treated as a security issue which development aid is expected to address.

Linking migration to security and development

The closer coordination between security and development actors gained prominence in the post-Cold War period of the 1990s. This closer relationship between security and development was a response to the proliferation of civil conflict in countries already suffering from development problems. There is disagreement in the literature as to the benefits of this relationship. Some scholars are optimistic that it can be mutually beneficial (Picciotto 2010; Stewart 2004) while others are critical, claiming that it has resulted in development goals being subordinated to the militaristic national security considerations of donor states (Abrahamsen 2005; Carmody 2005; Duffield 2006, 2007, 2010). The UK is an interesting case as its development agency DfID is viewed as one of the more progressive in the way that it has made poverty alleviation its core mandate and has untied its aid from the purchase of British goods and services (Baulch 2006, 940; Chhotray and Hulme 2009, 38). This is significant as previously the UK government viewed overseas aid as a means of promoting British industry abroad (Barder 2007, 286). UK development aid was seen as a way of maintaining closer relationships with former colonies and ensuring the continuation of trade practices into the post-colonial period (McKinlay and Little 1978, 323). While this tying of development aid to the purchase of British goods and services declined from 50% in the 1980s to 15% in the 1990s (Barder 2007, 287), the decision to eliminate tied aid in 2002 was a progressive step. It was ahead of other countries such as Canada, which took until 2015 to untie aid, and the US which still uses tied aid.

There is disagreement in the literature over the merits of DfID bringing security into its development policy. Some scholars argue that security in DfID's policy is still focused on the security of those in the developing world (Wild and Elhawary 2016; Pugh, Gabay, and William 2013) others argue that this move has led DfID to prioritise UK national security (Abrahamsen 2005; McConnon 2014, 2019). The term security-development nexus is a broad one encompassing many different actors. This article examines the migration-security-development nexus as it relates to the incorporation of security issues into the development policy of bilateral donors, specifically the UK. The difficulty with the literature in this area is that relatively few studies address how migration, development and security are inter-related. As Ninna Nyberg Sørensen asserts 'Migration, development and security are integrally linked but habitually studied in "pairs"' (Sørensen 2012, 62). There is a large body of work on how migration connects to security separately (Bigo 2001; Bourbeau 2015; Huysmans 2000; Sørensen 2012) and how migration connects to development separately (Beine, Docquier, and Rapoport 2008; de Haas 2012; Gamso and Yuldashev 2018; Lowell and Findlay 2001; Stark, Helmenstein, and Prskawetz 1997). However, while there are some key contributions (Smith 2016; Sørensen 2012, 2016; Tirtosudarmo 2018; Williams 2016) the linkages between all three remain underexplored.

How migration has become a security concern is challenged in the literature. It is argued to be a means through which security agencies compete with each other for prominence, rather than a new security threat in itself (Bigo 2001, 121). Furthermore, these associations between migration and insecurity for the host country are constructed through racist stereotypes (Bigo 2002, 66; Bourbeau 2015, 1970). This process is part of what Bello (2017) describes as the 'spiralling securitisation of migration' where both state and non-state actors contribute through policy, language, bureaucratic processes and practices to the framing of migrants as a security threat. These discourses connecting migration to security are also argued to be a means of asserting national identities in a diverse European Union without internal borders (Huysmans 2000, 770). Within these connections between security and migration there is little consideration given to the diverse types of migration for example whether asylum seeker, refugee or economic migrant. For example, Bello (2017, 60) highlights the way in which border control classifies people as eligible to claim asylum or not eligible. She disaggregates the numerous different types of migrant experience which are subsumed in this broad category of 'ineligible' including people who have never moved country and were born in the host country but do not have legal status.

One problematic view of the connection between development and migration is that investing development aid in building the capacity of a country will reduce the need for migration. Caselli (2019) refers to this as the 'help them at home approach'. This idea is contested because evidence suggests that as countries develop, migration actually increases due to raised standards of education, curiosity about the rest of the world and the desire to fulfil expanded ambitions (de Haas, Miller and Castles 2020; Clemens 2014; Collyer 2019, 171). Furthermore where migrant flows are from conflict affected countries or those under heavy authoritarian rule the conditions are not fruitful for the development process to begin (Caselli 2019, 984). This is an important point because many donors including the UK subscribe to the idea of capacity building as a means of reducing migration.

The arguments in the literature on linkages between migration and development disagree on the potential benefits of migration for poverty alleviation (Lowell and Findlay 2001; Stark, Helmenstein, and Prskawetz 1997) and the negative impact of brain drain that migration has on development (Beine, Docquier, and Rapoport 2008). The logic of the literature pessimistic about the development benefits of migration is that it is another form of exploitation of the Global South and the outward movement of human resources is a cause of underdevelopment in itself (Beine, Docquier, and Rapoport 2008). The optimistic view of the benefits of migration for development centre on two things: the large sums of remittances that migrants send back to their home country and the potential for returning migrants to bring about social and economic change based on their experiences of living in the West (Sørensen 2016, 65). de Haas (2012, 9) describes this as a pendulum of development thinking which has swung from being optimistic about the impact of migration on development to being negative about it and back to being positive. This narrative was driven largely by the World Bank's assertion of the positive impact of remittances on development in the late 1990s/early 2000s (Sørensen 2016, 71). This debate is relevant for this study of the UK as the New Labour government championed free-markets and freedom of movement (Driver and Martell 2002). DfID was balancing a belief in globalisation and the free-market with observations of the negative impact these were having in some developing countries. As discussed below, DfID references both these ideas of migration alleviating poverty and also causing a 'brain drain' for developing economies. As such both sides of the de Haas's pendulum swing are evident in DfID policy.

As Sørensen (2012, 63) points out the body of literature on the linkages between security, development and migration is not as comprehensive. There is more research on the theoretical and conceptual side of this relationship than on practical concrete examples. Duffield (2006, 77) argues that controlling migration is just one way in which security and development cooperation is a form of governmental control. Truong and Gasper (2011) explore how migration legislation priorities the nation state over people. Tirtosudarmo (2019) argues that the understanding of migration as a security problem is rooted in global inequality and Northern assumptions about the Global South as a source of danger. Furthermore, Adrian Smith (2016, 2130) argues that both positive and negative understandings of migration are rooted in global inequalities between North and South resulting from racialised global capitalist relations. While these works offer valuable theoretical insights they raise the question of how migration is framed as both a development and security issue in specific cases. How do donors engage with these arguments and has this changed over time?

Addressing these questions to some extent Sørensen (2012) gives an overview of how security has been brought into broader development policy considerations of the potential connections between migration and development. She raises the question of whether this connection has put development policy at the service of migration control (Sørensen 2012, 66). Sørensen (2012) proposes a view of migration that encompasses both migrants and their trans-border networks on one hand and the state policies and practices aimed at controlling that migration. In terms of studying this relationship in a specific context, Williams (2016) details the process by which the US-Mexico border has become increasingly militarised. She traces the process by which migrant deaths were framed as a safety issue and increased militarisation of the border was justified as a means of saving migrant lives (Williams 2016, 31). Sørensen's (2016) work on Denmark highlights how migration was brought into Danish development policy during the 2000s and the controversy this caused in political circles. Sørensen (2016, 72) links these changes in discourse on migration and development to political dynamics in Denmark. She argues that it led to policy incoherence with Denmark framing migration and resulting remittances as important for development while at the same time taking a hard line on migration domestically. While Sørensen's (2016) work provides an essential account of how Denmark brought migration into its development policy during the 2000s, it does not address the security aspect of this relationship in sufficient depth.

As a result, there is no in-depth study into how specific donors have brought the issue of migration into the security-development policy space over an extended period. Given the prominent position the UK plays as an aid donor and the pre-occupation with migration domestically it is an interesting case to explore the policy linkages between migration development and security. Abrahamsen (2005, 74) suggested back in the mid-2000s that presenting the developing world as a source of terrorism and danger for the UK has resulted in more exclusionary public attitudes to migrants based on fear. It is also a useful case to investigate the extent to which development policy contributes to what Bello (2017) refers to as either a securitisation or desecuritisation of migration. To build on these contributions, this article draws on a systematic analysis of key policy documents to better understand the changes in representations of migration as a development and security problem in DfID policy discourse. Exploring this case allows a number of questions to be addressed: how has the framing of migration as a development-security issue changed over time? Do these changes contribute to an upwarding or downwarding of the spiralling securitisation of migration as outlined by Bello (2022). How do these changes relate to broader changes in foreign and security policy?

Exploring UK development policy positions over time

This article explores the UK's framing of migration as both a development and a security issue through an analysis of key policy documents from DfID's founding in 1997–2019. This period saw greater efforts to coordinate policy across the UK government with departments working together (Barder 2007, 298). Resulting in a number of jointly published policy documents and coordinating institutions between DfID, the Ministry of Defence (MoD) and the Foreign and Common Wealth Office (FCO). Many of these institutions have endured beyond the life of the Labour government. In studying the UKs framing of migration as a development and security problem, it is, therefore, necessary to look beyond just DfID's documents and include relevant foreign policy and security documents that also address UK development policy.

Through a discourse analysis of 16 key documents from DfID including collaborative documents with the Ministry of Defence (MoD) and the Foreign and Common Wealth Office (FCO), detailed in Table 1 below, this article examines how migration is understood as a security, and development issue. This time period allows an observation of contrasting perspectives between different governments with Labour in power from 1997 to 2010, the Conservative/Liberal Democrat coalition in charge from 2010 to 2015. From this empirical analysis this article argues that in this security/development space, migration is framed in different ways over this period of time. Drawing on this empirical analysis of documents, this article identifies three frames which are used in UK development policy: (1) movement as opportunity – migration is seen in a positive way having economic benefits; (2) movement as disruption – migration is seen as destabilising for neighbouring countries; (3) movement as danger – migration is seen as a security risk not just for developing countries but for the UK. The identification of these three different ways in which migration is represented allows a nuanced analysis of the process by which migration has come to be framed as a national security risk in UK development policy. This article adds to the existing literature an empirical contribution through this in-depth analysis of the case of the UK over a 20 year period and also a theoretical one by couching this analysis within the broader context of the spiralling securitisation of migration.

Movement as opportunity

From a development perspective in UK policy, the movement of people is at times considered a positive thing. Migration is argued to have economic benefits for developing countries as a means of alleviating poverty where a family member will migrate seasonally in order to cope during times of distress or shortage 'Poor people typically engage in a diverse range of economic activity … often migrating seasonally or longer term between rural and urban economies, in order to find the best opportunities for improving their livelihoods' (DfID 2000, 32). This position is clearly articulated in the 2007 policy

Table 1. Sample of UK documents.

Agency	Year	Publication Title
DfID	1997	Eliminating World Poverty: A Challenge for the Twenty-First Century
DfID	1999	Poverty and the Security Sector
DfID	2000	Eliminating World Poverty: Making Globalisation Work for the Poor
DfID MoD FCO	2001	The Causes of Conflict in Sub Saharan Africa
DfID MoD FCO	2003	The Global Conflict Prevention Pool: A Joint UK Government Approach to Reducing Conflict
DfID MoD and FCO	2004	The Africa Conflict Prevention Pool: An Information Document
DfID	2005a	Fighting Poverty to Build a Safer World: A Strategy for Security and Development
DfID	2005b	Failed States Strategy
DfID	2007	Moving out of Poverty: Making Migration Work Better for Poor People
DfID	2006	Eliminating World Poverty: Making Governance Work for the Poor
DfID	2009	Eliminating World Poverty: Building Our Common Future
DfID MoD and FCO	2011	Building Stability Overseas Strategy
DfID	2011	UK aid: Changing Lives, Delivering Results
DfID	2015	UK Aid: Tackling Global Challenges in the National Interest.
Her Majesty's Government	2015	National Security Strategy and Strategic Defence and Security Review 2015: A Secure and Prosperous United Kingdom
DfID	2019	Governance for Growth, Stability and Inclusive Development

document on migration and poverty 'migration has the potential to support the achievement of the Millennium Development Goals (MDGs) and to improve poor people's lives' (DfID 2007, 2). In this frame, migration is viewed as a necessary coping mechanism for dealing with poverty and economic distress. During times of shortage, a family member migrating either seasonally or long-term will be able to provide income to help get through a period of difficulty. Mobility is not only necessary but is also beneficial with remittances serving as a source of income and new ideas brought by returning migrants a source of economic stimulus:

> Planning for and managing migration can help both to reduce poverty and meet the demand for labour in developed countries. It can also have a positive social and political impact as successful migrants return home. Money sent back by migrants plays an important part in sustaining the local economy. (DfID 2006, 69)

Mobility is essential as a means of poverty alleviation, which is DfID's primary mandate. When a single family member migrates, the resources generated by this allow the rest of the family to remain in their area. Without this relief, mass migration is a possibility with whole families being forced to move during times of distress.

Following on from this it is argued that barriers to the movement of people are problematic and should be improved. DfID asserts that more modern airports and easier customs and immigration procedures are essential for allowing the movement of people between developing countries (DfID 2000, 42). In contrast to the 3rd framing, openness and ease of movement are desirable and essential for economic growth and poverty alleviation. This is a clear example of what de Haas (2012, 9) describes as the policy swing to highlighting the benefits of migration. Grounded in the neo-liberal understanding of economic development migration is framed as mutually beneficial for all parties. It is also an instance of what Bello (2017, 66) describes as the use of language which has the potential to desecuritise migration. By highlighting the positive benefits of migration for both host countries and countries of origin at this point DfID challenges the spiralling securitisation of migration.

When conflict is discussed it is in terms of how it disrupts this necessary movement of people 'The interrelated nature of African economies also means that the costs of war within a region generally result in economic costs for neighbouring countries. These include production losses through the loss of opportunities for migration' (DfID, MoD, FCO 2001, 12). Rather than migration being a negative consequence of conflict, at this stage that lack of opportunity to migrate is a negative outcome of conflict. The only negative associated with migration in this frame is the possible drain of resources on developing countries with migration to wealthier countries. The benefits for developing countries receiving migrants is highlighted, but also the negative consequences of a drain of talent from developing countries 'But these outflows (of migrants) can also be a drain on human resources in critically short supply. We are undertaking more research on this issue' (DfID 2000, 43). The proposed solution to this is greater development efforts targeted at out-migration countries. Again this shows a recognition of what de Haas (2012, 9) calls the policy swing to a pessimistic view of the negative development effects of migration.

This understanding of migration is consistent with the Labour government's broader socio-economic policy during this period. Tony Blair led Labour to power in 1997 on a platform that proposed a 'Third Way' which combined socialist issues such as social justice and equal opportunity with neoliberal issues such as globalisation and open markets (Rose 2000). One of Labour's campaign promises was the establishment of DfID as a separate government department with the aim of refocusing UK development policy on poverty reduction rather than on a trade or foreign policy agenda (Short 2004). Evident in this article's analysis is the tension between the positive framing of migration a driver of development through remittances coupled with a concern that migration is a drain on human resources in origin countries leading to further restrictions on development. This tension is indicative of New Labour's attempts to find a 'third way'. This assertion of the positive benefits of migration is important because they do not appear in any documents later than 2007 and are markedly different to later understandings of migration as an overwhelmingly negative.

Movement as disruption

When the movement of people is framed in a negative way it is mostly in terms of the forced movement of refugees by conflict. In this frame, mobility is negative because of the disruption it causes to neighbouring countries: 'Instability in one country can spill over to the region. So can refugees, disease, and crime' (DfID 2005b, 3) When migration is discussed in this way it is to highlight core development problems of poverty, inequality and climate change as causes of forced migration (DfID 2000, 14). The threat and danger caused by the movement of people in this frame is to developing countries that receive migrants (DfID 1997, 67; DfID, MoD, FCO 2001, 12) and the migrant populations themselves who are at risk of disease and illness

> Increased migration, whether for economic or political reasons, conflict or natural disasters, has also caused health problems arising from the loss of traditional safety nets and the adaptation to new environments. Displaced populations tend to be particularly vulnerable to communicable diseases such as malaria, meningitis, pneumonia and diarrhoea. (DfID 2000, 32)

Even when migration is understood as a risk in this way the potential benefits are still highlighted:

> Developed countries can help poor people make the most of migration by: helping countries plan for and manage the consequences of it; understanding better the impact of their own immigration policies on development; supporting the efforts of migrant groups to help their home communities; and helping people to invest at home by making money transfers easier. (DfID 2006, 70)

In this frame, there is still a positive relationship between migration and development and if it is a problem, it is a problem to be managed rather than prevented outright. While the dangers of migration are recognised, these are only discussed in terms of the negative impact on developing countries receiving migrants and on migrant populations themselves. In this frame, when security and development overlap, the referent object of security is people experiencing poverty in the Global South.

A key feature of DfID policy during this time was not just to react to development problems but also to engage with the broader global problems behind them. This was part of DfID's expanded remit and it involved conflict being brought into development policy.

The UK became involved in a number of conflicts over this period including interventions in Kosovo in 1999 and the Sierra Leone in 2000. These were presented as humanitarian in nature and required limited military involvement. However, subsequent UK military interventions in Afghanistan in 2001 and Iraq in 2003 were far more complex involving lengthy involvement and significant resources. The Iraq conflict was a source of significant public and political opposition, especially when no weapons of mass destruction were found (Roe 2008, 624). It meant that DfID's involvement in conflict was no longer confined to limited, short-term humanitarian interventions but also as part of post-invasion state-building in Iraq and Afghanistan alongside a military still actively engaged in combat (McConnon 2019). The awareness of conflict as an issue in migration and the disruptive effects that mass migration can have on development are indicative of DfID's direct engagement with security and conflict issues during this time. This second frame introduces the idea of migration as a danger albeit as a danger to those living in the Global South. Importantly, there is no reference to the national security of the UK as a priority in migration as a development and security issue. The referent object of security is still people living in the Global South. However, this changes in the next phase and the referent object of security is the UK itself. When the migration is framed as a danger it is now a danger to UK national security. This shift is consistent with a broader change in UK development policy of arguing that development policy should address UK national security needs.

Movement as danger

Within this frame, the movement of people is understood as a danger to international security and UK national security in particular. The trope that conflict in faraway places can result in security risks for the UK is consistently highlighted. This danger comes from conflict in the developing world which results in the movement of people to the UK:

> Our common security depends on the emergence of stable and effective states around the world. Instability of fragile countries does not respect international borders. Eight of the top ten UK asylum applicant nationalities are from fragile countries. (DfID 2009, 16)

In this frame, weak/fragile/failed states are singled out as the cause of large scale movement of people. The point that fragile states are providing the majority of asylum applicants to the UK is blunt in identifying asylum seekers as a source of 'instability' for the UK.

This flow of people is also placed in the same category as other problems caused by state fragility such as terrorism, criminality and drug trafficking

> In our interconnected world, the effect of violence in one region can spread to other more stable areas through refugee flows, terrorist activity, and organised crime groups, all of which can have an impact on our own security. Five countries -all in the midst of conflict -produced 60% of the world's refugees in 2009. (DfID, MoD, FCO 2011, 8)

Placing migration alongside these security problems of terrorism, drugs and criminality is a big shift from highlighting the benefits of migration. This connection between migration and threats to UK national security is repeated consistently in development policy over this time (DfID 2015, 13, 17; DfID 2019, 22; HMG 2015, 48). This connection is even made by Prime Minister Teresa May during her state visit to South Africa in 2018:

> I'm all too aware that our domestic security is reliant on stability worldwide, not just in our immediate neighbourhood. From reducing drivers of illegal migration to denying refuge to terrorists who would strike our shores, in 2018 African and British security are inextricably linked and mutually dependent. (May 2018)

These remarks again make this connection between instability and insecurity in Africa, migration, terrorism and UK national security. While the potential dangers of migration are highlighted earlier than 2009 (DfID, MoD, FCO 2001, 12) in previous phases they are also offset by reiteration of the positive aspects of migration. However, in this third phase migration is only mentioned as a problem and discussed as a danger caused by conflict and state fragility in the Global South. This connection of migration to conflict and insecurity in the Global South and security threats to the UK represents a shift away from DfID's earlier position of desecuritising language towards the securitisation of migration. How this shift to framing migration as a national security issue to be addressed by development policy and how it relates to these domestic political changes requires further discussion and is the subject of the next section.

'Development in the national (security) interest'

A key question raised by this finding is what has driven this shift? This frame also coincides with a time-period of significant political upheaval in the UK. The Labour Party's 13 years in power came to an end in 2010 with the election of the Conservative-Liberal Democrat coalition government led by Prime Minister David Cameron. The Conservative Party were returned with a majority in the 2015 election and have had three different Prime Minister's following the public vote to leave the EU in 2016. In addition to these political changes, the UK also experienced terrorist attacks from militant Islamist groups over this time, beginning in London on 7 July 2005 with bombings taking place on buses and trains. These factors all influence the direction of the UK's development, security and foreign policy over this time. If the period of the late 1990s to late 2000s was one of looking outwards and finding the UKs place in the world, the late 2000s to the late 2010s has been one of looking inwards with political instability, uncertainty over Brexit, a concern with domestic terrorist attacks and a preoccupation with migration and border control.

Over this same time period, DfID has increasingly brought the idea of security into its development policy. Initially 'security' was very strictly defined as the security of people in the developing world and DfID's involvement in security activities was conditional on a clear benefit to poverty alleviation (McConnon 2014, 1139; 2019, 125–129). Over the period of the 2000s and 2010s this definition of 'security' expanded to include the national security of the UK as a development issue (McConnon 2014, 1143; 2019, 129–132). This move to bring national security into development policy coincides with the framing of migration as a national security issue in development policy. In turn, this idea of national security has been broadened to include the 'national interest'. This has been used as a means of the UK justifying the protection of its aid budget during recession, while other ministries underwent cuts in order to meet the .7% of GNI target for overseas development aid.

The extent to which this has been adopted is evident in the subtitle of DfID's most recent major policy statement in 2015 'Tackling global challenges in the national interest'. The rationale behind this is the claim to common security interests between all parts of the globe due to the interconnected nature of security risks. Conflict and instability in distant parts of the world can result in risks to UK national security, therefore, spending development aid addressing these conflicts benefits both people in these countries but also the UK national interest. Shifting the discourse in this way is resonant with Williams's (2016, 28) work on how the militarisation of the US border with Mexico is framed in humanitarian terms of making the border 'safer' for both migrants and for the US. Similarly, DfID suggests that development policy can make Britain safer by offsetting the need for migrants to move in the first place. As discussed above, the idea that development spending can reduce migration is extremely problematic with evidence suggesting the opposite in fact (Caselli 2019; de Haas, Miller and Castle 2020; Collyer 2019). This switch to selling the ideas of development aid in realist terms of self-interest is quite profound and suggests an inward looking focus to development policy rather than an outward looking one.

These changes certainly coincide with significant political change in the UK and a reassessment of its place in the world. It is not possible to pick out a clear, linear cause and effect relationship between these issues. Even after the 2005 London bombings, DfID continued to frame migration in development terms only and not as a national security issue for several years. Similarly, the change in government from Labour to Conservative in 2010 also seems like an obvious catalyst, but the shift to security was evident in the latter stages under Labour also. However, the current Conservative government has accelerated this move to framing migration as a national security problem offering development aid as a solution. It has also overseen a period of upheaval for DfID with 5 different heads in four years. A number of these choices were notable for their strong position on using development aid for UK national interests. Priti Patel was appointed DfID Head in 2016 even though she had previously asserted that DfID should be disbanded in its current form and that development aid should be used to advance Britain's trade interests (Stone 2016). Similarly, her successor Penny Mordaunt, appointed in 2017, is a strong supporter of Brexit and suggested radical changes to DfID including using it as a conduit to raise private donations rather than spending from the national budget (Elgot 2019). Furthermore, Prime Minister Boris Johnson wrote the Foreword to a report by The Henry Jackson Society calling for aid to fund peacekeeping operations and for DfID to be brought back into the Foreign Office (Seely and Rogers 2019). A suggestion that was put into action in June 2020. The UK government previously had people at the top level who bought into the core values of development aid as separate from UK commercial and security interests and focused solely on poverty reduction. Evident in the 2002 Development Act. In contrast today, these values no longer have the same support and even those that support aid publicly do so in terms of its benefit to the national interest.

The way in which the UK brings together migration, security and development contrasts with that of other donors. Firstly, the UK brought migration into development policy at an earlier point than most donors. Whereas the UK did this in the late

1990s, Sweden, Denmark and Germany and the EU brought migration into development policy in the 2000s (Koff 2017, 11–13; Sørensen 2012, 65; Sørensen 2016, 66). Secondly, while the US and the EU have used development aid as a means of externalising border controls in third countries (Koff 2017; Sørensen 2012) the UK has not gone as far as this yet, although it may do so in time. Thirdly, up until 2009, the UK framed migration in a positive way, as a driver of development similar to Denmark (Sørensen 2016, 67). However, Denmark continues to frame migration as a positive force for development and the UK now only frames migration as a national security threat in its development policy.

What this research demonstrates is that this securitisation of migration has taken place incrementally over an extended period of time. In the context of the spiralling securitisation of migration, development discourse has in the past been what Bello (Bello 2022) would describe as an 'upwarding influence' presenting a positive view of migration. When even development policy discourse frames migration as a national security problem this is an indication of the pervasive securitisation of migration that Bello (Bello 2022) highlights. Migration is an essential part of the connection of UK development spending to UK national security problems because the movement of people is something that directly connects the UK with parts of the world deemed to be dangerous. This now means that development policy is expected to manage the movement of people as an issue that exists within the security-development space. Migration is placed alongside violent extremism as a problem for the UK. This is an example of what Bello (2017, 59) describes as how 'both language and facts translate into perceptions of threats'. The concrete events of violent extremist attacks and state collapse in the Global South are connected to UK national security through the language of securitised migration. Implied in this connection is the possibility that people themselves are dangerous and can bring violent extremism among other things with them when they move and manage to reach the UK. Within this framing, there are no positive benefits to the movement of people.

If migration is something that carries an intrinsic national security risk within it, then the role of development in prevention is still unclear. In November 2015, the UK announced that it would divert £475 million in development funding to respond to the migrant crisis.[1] The description of how this funding will be used is not specific and largely describes mainstream development work of addressing poverty, creating employment, encouraging migrants to stay in their host country by giving them access to services, and humanitarian aid for migrant emergencies. There is also a desire to assist countries with absorbing large numbers of migrants: 'This is building resilience to the conflict in neighbouring countries and preventing regional collapse, including supporting countries to absorb the massive influx of refugees' (DfID 2015, 14). This is problematic as supporting countries to absorb large influxes of people is similar to the 'help them at home' approach of capacity building critiqued by Caselli (2019). This policy of externalising the management of immigration to countries receiving development aid is problematic on a number of levels. On one level it is unlikely to be effective as evidence suggests that advances in development lead to an increase in migration (de Haas, Miller and Castles 2020; Clemens 2014; Collyer 2019, 171). On another level, development aid is supposed to be primarily focused on poverty alleviation. The externalisation of migration control can lead to more militarised and repressive containment solutions which are inconsistent with development values and negatively impact on the poorest and most vulnerable (Collyer 2019, 176). These type of aid for migration containment agreements are a further deviation from DfID's original core values of prioritising poverty reduction above all else.

One change is the increase in development aid remaining in the UK because it is being used to host incoming refugees. As articulated by Chancellor of the Exchequer George Osborne:

> But let me say this, the foreign aid budget we have – and we've increased this foreign aid budget – can provide the support in the first year for these refugees, can help local councils with things like housing costs. (George Osborne BBC's Andrew Marr Show 6 September 2015)

DfID previously sought to spend as much of its budget as possible outside of the UK and took the step to untie aid from the purchase of British goods and services back in 2002. This is another deviation from the core DfID aim of spending money on poverty alleviation. This push to addressing migration in addition to broader national security issues will create further uncertainty as to what development aid is expected to achieve. It is likely to lead DfID further down the path of using aid in an instrumental way of addressing UK national interests.

Conclusion

This article argues that in UK development policy the migration of people is treated as a danger to the UK national security. This understanding of migration represents a break with DfID's previous positive framing of migration as necessary for development. This article provides an in-depth exploration of the interconnections of migration, development and security in UK policy over a period of two decades. It provides original insight through a detailed exploration of this process and the identification of three different ways in which migration, development and security are framed over this period of time. This shift can be understood in the context of the increasing importance of UK national security in development policy and broader UK political changes over this time. With the discursive focus increasingly on the UK as the referent object of security rather than people in the Global South the potential benefits of migration for those living in poverty are no longer acknowledged. Instead, migration is understood as the means through which danger from one part of the world can directly impact on the security of the UK. This is an example of the spiralling securitisation of migration, the key theme of this Special Issue. In this understanding of migration, people who move from the Global South to the UK are a security risk in and of themselves due to the presumed connection to terrorism, religious extremism and disease that they represent. The diversion of development funding to address the Mediterranean migrant crisis are largely a continuation of existing development policies, with the exception of increased funding for local councils in Britain who will receive refugees. However, this represents one more way in which the remit of UK development aid is being increasingly expanded to address broad national security problems both concrete and immediate and speculative representing future risk.

Note

1. These figures are taken from a UK government press release "UK aid for Turkey to help address impact of the Syria conflict" 13 November 2015 https://www.gov.uk/government/news/uk-aid-for-turkey-to-help-address-impact-of-the-syria-conflict.

Disclosure statement

No potential conflict of interest was reported by the author(s).

References

Abrahamsen, Rita. 2005. "Blair's Africa: The Politics of Securitization and Fear." *Alternatives: Global, Local, Political* 30 (1): 55–80. doi:10.1177/030437540503000103

Barder, Owen. 2007. "Reforming Development Assistance: Lessons from the U.K. Experience." In *Security by Other Means*, edited by Lael Brainard. 277–320. Washington, D.C.: Brooking Institution Press.

Baulch, Bob. 2006. "Aid Distribution and the MDGs." *World Development* 34 (6): 933–950. doi:10.1016/j.worlddev.2005.11.013

Beine, Michel, Fréderic Docquier, and Hillel Rapoport. 2008. "Brain Drain and Human Capital Formation in Developing Countries: Winners and Losers." *The Economic Journal* 118 (528): 631–652. doi:10.1111/j.1468-0297.2008.02135.x

Bello, Valeria. 2017. *International Migration and International Security: Why Prejudice is a Global Security Threat*. London: Routledge.

Bello, V. 2022. "The Spiralling of the Securitisation of Migration in the EU: From the Management of a "Crisis" to a Governance of Human Mobility?" *Journal of Ethnic and Migration Studies* 48 (6): 1327–1344. https://doi.org/10.1080/1369183X.2020.1851464.

Bigo, Didier. 2001. "Migration and Security." In *Controlling a New Migration World*, edited by Virginie Guiraudon and Christian Joppke. 121–149. London: Routledge.

Bigo, Didier. 2002. "Security and Immigration: Towards a Critique of the Governmentality of Unease." *Alternatives: Global, Local, Political* 27 (S1): 63–92. doi:10.1177/03043754020270S105

Bourbeau, Philippe. 2015. "Migration, Resilience and Security: Responses to New Inflows of Asylum Seekers and Migrants." *Journal of Ethnic and Migration Studies* 41 (12): 1958–1977. doi:10.1080/1369183X.2015.1047331

Brocza, Stephan, and Katharina Paulhart. 2015. "EU Mobility Partnerships: A Smart Instrument for the Externalization of Migration Control." *European Journal of Futures Research* 15 (3): 1–7. doi:10.1007/s40309-015-0073-x

Carmody, Padraig. 2005. "Transforming Globalization and Security: Africa and America Post-9/11." *Africa Today* 52 (1): 97–120. doi:10.1353/at.2005.0052

Carrera, Sergio, Jean-Pierre Cassarino, Nora El Qadim, Mehdi Lahlou, and Leonhard Den Hertog. 2016. "EU-Morocco Cooperation on Readmission, Borders and Protection: A Model to Follow?" *CEPS Papers in Liberty and Security in Europe*, 87, 1–18.

Carrera, Sergio, Leonhard Den Hertog, and Joanna Parkin. 2012. "EU Migration Policy in the Wake of the Arab Spring What Prospects for EU-Southern Mediterranean Relations?" *MEDPRO Technical Report* 15: 1–29.

Caselli, Marco. 2019. "Let Us Help Them at Home: Policies and Misunderstandings on Migrant Flows Across the Mediterranean Border." *Journal of International Migration and Integration* 20: 983–993. doi:10.1007/s12134-018-00645-w

Chhotray, Vasudha, and David Hulme. 2009. "Contrasting Visions for Aid and Governance in the 21st Century: The White House Millennium Challenge Account and DFID's Drivers of Change." *World Development* 37 (1): 36–49. doi:10.1016/j.worlddev.2007.11.004

Clemens, Michael A. 2014. "Does Development Reduce Migration?" In *International Handbook on Migration and Economic Development*, edited by Robert E. B. Lucas, 152–185. Cheltenham: Edward Elgar Publishing.

Collyer, Michael. 2019. "From Preventive to Repressive: The Changing Use of Development and Humanitarianism to Control Migration." In *Handbook on Critical Geographies of Migration*, edited by Katharyne Mitchell, Reece Jones, and Jennifer L. Fluri, 170–181. Cheltenham: Edward Elgar Publishing.

de Haas, Hein. 2012. "The Migration and Development Pendulum: A Critical View on Research and Policy." *International Migration* 50 (3): 8–25. doi:10.1111/j.1468-2435.2012.00755.x

de Haas, Hein, Mark J. Miller, and Stephen Castles. 2020. *The Age of Migration: International Population Movements in the Modern World*. London: Red Globe Press.

DfID. 1997. *Eliminating World Poverty: A Challenge for the 21st Century, White Paper on International Development*. London: Department for International Development.

DfID. 1999. *Poverty and the Security Sector, Policy Statement*. London: Department for International Development.

DfID. 2000. *Eliminating World Poverty: Making Globalisation Work for the Poor. White Paper on International Development*. London: Department for International Development.

DfID. 2005a. *Fighting Poverty to Build a Safer World. A Strategy for Security and Development*. London: Department for International Development.

DfID. 2005b. *Why We Need to Work More Effectively in Fragile States*. London: DfID.

DfID. 2006. *Eliminating World Poverty: Making Governance Work for the Poor. White Paper on International Development*. London: Department for International Development.

DfID. 2007. *Moving out of Poverty: Making Migration Work Better for Poor People*. London: Department for International Development.

DfID. 2009. *Eliminating World Poverty: Building Our Common Future. White Paper on International Development*. London: Department for International Development.

DfID. 2015. *UK Aid: Tackling Global Challenges in the National Interest*. London: Department for International Development.

DfID. 2019. *Governance for Growth, Stability and Inclusive Development*. London: Department for International Development.

DfID, FCO and MoD. 2001. *The Causes of Conflict in Sub-Saharan Africa*. London: Department for International Development.

DfID, FCO and MoD. 2011. *Building Stability Overseas Strategy*. London: DfID, FCO and MoD.

Driver, Stephen, and Luke Martell. 2002. *Blair's Britain*. London: Polity Press.

Duffield, Mark. 2006. "Human Security: Linking Development and Security in an age of Terror." *New Interfaces Between Security and Development: Changing Concepts and Approaches, German Development Institute, Study* 13: 11–38.

Duffield, Mark. 2007. "Racism, Migration and Development: the Foundations of Planetary Order." *Progress in Development Studies* 6 (1): 68–79. doi:10.1191/1464993406ps128oa

Duffield, Mark. 2010. "The Liberal Way of Development and the Development – Security Impasse: Exploring the Global Life-Chance Divide." *Security Dialogue* 41 (1): 53–76. doi:10.1177/0967010609357042

Elgot, Jessica. 2019. "Penny Mordaunt Criticised Over Call for aid to Come from Private Sector." *The Guardian*.

Evans, Gillian. 2017. "Brexit Britain: Why we are all Postindustrial now." *American Ethnologist* 44 (2): 215–219. doi:10.1111/amet.12470

Gamso, Jonas, and Farhod Yuldashev. 2018. "Does rural development aid reduce international migration?." *World Development* 110: 268–282.

Glencross, Andrew. 2016. *Why the UK Voted for Brexit: David Cameron's Great Miscalculation*. London: Palgrave Macmillan.

HMGovernment. 2015. *National Security Strategy and Strategic Defence and Security Review 2015: A Secure and Prosperous United Kingdom*. London: The Cabinet Office.

Hobolt, Sarah. 2016. "The Brexit Vote: A Divided Nation, a Divided Continent." *Journal of European Public Policy* 23 (9): 1259–1277. doi:10.1080/13501763.2016.1225785

Huysmans, Jef. 2000. "The European Union and the Securitization of Migration." *JCMS: Journal of Common Market Studies* 38 (5): 751–777. doi:10.1111/1468-5965.00263

Koff, Harlan. 2017. "Policy coherence for development and migration: Analyzing US and EU policies through the lens of normative transformation." *Regions and Cohesion* 7 (2): 5–33.

Lowell, B. Lindsay, and Allan Findlay. 2001. "Migration of Highly Skilled Persons from Developing Countries: Impact and Policy Responses." *International Migration Papers* 44: 25.

May, Theresa. 2018. "PM's Speech in Cape Town: 28 August 2018" https://www.gov.uk/government/speeches/pms-speech-in-cape-town-28-august-2018.

McConnon, Eamonn. 2014. "Security for all, development for some? The incorporation of security in UK's development policy." *Journal of International Development* 26 (8): 1127–1148.

McConnon, Eamonn. 2019. *Risk and the Security-development Nexus: The Policies of the US, the UK and Canada.* London: Springer.

McKinlay, Robert D, and Richard Little. 1978. "The French aid relationship: a foreign policy model of the distribution of French bilateral aid." *Development and Change* 9 (3): 459–478.

Picciotto, Robert. 2010. "Conflict Prevention and Development Co-Operation in Africa: An Introduction." *Conflict, Security and Development* 10 (1): 1–25. doi:10.1080/14678800903553787

Pugh, Jonathan, Clive Gabay, and Alison J. William. 2013. "Beyond the Securitisation of Development: The Limits of Intervention, Developmentisation of Security and Repositioning of Purpose in the UK Coalition Government's Policy Agenda." *Geoforum; Journal of Physical, Human, and Regional Geosciences* 44: 193–201. doi:10.1016/j.geoforum.2012.09.007

Roe, Paul. 2008. "Actor, Audience(s) and Emergency Measures: Securitization and the UK's Decision to Invade Iraq." *Security Dialogue* 39 (6): 615–635. doi:10.1177/0967010608098212

Rose, Nikolas. 2000. "Community, Citizenship, and the Third Way." *American Behavioral Scientist* 43 (9): 1395–1411. doi:10.1177/00027640021955955

Seely and Rogers. 2019. *Global Britain: A Twenty-First Century Vision.* London: The Henry Jackson Institute.

Short, Clare. 2004. *An Honourable Deception: New Labour, Iraq and the Misuse of Power.* London: The Free Press.

Smith, Adrian A. 2016. "Migration, development and security within racialised global capitalism: refusing the balance game." *Third World Quarterly* 37 (11): 2119–2138.

Sørensen, Ninna Nyberg. 2012. "Revisiting the Migration–Development Nexus: From Social Networks and Remittances to Markets for Migration Control." *International Migration* 50 (3): 61–76. doi:10.1111/j.1468-2435.2012.00753.x

Sørensen, Ninna Nyberg. 2016. "Coherence and Contradictions in Danish Migration-Development Policy and Practice." *The European Journal of Development Research* 28 (1): 62–75. doi:10.1057/ejdr.2015.73

Stark, Oded, Christian Helmenstein, and Alexia Prskawetz. 1997. "A Brain Gain with a Brain Drain." *Economics Letters* 55 (2): 227–234. doi:10.1016/S0165-1765(97)00085-2

Stewart, Frances. 2004. "Development and Security." *Conflict, Security and Development* 4 (3): 261–288. doi:10.1080/1467880042000319863

Stone, Jon. 2016. "The New International Development Secretary Wanted to Scrap What is Now her Department." *The Independent.* http://www.independent.co.uk/news/uk/politics/new-international-development-secretary-priti-patel-called-for-department-for-international-a7137331.html

Tirtosudarmo, Riwanto. 2018. "The Migration-Development-Security Nexus: In Search of New Perspectives in the Changing East Asian Context." In *The Politics of Migration in Indonesia and Beyond*, edited by Riwanto Tirtosudarmo. 197–223. Singapore: Springer.

Truong, Thanh-Dam, and Des Gasper. 2011. "Transnational Migration, Development and Human Security." In *Transnational Migration and Human Security*, edited by Truong, Thanh-Dam, and Des Gasper. 3–22. Berlin: Springer.

Wild, Leni, and Samir Elhawary. 2016. "The UK's Approach to Linking Development and Security: Assessing Policy and Practice." In *The Securitization of Foreign aid*, edited by Stephen Brown and Jörn Grävingholt. 42–63. London: Palgrave.

Williams, Jill M. 2016. "The Safety/Security Nexus and the Humanitarianisation of Border Enforcement." *The Geographical Journal* 182 (1): 27–37. doi:10.1111/geoj.12119

The EU and migration in the Mediterranean: EU borders' control by proxy

Stefania Panebianco ⓘ

ABSTRACT
The year 2015 is often labelled as the year of the Mediterranean migration crisis, with the Central Mediterranean route heavily weighting the humanitarian crisis in terms of victims. Migration and border control have then become a highly politicised issue both at European and national level entrapping the European Union (EU) in contradictory political strategies. On the one hand, the duty to protect people on the move puts the humanitarian dimension at the centre of the crisis management. On the other, the border control argument brought about by European leaders assumes defence of state frontiers as the main goal to be achieved, irrespective of individual needs. Closing the borders to protect EU member states' (EUMS) sovereignty and their supposed national homogeneity has become a prevailing political argument conducive to the externalisation of the migration management. This article investigates the contradictions of the EU response to address migration in the Mediterranean and focuses on the burden-shifting of the Mediterranean migration management which involves non-EU actors as migration crisis managers to provide EU borders' control. This political process has exploded in the EU since 2015 favouring the upward spiralling of the securitisation of migration which is explored in this SI.

Introduction

Since the 1990s security discourses have dominated the academic debate on migration (among others, Buzan, 1991; Wæver et al., 1993; Huysmans, 2000; Lazaridis and Wadia, 2015). In the last decade, the political debate in the European Union (EU) has been strongly influenced by the migration-security nexus, overshadowing the humanitarian dimension of the phenomenon. Over time, migration to Europe has become a highly politicised issue framed by security considerations often portraying migrants as a security threat. Being an object of lively debate at domestic and EU level, migration is a highly divisive issue that animates EU politics. Migration has been constructed as a threat to national identity by those European political leaders who pledge for the closure of the EU borders and seek the shifting of the management of the migration crisis outside the EU borders to preserve the state's integrity.

Due to diverging visions and priorities between different actors and among EU member states (EUMS), the EU has found a common ground in border closure strategies. The analysis of the EU approach(es) to address the Mediterranean migration crisis points out the burden-shifting process that the EU is experiencing via a stronger involvement of non-EU actors and border countries, Libya in particular, to address unsolicited human mobility. Although a humanitarian approach is practiced on the ground by NGOs and civil society organisations engaged in the Mediterranean migration crisis, the EU is entrapped in the intergovernmental logics dominated by EUMS keen of protecting their own borders, unable to provide human protection to people in trouble. The migration crisis has demonstrated that burden-sharing is unfeasible and the 'externalisation of adjustment burdens to non-EU actors [is] necessary by default' (Genschel and Jachtenfuchs, 2018, 178).

The migration crisis has provoked an intergovernmental turn at EU level (Biermann et al., 2019), halting the reform of the Dublin Regulation (consensus to reform still needs to be found) or introducing a voluntary resettlement mechanism replacing the controversial quota system to relocate migrants within the EU territory according to a pre-set scheme (European Council, 2018a). Therefore, closing the EU borders and externalising the management of migration to non-state actors and to neighbour countries – via, for instance, disembarkation platforms potentially outside of the EU, has become the lowest common denominator agreed by the EU to address irregular migration in the Mediterranean. Disrespectful of the needs and security of people on the move across the Mediterranean Sea.

Several European leaders such as Matteo Salvini or Giorgia Meloni in Italy or Victor Orban in Hungary depict migration as a threat to state security and national sovereignty and act as 'upwarding forces' of securitisation (Bello, 2017, 2022). According to the model adopted in this Special Issue, phenomena such as securitisation of migration may spiral over time, i.e. the intensity of the phenomenon can increase in an upward direction, or decrease in a downward direction (Bello 2022). The spiralling model provides an analytical framework that timely explains the upwards and downwards of the migratory issue. Assuming that securitisation of migration is not a linear process but a *spiralling* phenomenon (Bello, 2017), this articles seeks to explain the reasons why securitisation of migration has spiralled after 2015. Why has the securitisation spiralled at a certain point and who has favoured this process? It is necessary to investigate whether the intensity of this phenomenon has increased in an upward direction because of domestic political discourses imbued with security concerns claiming for EU borders' closure irrespective of the humanitarian dimension. The last 10 years have experienced securitisation of migration as a spiralling phenomenon. The discourse on the 'humane' management of the Mediterranean migration crisis that was defended by the Italian *Mare Nostrum* operation (MNO) (2013–2014) or by the European Agenda for Migration (2015) has been progressively replaced by control of human mobility achieved through EU borders' closure and agreements with border countries (i.e. Libya and Turkey).

This article explores the EU response to the migration wave that since 2011 has characterised the Mediterranean region with a peak in 2015. It zooms into the protection of the borders rhetoric that provides a sound reason to externalise the management of the flows to bordering countries and to third parties – with Libya representing a meaningful case on this point. It explains why the EU has progressively adopted an approach of 'borders' control by proxy' departing from an approach permeated by the humanitarian dimension. The politicisation of migration based upon security speech acts in most EUMS has been detrimental to the communitarisation of the European external migration policy. EUMS acting as veto-powers within the European Council have framed EU migration policy-making departing from the burden-sharing approach set by the European Agenda on Migration adopted in 2015. The EU is currently investing on the externalisation of migration management disregarding the implications of this choice in humanitarian terms or its political costs.

The article proceeds as follows. Section one defines Mediterranean migration and the humanitarian crisis at the EU Southern borders. Section two focuses on the European response to the migration crisis and the change of rhetoric and strategies since 2015. Section three investigates the politicisation of migration that accompanied the construction of migration as a security threat. Section four identifies patterns of externalisation, focusing on Libya in particular. The main argument is that the EU is investing in the involvement of third parties in the management of migration in the Mediterranean area to achieve borders' control by proxy. This analysis provides substance to the upwards set by the spiralling model.

Contextualising Mediterranean migration: a massive humanitarian crisis at EU southern borders

The EU is currently faced with a massive humanitarian crisis at its borders. Not just in terms of arrivals, but primarily regarding the (in)security of people on the move. Although an emergency frame has often been applied to explain the current migration flows across the Mediterranean seawaters, Mediterranean migration is rather a structural condition of this 'age of migration' (Attinà, 2018, 50). The phenomenon of irregular migration from the Global South to the Global North renders this long-lasting multidimensional crisis one key feature of our times.

Scholars generally agree that migration is a global phenomenon which has multiple causes (Attinà, 2016; Bettini, 2017; Carling and Schewel, 2018; De Haas, 2011; Geddes, 2015; Van Hear et al., 2018). Alongside people fleeing from armed conflicts and persecutions for political opinions, religion, sexual orientation, or nationality, which entitle to legal protection according to the Geneva Convention of 1951, there are also other causes forcing people to move and leave their home country, such as environmental change, demographic pressure, or structural poverty. The traditional legal distinction between refugees and economic migrants does not acknowledge this complexity. This is even more the case in the Mediterranean region, being a crossroad of people on the move to Europe with different reasons to leave their countries, elicited by global and local migration drivers. This variety of push factors triggers several actors in the management of migration, which is per definition a trans-boundary issue (Attinà, 2018, 62).

Although migration is a global issue and maritime migration has always existed, over time migratory routes have changed according to contingent conditions. In the last 30 years, migration flows across the Mediterranean Sea have experienced various routes and exploited different entry points to Europe depending on specific circumstances: through the Gibraltar Straits and the Adriatic in the 1990s, via the Canary Islands in the 2000s, increasingly from North Africa since 2011, and massively through the

Eastern Mediterranean in 2015. Libya in particular, being a failed state, plays a crucial role as a transit country, acting as gatekeeper for migration flows to Europe via the Central Mediterranean route.

In 2015, Mediterranean arrivals were more than 1 million, involving primarily Greece and Italy as frontline southern EUMS (Figure 1). However, figures on Mediterranean migration flows do not say that people forced to embark on a long risky journey across the Mediterranean are a small proportion compared to those displaced people who remain in the neighbourhood of a state in wa[1] or detained in camps waiting for accessing Europe.

Figure 2 provides a breakdown of arrivals to Europe in 2014–2018 via the three main Mediterranean routes, the Eastern, Central and Western ones. Greece – the gateway to Europe via the Eastern route, was faced with an unprecedented number of arrivals in 2015 (856,723), while Italy registered the peak of arrivals in 2016 (181,436). In 2018, the Italian Minister of the Interior, Matteo Salvini, closed ports to migrants arriving with *Search and Rescue* operations (SARs) determining a drop in the arrivals via the Central Mediterranean route (23,370). The year 2018 was then characterised by an increase of sea arrivals to Spain (58,569) via the Western Mediterranean route. Being migration a global phenomenon triggered by multiple causes, migration flows cannot be arrested, but merely diverted due to contingent situations.[2]

These figures suggest that migration triggers such as territorial disputes, state failure and civil unrest, together with structural poverty and environmental change are exploited by smugglers' networks that adapt their strategies to contingent factors and divert flows searching for accessible entry-points.

Figure 2 also shows data on dead and missing people in the Mediterranean distinct per routes. Since 2011, the number of migrants smuggled to the EU via the Mediterranean routes has consistently increased and inevitably the number of dead and missing persons on maritime routes has risen dramatically, with a peak of 5096 in 2016

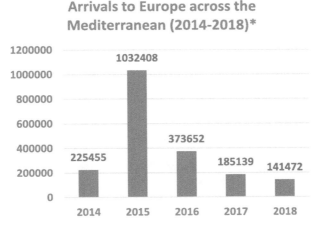

Figure 1. *Mediterranean arrivals include sea arrivals to Italy, Cyprus and Malta, and both sea and land arrivals to Greece and Spain. Source: *Mediterranean Migration Portal*, UNHCR (Accessed March 22, 2019).

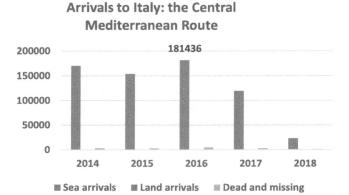

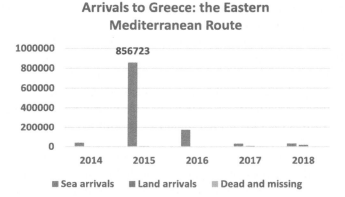

Figure 2. Source: *Mediterranean Migration Portal*, UNHCR (Accessed March 22, 2019).

(Figure 3). With these data on dead and missing people, the Mediterranean is the most lethal route in the world.

At the time of the peak of arrivals, in 2015, EUMS – with Greece and Italy on the fore-front – struggled to find a common solution, and a South *versus* Central and Eastern

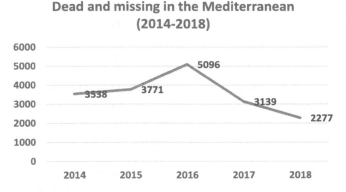

Figure 3. Source: *Mediterranean Migration Portal,* UNHCR (Accessed March 22, 2019).

European cleavage soon emerged (Panebianco, 2016). Physical burden-sharing was contested by some European leaders, in particular those less confronted directly with the crisis. Repeated shipwrecks and mass drownings forced member states at the EU southern borders to address the crisis in the absence of solidarity of other EUMS. This was the case of Italy, that in 2013 launched *Mare Nostrum* to face the unprecedented number of arrivals and of shipwrecks that were provoking a humanitarian crisis (Panebianco, 2017).

Of course, migration in the Mediterranean triggers several facets of crisis. This is primarily a humanitarian crisis due to its dramatic death toll. Furthermore, Mediterranean migration can be framed as a crisis because it origins in region/states of crisis (Attinà, 2016). Moreover, it is a crisis because it is 'popularly understood to demand immediate policy response' (Bilgin, 2017, 57). In addition to that, it is *constructed* as a crisis due to the involvement of media framing this phenomenon as dramatically unexpected and new (Harteveld et al., 2018). Or, more simply, the crisis is to be expected due to the features of EU border policy (Guiraudon, 2018, 152). Confronted with the drastic increase of arrivals registered in 2015, the EU showed its policy *inertia* (Guiraudon, 2018) and proved unable to address the humanitarian crisis at its borders. In addition to this, since 2015 upwarding forces of securitisation emerged. European political leaders such the Hungarian Victor Oban or the Italian Matteo Salvini favoured the spiralling of the securitisation of migration. Being obsessed with the defence of the EU borders, they constructed a rhetoric of state's protection from the security threats (migration included) that clearly emerged at the (intergovernmental) institutional level, overwhelming the humanitarian dimension of the crisis.

The European response to the migration crisis: contradictory strategies

April 2015 can be regarded as the 'Black April' of migration across the Mediterranean seawaters, with victims mounting to 1240 in one month only. At that time among EU institutions, EUMS and European public there was a widespread consensus that common action was needed to face the humanitarian crisis. The EU then tried to launch an EU migration governance[3] motivated by the principles of solidarity and responsibility which are expressed in the EU treaties.[4] In reaction to these dramatic shipwrecks, the High Representative for the Union of Foreign Affairs and Security Policy called upon the human protection and the 'duty to intervene' to save people in distress in the Mediterranean to avoid a humanitarian disaster (Mogherini, 2015).

In May 2015, the European Commission adopted the European Agenda on Migration listing various proposals for reforming, extending and better implementing the Schengen regulatory framework (European Commission 2015). The Agenda on Migration launched the 'hotspot approach' setting up hotspots in frontline EUMS as 'identification' centres in order to select those who are entitled to apply for asylum and those who are not.[5] The Agenda proposed also a redistribution of migrants according to a 'quota system'.[6] But the plan did not work out due to the opposition of central and eastern European countries.[7] The governments of the so-called Visegrad countries (Czech Republic, Hungary, Romania and Slovakia) soon announced that they did not intend to comply with the relocation scheme and refused to accept the number of assigned migrants set by the European Council upon proposal of the European Commission .[8] Opposing the quotas, the Visegrad countries were *de facto* questioning EU norms.[9]

In the midst of the crisis, a cleavage between Mediterranean border countries as first entry EU countries, carrying the highest burden of arrivals, and the Visegrad countries became evident (Panebianco, 2016). Central and Eastern European leaders were reluctant to share the migrants' burden. They pronounced instead discourses in defence of the nation-state's integrity and launched initiatives to physically protect the borders with walls and barbed wires, in Hungary as in Bulgaria, but also in Slovenia and Austria, paving the way for the closure of the external and internal EU borders.

The initial controversy South *versus* Eastern Europe was reshuffled when Italy joined the group of EUMS pleading for 'closing the EU borders'. The humanitarian approach that the Italian government had defended in 2013 with the MNO was fading away (Panebianco, 2017), overwhelmed by a political construction of the migration crisis within the security framework. In February 2017, the Italian government signed the Memorandum of Understanding (MoU) with Libya and in July 2017 Italy approved the Code of Conduct for NGOs conducting SAR operations in the Mediterranean, thus reducing SAR NGOs' activity. In the summer 2018, the government led by Giuseppe Conte, following the political stances of the Minister of the Interior Matteo Salvini, launched the Italian strategy of 'closed ports', emblematically preventing a vessel of the Italian Coast Guard (2017) to disembark migrants. Afterwards, Salvini closed the Italian ports to several NGOs (Sea Watch, Open Arms, Ocean Viking).

The European leaders and EU institutions were unable to Europeanize the refugee crisis, and showed instead the inadequateness of the EU legal framework for a common asylum and migration policy. The refusal to redistribute migrants, the construction of internal physical barriers, the restoration of controls at the borders and a general decline of cooperation among EUMS marked a severe crisis of the EU (Bauböck, 2018, 142).

Many scholars claim that the EU is having hard times in finding effective strategies and tools to face migration to and across Europe, thus revealing a much deeper internal crisis.[10] The EU proved to be unable to face refugees and migrants' flows in a coherent and effective way, producing strategies and tools detrimental to the *acquis communautaire*. The migrants' wave provoked a serious 'governance failure of the EU in coming to terms with the refugee flows' (Börzel and Risse, 2018, 90). 'The Schengen crisis [...]

has been marked by the EU's continued inability to respond effectively and in a co-ordinated manner to the unprecedented influx of refugees and migrants' (Börzel and Risse, 2018, 84).

When dealing with migration, domestic and EU levels are strictly intertwined and diverging interests easily arise because core state's issues are at stake. The collective action foreseen at EU level to face the migration crisis has been frozen by colliding interests of EUMS and the mounting of populism. As Caporaso argues, there are 'institutional fixes': '[w]hen preferences of Member States diverge, institutions may prove to be of little help' (Caporaso, 2018, 1345). The explanation for this stalemate is to be found in 'divergent preferences among key Member States, domestic political processes that reward anti-immigrant behaviour, and demanding EU voting rules' (Caporaso, 2018, 1354).

Decisions taken at European Council level since 2015 indicate that an intergovernmental turn is currently shaping the EU migration policy. EUMS acted as veto-powers by opposing the implementation of the quota system. Quotas to relocate migrants within the EU were then turned into voluntary mechanisms, since transfer has to apply 'on a voluntary basis' (European Council 2018a). In 2017, the EUMS' opposition to the quota system and the refusal to relocate migrants was openly acknowledged by the President of the European Union, Donald Tusk, after and even before the European Council of December 2017.[11] It was evident that the issue of mandatory quotas proved to be highly divisive and turned to be ineffective. To overcome the political stalemate, in the Final Conclusions of the European Council of specific reference to migration was omitted, although the EU leaders had held a lively debate on the external and internal dimensions of the EU migration policy to assess what had or had not worked in the previous two years, and had discussed how to strengthen the policy (European Council, 2017). The EU's relocation scheme had failed and EUMS were unprepared to respect the principle of burden-sharing which is at the basis of the European external migration policy.

EUMS acted as veto-powers also regarding the reform of the Dublin Regulation that imposes the state of first entry to identify migrants and handle their asylum applications. According to the so-called Dublin system set up from the late 1990s onwards by the Dublin Conventions I, II and III, migrants entering the EU have to be identified in the first-entry member state. Each Member State must control access to EU territory and handle issues of immigration, refugee protection and asylum provision. Therefore, states of first entry have to carry hugely disproportionate burdens. During the peak of arrivals across the Mediterranean (2014–2018), states of first entry like Italy or Greece lacked capacities and incentives to fully implement the Dublin Regulation. The Dublin Regulation assigns responsibility exclusively to the first safe EU country, but the common control of EU external borders and open internal ones imply that asylum seekers do not enter just Greece or Italy, but rather EU territory. The EU had adopted the CEAS, with the Dublin Regulation being one of the pillars of EU common policy (Kaunert and Leonard, 2012). But that was under normal conditions. Faced with the high numbers registered the migration crisis of the 2010s, the situation changed dramatically.

The EU has found it hard to move in the direction set by the European Commission in the European Agenda on Migration by reforming the Dublin Regulation and implementing the principles enshrined in the Treaties that were to accompany the migration system.

Some EUMS rejected EU instruments such as the quota system to relocate migrants across the EU; the European Council revealed unable to ensure the implementation of these EU tools, and the Council of the EU did not proceed with the reform of the Dublin Regulation despite the favourable vote of the European Parliament on 16 November 2017. Assuming that refugee protection is a 'legitimacy repair mechanism', refugee protection should abide by burden-sharing (Bauböck, 2018, 143 ss). Yet, in 2015 the EU has failed the 'burden-sharing test'.

Regulatory integration to ensure effective policy co-ordination had failed, leaving the Schengen system fragile and vulnerable to shock (Genschel and Jachtenfuchs, 2018, 183). Severe distributive conflicts among the Member States, and high levels of constraining dissent within them, prevented an adequate supply of European burden-sharing capacities. Schengen proved to be a 'fair weather system': 'when the refugee crisis broke, the EU was unprepared and had to develop coping strategies on the hop' (Genschel and Jachtenfuchs, 2018, 185).

On the burden-sharing principle there still is a cleavage to overcome. The Visegrad leaders contest the principle of burden-sharing because conceptually they find it atypical that one Member State lets migrants access its territory to distribute them among other EUMS afterwards. They insist on the responsibility of each EUMS to protect (i.e. close) their borders and assume that this is a matter of defending the member state-borders, not EU borders, with any means available to be adopted at local/national level. Therefore, instead of supranationalising the EU's response to the refugee crisis, the '[m]ember states reverted to national solutions, non-compliance with EU policies during the Schengen crisis [...] and calls for changing the treaties to exempt asylum and immigration rules' (Börzel and Risse 2018, 92).

Most recent literature contradicts pre-2015 migration crisis arguments on the expansive potential of the EU asylum system (Zaun, 2016). European states and policy-makers play a crucial role in blocking the refugee quota system (Zaun, 2018), in pursuing a bold return policy and invest in externalisation (Slominski and Trauner, 2018), or in halting refugee burden-sharing initiatives in favour of free-riding initiatives, i.e. burden-shifting (Thielemann, 2018). In the migration field, there is less Europe instead of more Europe, or simply non-use of Europe (Slominski and Trauner, 2018).

Politicising migration: when populist European politics unmakes EU policies

Migration has become a 'hot topic' in West European politics (Grande et al., 2019). In the last years, public attention to migration has increased in several western countries, with media actively contributing to politicising this issue (Harteveld et al., 2018; Krzyżanowski et al., 2018). Political support to populist political forces claiming to defend the domestic borders has also increased (Conti, 2018).

Several political parties in Europe nowadays share a hard line towards migration and display fierce opposition to migrants' entry into Europe: the UK Independence party (UKIP), in Germany *Alternative für Deutschland*, in France *Le Front National*, in Italy *Lega*, in Hungary *Fidesz*, in Austria the *Freiheitliche Partei Österreichs* (FPÖ), in Poland *Prawo i Sprawiedliwość* (PiS), in Finland The Finns Party. These parties have gained large electoral support with anti-migration political discourses, focused on the firm defence of state sovereignty. They can prevent action towards joint initiatives other than the closure of the borders (external and internal). After all, the European response to the migration crisis reflects the preferences of European governments that are accountable to electorates very often enchanted by extremisms, intolerance and xenophobia, as most recent elections in Europe indicate.

There is a populist 'voice' conveying anger and fierce opposition against migrants, asylum-seekers or refugees, to any type of people on the move irrespective of considerations of humanitarian concerns. The migration crisis has produced populist stances against *people on the move,* whether or not entitled to humanitarian protection. In just few years, European leaders dominating the public opinion with the nation-state rhetoric have overshadowed solidarity and burden-sharing.

The politicisation of migration at EU and domestic level has often been framed within a security discourse. Populist parties and European political leaders who defend the national security and state-borders are inclined to portray migrants as a security threat. Therefore, this politicisation process goes hand to hand with a securitisation one, in a mutual reinforcing relation the former sustains the latter and *vice-versa.* The literature on securitisation has widely acknowledged that some European governments attempted to present migrants as a threat to national cohesion, culture and welfare systems, and that migration has been given sufficient saliency to win the assent of the audience enabling those who are authorised to handle the issue to use appropriate means (Balzacq et al., 2016, 495). For several years, in the political science literature migration has been portrayed as a security issue, as a threat to the security of states, societies and individuals within them.

The securitisation of migration goes back to the early 1990s when the so-called Copenhagen School sought to understand how some political actors socially construct migration as a security issue (Waever et al., 1993; Huysmans, 2000). More recently, the so-called Paris School has focused on the relevance of *routinised practices,* i.e. practices of borders' surveillance and control (Bigo, 2000; Bigo and Tsoukala, 2008). Research has also explored the humanitarian approach that considers first and outmost human beings' security (Cuttitta, 2017). The Italian MNO has drawn the attention on initiatives aimed at protecting migrants as alternatives to approaches focused on state security issues. More recently, the academic discourse has focused on the contradictions between the humanitarian approach and the border controls' strategies in the name of the defence of states' frontiers. Some scholars have stressed that sometimes the human security discourse has also been used to legitimise the tightening of borders in the name of migrants' own security (Moreno-Lax, 2018; Cusumano, 2019).

Departing from a humanitarian approach putting migrants as human beings at the centre of policy action as outlined in 2015 by the High Representative Federica Mogherini, in just a few years the EU has turned to the defence of the borders relying upon burden-shifting rather than respecting the burden-sharing principle enshrined in the treaties and recalled by the European Agenda on Migration. Pushing the problem of migration management beyond the EU borders (see *infra*), the existing framework is conducive to more human insecurity with no tools to control the respect of migrants' rights.

Political discourses focused on a homogeneous nation-state have become very popular in several EUMS and societies have started supporting populist right parties pledging for the preservation of European societies from external contaminations. For instance, the populist discourse has flourished in Italy (Conti, 2018; Orsina, 2019), where a politicisation process favoured by populist parties focused on migration to divert political attention from other relevant issues.[12] In 2018–2019, the Italian government – urged by the Minister of the Interior, Matteo Salvini, addressed migration as a major security threat. In 2019, the government led by Giuseppe Conte adopted a 'closing the ports' policy aimed at guaranteeing more security to citizens, in neat contrast to the humanitarian approach previously sustained by the Italian government with the MNO. With the decision to close Italian ports to any SAR NGO to avoid disembarking migrants in Europe, Italy provided a meaningful example of populist political claims and policy initiatives to defend the European citizens by closing the Italian borders.

European politics is facing mounting populist and Eurosceptic parties such as the Italian Lega that address migration with the political rhetoric of borders' defence by evoking a fortress Europe closed to migratory flows, either spontaneous, irregular or regulated. This border closure strategy brings back in the political debate the fortress Europe concept that for several years the EU had struggled to wipe out, to create instead a Euro-Mediterranean region via Euro-Mediterranean cooperation (Bicchi, 2018). Exclusion discourses have become very popular at domestic level and often prevail over inclusion ones contributing to the definition of European interests.

On the one hand, with the politicisation of the migration issue, EU institutions and politics entered the public debate producing high levels of polarisation, increase of mobilisation and the expansion of actors in various public domains (Börzel and Risse, 2018, 85). On the other, this phenomenon has not produced more European integration, but rather a public debate on the essence of the EU, on its effectiveness and *raison d'etre*. As if European electorates requested more control rather than more integration.

To a large extent, the migration crisis has produced high levels of politicisation, expressing the centrifugal forces of Eurosceptic populism. Euro-scepticism (or even euro-criticism) is mounting all over Europe and European public opinion is becoming more attentive to gaining direct advantages from European integration while avoiding disadvantages (or what are perceived as such) (Börzel and Risse, 2018). A widespread resentment on migrants characterises domestic debates on refugees and the migration crisis (Börzel and Risse, 2018). Eurobarometer data denounce a widely shared attitude of the European public opinion that associate migration to a big problem that requires effective solutions (Eurobarometer 2018a), irrespective of the real number of migrants living in their countries (Eurobarometer 2018b).

The absence of a common response to the migration crisis can be regarded as a result of a 'constraining dissensus' and the rise of Eurosceptic parties (Börzel and Risse, 2018, 84). According to this post-functionalist explanation of the Schengen crisis 'Eurosceptic attitudes of citizens in national elections and referenda on EU affairs limit the room of manoeuvre for national governments and European élites searching for functional solutions to Europe's pressing problems' (Börzel and Risse 2018, 86).

European politics is currently affected by extremist populist and xenophobic parties; this inevitably impacts on the EU migration policy and the political preference for protecting the EU borders. Considering that politics matter and determines *who* decides (Geddes and Scholten, 2016) and (on) *what*, the analysis of European politics, the advancement of extremist right parties, the mounting Euroscepticism/Euro-criticism and the political rhetoric of guaranteeing state's security via border closure demonstrates that, as far as migration is concerned, *politics unmakes policy*. A mix of political leaders, political parties, public opinion and media can easily pull down EU policy-making.

Externalising migration management: EU borders' control by proxy

Even before the 2010s, migration was an issue of concern with regard to the externalisation of EU internal policies (Del Sarto, 2010, 156). Externalisation, i.e. outsourcing the EU's external border management to neighbouring countries (Del Sarto, 2010, 159), was attempted already in the mid-1990s. Since the setting-up of the Euro-Mediterranean Partnership in 1995, and more specifically with the adoption of the European Neighbourhood Policy in 2004, the EU conceived stronger cooperation with Mediterranean neighbours as a way to address migration (Del Sarto, 2010, 160). Focusing on EU Mediterranean borders, Del Sarto suggested the existence of a 'borderland', i.e. a hybrid area of transition, 'characterised by a net of different boundaries according to different functional and territorial lines within which the Union's rules and regulations apply' (Del Sarto, 2010, 165).

When the migration crisis exploded the EU tried to turn states in North Africa and the Middle East into a buffer zone, co-opting their governments into the control of migration and the fight to organised crime by offering an array of incentives. With EURONAVFOR MED and the establishment of the European Border and Coast Guard, financial and technical support have been provided to Mediterranean neighbours to strengthen the EU external borders. Also, paramilitary actors such as the Libyan Coast Guard, International Organisations and NGOs are involved in the management of the crisis outside the EU borders.

In March 2016, the EU signed an agreement with Turkey and in February 2017 the Italy-Libya MoU was signed – straight afterwards endorsed by the EU. The EU-Turkey deal addresses the so-called Eastern route, while the MoU tackles the central Mediterranean route. With these instruments the EU is investing on the direct involvement of transit countries or temporarily destination countries such as Libya or Turkey in the management of migration. However, the content of these cooperation frameworks is rather different.

Under the terms of the EU-Turkey 'Joint Action Plan', the EU promised Turkey up to 6 billion euros, visa liberalisation, and a reinvigoration of the accession talks in return for its assistance in guarding EU borders from irregular migration. The EU-Turkey agreement allows Greece to return to Turkey irregular migrants arrived after 20 March 2016. In exchange, EUMS have agreed to increase resettlement of Syrian refugees residing in Turkey, accelerate visa liberalisation for Turkish nationals and boost existing financial support for Turkey's refugee population. According to the Plan, Turkey can be regarded as a 'safe third country', a condition that is much more controversial in the Libyan case.

In early 2017, Italy has been a promoter of the externalisation of migration management to Libya. With the MoU the Italian government decided to devote large resources to train the Libyan Coast Guard and to the control of the land-borders; cooperation has been established at all institutional levels, including local authorities and mayors in the southern part of the country. The EU has fully endorsed the MoU and is cooperating with the Libyan Coast Guard, trained by European forces within EUNAVFOR MED; also FRONTEX, transformed in the European Border and Coast Guard Agency, conducts maritime operations at the EU borders and cooperates with the Libyan Coast Guard.

In June 2018, the European Council agreed on launching the second tranche of the Facility for Refugees in Turkey and at the same time on transferring 500 million euro from the 11th EDF reserve to the EU Trust Fund for Africa (European Council 2018a). Moreover, EUMS regarded the EU Trust Fund for Africa as a crucial multi-dimensional instrument to address Mediterranean migration.

Although key aspects of the EU's external border management are physically trans-ferred to the territory of the southern neighbours and partially 'outsourced' in terms of personnel, cooperation has never been so close to set up a real governance of migration. It is more a strategy of 'EU borders' control by proxy', i.e. a delegation to non-EU parties without requesting guarantees of human rights' respect. In so far as migration has become a 'hot political issue' and requires to be delegated to other actors so to provide states' and societal security, other actors or third states are assumed *a priori* to be 'safe countries'. This raises serious concerns in terms of human security considering that IOs and NGOs regularly denounce migrants' inhuman con-ditions during their journey (e.g. see the reports on Libya issued by the International Organisation for Migration (IOM), the United Nations High Commissioner for Refugees (UNHCR) or Amnesty International).

The active – although reluctant – involvement of the Libyan Coast Guard in patrolling the Mediterranean in a portion of sea recently identified as the 'Libyan maritime zone', allows for the delegation of the 'dirty work'. Managing migration at the EU borders con-sists in preventing migrants from crossing the Central Mediterranean with any possible means. Once migrants are disembarked on the Libyan territory, they are brought back to detention centers that are often inaccessible to any control from the international com-munity.[13] This represents a clear violation of the international maritime law, that requires that people in distress at sea must be provided with a 'safe port', and of the *non-refoulement* principle stating that people entitled to humanitarian protection cannot be returned to countries where their life is in danger.

Over the years, the principle of solidarity and the duty to protect human beings have been overwhelmed by a 'fencing Europe' strategy (Attinà, 2018). The EU external migratory policy is currently embedded in a European framework of *stop-and-return* (Attinà, 2018, 65). *Stop* at the external borders is guaranteed via externalisation of migration flows via agreements with border countries. *Returns* can be 'forced' by first entry countries, if they verify that migrants do not respect the rule to apply for asylum and there are no legal basis to stay in the European territory, they are repatriated (Slo-minski and Trauner, 2018). *Returns* can be 'voluntary' if migrants apply for voluntary return programmes such as the IOM ones.[14] A more effective and coherent European return policy is one of the pillars of the EU new approach to migration (European Council 2018a).

The closure of EU borders to migrants and the externalisation of migration manage-ment has been progressively identified by the European Council as a way to overcome the stalemate on migration that had emerged in December 2017 (European Council 2017). In June 2018, the European Council has envisaged a 'comprehensive approach to migration which combines more effective control of the EU's external borders, increased external action and the internal aspects, in line with our principles and values'; this includes fight to smuggling – in Libya or elsewhere, support to frontline Member States such as Italy, cooperation with countries of origin such as the Sahel region or transit such as Libya (European Council 2018a). The Libyan Coastguard, but also coastal and Southern communities have been identified as crucial actors to cooperate with. With the involvement of third parties in the migration governance the EU is investing on borders' control by proxy.

To prevent illegal migration and strengthening cooperation with countries of origin and transit, North Africa in particular, has become a key priority of the EU comprehensive approach to migration. The European Council meeting of 18 October 2018, following the informal leaders' discussion in Salzburg, indicated the strong intergovernmental stance of EU external migration policy (European Council 2018b). The EU has envisaged a 'new approach' based on shared and complementary action among EUMS and non-EU parties to explore the setting up of 'disembarkation platforms' in close cooperation with relevant third countries as well as UNHCR and IOM.

External migration management remains a pillar of what the EU considers a 'new approach to migration'. Effective control of the EU's external borders remains at the heart of the EU comprehensive approach to migration. The reduction of illegal border crossings is regarded as a direct result of the external migration policy of the Union and its Member States, based, in particular, on control of the external borders, the fight against smugglers and cooperation with countries of origin and transit, which has been intensified (European Council 2018c).

The EU approach to migration based upon effective control of EU borders has been reaffirmed in June 2019. The *New Strategic Agenda 2019–2024* adopted by the European Council focuses on four main priorities: (1) protecting citizens and freedoms; (2) developing a strong and vibrant economic base; (3) building a climate-neutral, green, fair and social Europe; (4) promoting European interests and values on the global stage (European Council 2019). The New Strategic Agenda sets effective control of the external borders as an absolute prerequisite for guaranteeing security and considers cooperation with countries of origin and transit as a key strategy to fight illegal migration and human trafficking, together with effective returns.

Control is not detrimental nor negative *per sè*, nor does it imply necessarily inhumane conditions. What is peculiar to European external migration policy today is that it mostly entails borders' control by proxy, i.e. delegating migration management to third actors with an open mandate. No human rights' respect is granted if migration flows are blocked at the EU borders. Despite the denounces of political actors such as NGOs and civil society associations, it is assumed by default that the EU is dealing with 'safe third countries'.

Conclusion

The EU Mediterranean borders have become the deadliest borders in the world. Since April 2015, the humanitarian crisis provoked by the high number of tolls due to several dramatic shipwrecks in the Mediterranean Sea has attracted the attention of European policy-makers, media and public opinion. The management of migration flows across the Mediterranean has entered the EU political agenda as a key priority. The mediatisation of the phenomenon – with rescue operations and disembarkations broadcasted while taking place and media reporting life conditions of hosting camps to denounce violence, abuses and inhumane living conditions – has ensured the politicisation of the migration phenomenon. However, strategies and practices carried on to face the migration crisis have been inconsistent and ineffective, non-existent is some respect.

By focusing on the EU external migration policy this article has demonstrated that EU migration policy-making is shaped by the intergovernmental method and EUMS act as veto powers at European Council level. Diverging strategic interests and disagreement on objectives *de facto* have led to policy inertia because EUMS often have diverging perceptions, values and ideas concerning migration (Caporaso talks about conflicting 'preferences among the actors', 2018, 1351).

This article has highlighted the contradictions of the EU response to Mediterranean migration focusing on political actors acting as upward forces of spiralling of securitisation. It has suggested to combine domestic politics, in particular the politicisation of the migration issue at domestic level, with the preferences within EU institutions (the European Council in particular) to provide an explanation of the EU migration policy fiasco.

This article has moved beyond the widely acknowledged phenomenon of securitisation of migration and investigated the outcomes of the securitisation of migration at the EU level considering that European political leaders of extreme right are behaving as securitising actors. It has assessed the impact of domestic political discourse on EU policy actions and established the linkage between domestic political discourse and EU policy (in)actions. It is the process by which highly politicised issues risk exiting the EU political agenda.

Notes

1. UNHCR reports that at least 5.6 million Syrian refugees have moved to Turkey, Lebanon, Jordan, Egypt or Iraq since the civil war erupted, while more than 6 million are displaced within the country and represent the category of 'internally displaced people' (UNHCR data accessed in April 2019).
2. Investigating personal motivations, a complex mixture of aspiration/ability to migrate arises (Carling and Schewel 2018).
3. EU migration governance draws from the definition of 'regional migration governance' provided by Lavenex (2019); it refers to '[r]egional institutions addressing mobility, asylum, migrant rights or migration control' and implies the complex interaction among various actors in the management of migration.
4. EUMS subscribed to a principle of sincere co-operation with regard to the tasks spelled out in the Treaty on the European Union (TEU Art. 4.3) and a principle of solidarity and fair sharing of responsibilities, including its financial implications, between the Member States in matters of border checks, migration and asylum (TFEU Art. 80).
5. Policy implementation remains a national responsibility and EUMS retain responsibility of granting asylum in the EU; however, several EU agencies - the EASO, Frontex, Europol and Eurojust, assist member states to identify, register and fingerprint incoming migrants in hotspot centres (Tazzioli 2018).
6. Following to the European Commission's proposal, in September 2015 the Council of the EU adopted an ambitious relocation plan to implement the quota system envisaged in the European Agenda on Migration. In this plan EUMS committed to relocating 160,000 persons from countries of first entry to other Member States over the course of two years.

7. The proposal on a temporary scheme to relocate refugees from Greece and Italy to other Schengen states had been formally adopted by a majority vote in September 2015, but remained factually irrelevant because eastern European countries continued to resist it.

8. In its progress report of September 2016, the Commission reported the gap between the number of relocation requests submitted and the acceptances by Member States. Austria and Hungary, for instance, had not submitted any pledge and Poland had suspended the processing of relocation requests (European Commission 2016).

9. In October 2016, the Hungarian government even held a referendum asking voters to reject the EU plan for relocation. The Hungarian and Slovak governments challenged the legality of the relocation plan before the Court of Justice of the EU.

10. On the current debate on the interaction between the migration crisis and the crisis of the fundamental principles leading to European integration see Bauböck (2018), Biermann et al. (2019), Börzel and Risse (2018), Caporaso (2018), Genschel and Jachtenfuchs (2018).

11. In his Remarks following the meeting, Donald Tusk defined quotas as 'a contentious issue' and explained the reasons why it was decided to assess progress in this respect later on and to post-pone any agreement on the reform of the asylum system to June 2018 (Tusk, 2017a). The preparatory documents circulated by President Tusk ahead of the summit had mentioned internal deadlocks hampering policy development (Tusk, 2017b). In a press release he had to admit that concerning migration 'a lack of unity is very visible'.

12. On the party competition dynamics over the migration issue see Urso (2018).

13. Interview, IOM, December 2018.

14. The IOM, with the support of the Italian Ministry of the Interior and thanks to EU funds, has launched 'Voluntary Return Programmes' aimed at favouring the socio-economic re-integration in countries of origin. Interview, IOM, December 2018.

Disclosure statement

No potential conflict of interest was reported by the author(s).

Funding

This research has been conducted within the project "The Italian Visa, Asylum and Migration policy between domestic and international constraints" financed by the University of Catania in the frame of the Research Plan 2017-2019; University of Catania.

ORCID

Stefania Panebianco ⓘ http://orcid.org/0000-0001-8284-5995

References

Attinà, Fulvio. 2016. "Migration Drivers, the EU External Migration Policy and Crisis Management." *Romanian Journal of European Affairs* 16 (4): 15–31.

Attinà, Fulvio. 2018. "Tackling the Migrant Wave: EU as a Source and a Manager of Crisis." *Revista Española de Derecho Internacional* 70 (2): 49–70. doi:10.17103/redi.70.2.2018.1.02

Balzacq, Thierry, Sarah Léonard, and Jan Ruzicka. 2016. "Securitization Revisited: Theory and Cases." *International Relations* 30 (4): 494–531. doi:10.1177/0047117815596590

Bauböck, Rainer. 2018. "Refugee Protection and Burden-Sharing in the European Union." *JCMS: Journal of Common Market Studies* 56 (1): 141–156. doi:10.1111/jcms.12638

Bello, Valeria. 2017. *International Migration and International Security. Why Prejudice is a Global Security Threat*. London: Routledge.

Bello, V. 2022. "The Spiralling of the Securitisation of Migration in the EU: From the Management of a "Crisis" to a Governance of Human Mobility?" *Journal of Ethnic and Migration Studies* 48 (6): 1327–1344. https://doi.org/10.1080/1369183X.2020.1851464.

Bettini, Giovanni. 2017. "Where Next? Climate Change, Migration, and the (Bio)politics of Adaptation." *Global Policy* 8 (S1): 33–39. doi:10.1111/1758-5899.12404

Bicchi, Federica. 2018. "The Mediterranean, Between Unity and Fault Line." *Global Affairs* 4 (2-3): 329–339. doi:10.1080/23340460.2018.1554394

Biermann, Felix, Guérin Nina, Jagdhuber Stefan, Rittberger Berthold, and Weiss Moritz. 2019. "Political (Non)reform in the Euro Crisis and the Refugee Crisis: A Liberal Intergovernmentalist Explanation." *Journal of European Public Policy* 26 (2): 246–266. doi:10.1080/13501763.2017.1408670

Bigo, Didier. 2000. "When Two Become One: Internal and External Securitisations." In *International Relations Theory and the Politics of European Integration*, edited by Morten Kelstrup and Michael C Williams, 320–360. London: Routledge.

Bigo, Didier, and Anastassia Tsoukala. 2008. "Understanding (In)Security." In *Terror, Insecurity and Liberty: Illiberal Practices of Liberal Regimes After 9/11*, edited by Bigo Didier, and Tsoukala Anastassia, 1–9. London: Routledge.

Bilgin, Pinar. 2017. "Resisting Post-Truth Politics, a Primer: Or, How *Not* to Think About Human Mobility and the Global Environment." *Global Policy* 8 (S1): 55–59. doi:10.1111/1758-5899.12411

Börzel, Tanja A., and Thomas Risse. 2018. "From the Euro to the Schengen Crises: European Integration Theories, Politicization, and Identity Politics." *Journal of European Public Policy* 25 (1): 83–108. doi:10.1080/13501763.2017.1310281

Buzan, Barry. 1991. *People, States & Fear. An Agenda for International Security Studies in the Post-Cold War Era*. 2nd ed. London: Harvester Wheatsheaf.

Caporaso, James A. 2018. "Europe's Triple Crisis and the Uneven Role of Institutions: the Euro, Refugees and Brexit." *JCMS: Journal of Common Market Studies* 56 (6): 1345–1361. doi:10.1111/jcms.12746

Carling, Jørgen, and Schewel, Kerilyn. 2018. "Revisiting Aspiration and Ability in International Migration." *Journal of Ethnic and Migration Studies* 44 (6): 945–963. doi:10.1080/1369183X.2017.1384146

Conti, Nicolò. 2018. "National Political Elites, the EU, and the Populist Challenge." *Politics* 38 (3): 361–377. doi:10.1177/0263395718777363

Cusumano, Eugenio. 2019. "Migrant Rescue as Organized Hypocrisy: EU Maritime Missions Offshore Libya Between Humanitarianism and Border Control." *Cooperation and Conflict* 54 (1): 3–24. doi:10.1177/0010836718780175

Cuttitta, Paolo. 2017. "Delocalization, Humanitarianism, and Human Rights: The Mediterranean Border Between Exclusion and Inclusion." *Antipode* 50 (3): 783–803. doi:10.1111/anti.12337

De Haas, Hein. 2011. "Mediterranean Migration Futures: Patterns, Drivers and Scenarios." *Global Environmental Change* 21 (S1): S59–S69. doi:10.1016/j.gloenvcha.2011.09.003

Del Sarto, Raffaella A. 2010. "Borderlands: The Middle East and North Africa as the EU's Southern Buffer Zone." In *Mediterranean Frontiers: Borders, Conflicts and Memory in a Transnational World*, edited by Dimitar Bechev, and Kalypso Nicolaïdis, 149–167. London: I.B. Tauris.

Eurobarometer. 2018a. *Standard Eurobarometer 90*. Autumn 2018.

Eurobarometer. 2018b. *Integration of immigrants in the European Union*. Special Eurobarometer 469.

European Commission. 2015. *Communication from the Commission to the European Parliament, the European Council and the Council. A European Agenda on Migration*. Brussels, 13.5.2015, COM(2015) 240 final.

European Commission. 2016. *Communication from the Commission to the European Parliament, the European Council and the Council. Sixth Report on Relocation and Resettlement*. Brussels, 28.9.2016 COM(2016) 636 final.

European Council. 2017. *European Council Meeting Conclusions*. Brussels, 14 December 2017, EUCO 19/1/17 REV 1, CO EUR 24 CONCL 7.

European Council. 2018a. *European Council Meeting Conclusions*. Brussels, 28 June 2018, EUCO 9/18, CO EUR 9 CONCL 3.

European Council. 2018b. *European Council Meeting Conclusions*. Brussels, 18 October 2018, EUCO 13/18, CO EUR 16, CONCL 5.

European Council. 2018c. *European Council Meeting Conclusions*. Brussels, 13-14 December 2018, EUCO 17/18, CO EUR 2, CONCL 7.

European Council. 2019. "A New Strategic Agenda, 2019–2024." *Adopted at the Special European Council Meeting, 30 June 2019*.

Geddes, Andrew. 2015. "Governing Migration from a Distance: Interactions Between Climate, Migration, and Security in the South Mediterranean." *European Security* 24 (3): 473–490. doi:10.1080/09662839.2015.1028191

Geddes, Andrew, and Peter Scholten. 2016. *The Politics of Migration and Immigration in Europe*. 2nd ed. London: Sage.

Genschel, Philipp, and Markus Jachtenfuchs. 2018. "From Market Integration to Core State Powers: The Eurozone Crisis, the Refugee Crisis and Integration Theory." *JCMS: Journal of Common Market Studies* 56 (1): 178–196. doi:10.1111/jcms.12654

Grande, Edgar, Tobias Schwarzbözl, and Matthias Fatke. 2019. "Politicizing Immigration in Western Europe." *Journal of European Public Policy* 26 (10): 1444–1463.

Guiraudon, Virginie. 2018. "The 2015 Refugee Crisis was not a Turning Point: Explaining Policy Inertia in EU Border Control." *European Political Science* 17 (1): 151–160. doi:10.1057/s41304-017-0123-x

Harteveld, Elco, Schaper Joep, Sarah L. De Lange, and Wouter Van Der Brug. 2018. "Blaming Brussels? The Impact of (News About) the Refugee Crisis on Attitudes Towards the EU and National Politics." *JCMS: Journal of Common Market Studies* 56 (1): 157–177. doi:10.1111/jcms.12664

Huysmans, Jef. 2000. "The European Union and the Securitization of Migration." *JCMS: Journal of Common Market Studies* 38 (5): 751–777. doi:10.1111/1468-5965.00263

Italian Coast Guard. 2017. *Attività SAR nel Mediterraneo Centrale*, Comando Generale del Corpo delle Capitanerie di porto – Guardia Costiera (MRCCR). http://www.guardiacostiera.gov.it/attivita/Documents/attivita-sar-immigrazione-2017/Rapporto_annuale_2017_ITA.pdf.

Kaunert, Christian, and Sarah Léonard. 2012. "The Development of the EU Asylum Policy: Venue-Shopping in Perspective." *Journal of European Public Policy* 19 (9): 1396–1413. doi:10.1080/13501763.2012.677191

Krzyżanowski, Michał, Anna Triandafyllidou, and Ruth Wodak. 2018. "The Mediatization and the Politicization of the "Refugee Crisis" in Europe." *Journal of Immigrant & Refugee Studies* 16 (1-2): 1–14. doi:10.1080/15562948.2017.1353189

Lavenex, Sandra. 2019. "Regional Migration Governance – Building Block of Global Initiatives?" *Journal of Ethnic and Migration Studies* 45 (8): 1275–1293. doi:10.1080/1369183X.2018.1441606

Lazaridis, Gabriella, and Wadia, Khursheed. 2015. *The Securitisation of Migration in the EU: Debates Since 9/11*. Basingstoke: Palgrave Macmillan.

Mogherini, Federica. 2015. *High Representative/Vice-President Federica Mogherini's remarks at the UN Security Council*. New York, 11/05/2015, EEAS, https://eeas.europa.eu/headquarters/headquarters-homepage/5570_fr.

Moreno-Lax, Violeta. 2018. "The EU Humanitarian Border and the Securitization of Human Rights: The 'Rescue-Through-Interdiction/Rescue-Without-Protection' Paradigm." *JCMS: Journal of Common Market Studies* 56 (1): 119–140. doi:10.1111/jcms.12651

Orsina, Giovanni. 2019. "Genealogy of a Populist Uprising. Italy, 1979–2019." *The International Spectator* 54 (2): 50–66. doi:10.1080/03932729.2019.1603896

Panebianco, Stefania. 2016. "The Mediterranean Migration Crisis: Border Control *Versus* Humanitarian Approaches." *Global Affairs* 2 (4): 441–445. doi:10.1080/23340460.2016.1278091

Panebianco, Stefania. 2017. "The EU and Migration in the Mediterranean. Entrapped Between the Humanitarian Approach and Border Security." In *Migrants and Refugees Across Europe*, edited by Moccia Luigi, and Pop Lia, 139–168. Boschum: European University Press.

Slominski, Peter, and Florian Trauner. 2018. "How do Member States Return Unwanted Migrants? The Strategic (Non-)use of 'Europe' During the Migration Crisis." *JCMS: Journal of Common Market Studies* 56 (1): 101–118. doi:10.1111/jcms.12621

Tazzioli, Martina. 2018. "Containment Through Mobility: Migrants' Spatial Disobediences and the Reshaping of Control Through the Hotspot System." *Journal of Ethnic and Migration Studies* 44 (16): 2764–2779. doi:10.1080/1369183X.2017.1401514

Thielemann, Eiko. 2018. "Why Refugee Burden-Sharing Initiatives Fail: Public Goods, Free-Riding and Symbolic Solidarity in the EU." *JCMS: Journal of Common Market Studies* 56 (1): 63–82. doi:10.1111/jcms.12662

Tusk, Donald. 2017a. *Remarks by President Donald Tusk following the European Council meetings on 14 and 15 December* 2017. Statements and Remarks, 813/17-15/12/2017.

Tusk, Donald. 2017b. *Remarks by President Donald Tusk ahead of the European Council meetings.* Press Release, 14/12/2017.

Urso, Ornella. 2018. "The Politicization of Immigration in Italy. Who Frames the Issue, When and How." *Italian Political Science Review/Rivista Italiana Di Scienza Politica* 48 (3): 365–381. doi:10.1017/ipo.2018.16

Van Hear, Nicholas, Bakewell Oliver, and Long Katy. 2018. "Push-Pull Plus: Reconsidering the Drivers of Migration." *Journal of Ethnic and Migration Studies* 44 (6): 927–944.

Wæver, Ole, Buzan Barry, Kelstrup Morten, and Lemaitre Pierre. 1993. *Identity Migration and the New Security Agenda in Europe.* New York: St. Martins Press.

Zaun, Natascha. 2016. "Why EU Asylum Standards Exceed the Lowest Common Denominator: The Role of Regulatory Expertise in EU Decision-Making." *Journal of European Public Policy* 23 (1): 136–154. doi:10.1080/13501763.2015.1039565

Zaun, Natascha. 2018. "States as Gatekeepers in EU Asylum Politics: Explaining the Non-Adoption of a Refugee Quota System." *JCMS: Journal of Common Market Studies* 56 (1): 44–62. doi:10.1111/jcms.12663

The securitisation of migration in the European Union: Frontex and its evolving security practices

Sarah Léonard and Christian Kaunert

ABSTRACT

This article investigates the evolving security practices of one of the key actors in the handling of asylum-seekers and migrants at the external borders of the European Union (EU) Member States, the European Border and Coast Guard Agency, widely referred to as 'Frontex'. It does so by applying a revised version of the Copenhagen School's securitisation framework, which focuses on security practices and is underpinned by an understanding of security as belonging to a continuum. The article compares and contrasts the practices of Frontex in the context of two significant 'migration crises' in the Mediterranean, in 2005–2006 and 2015–2016, respectively. The analysis of the more recent practices of the Agency following the 2015–2016 'migration crisis' shows that this 'crisis' has led to an intensification of the security practices of the Agency. Frontex has moved towards the end point of the continuum, which is characterised by survival, existential threats, and militarisation. This has contributed to a spiralling of the securitisation of migration in the EU.

Introduction

Asylum and migration matters have increasingly given rise to intense political debates in Europe, especially in the aftermath of 9/11 (Lazaridis and Wadia 2015). They have been at the heart of several electoral campaigns over the last few years, notably in Germany. This country became the most popular final destination for asylum-seekers and migrants in the context of the 2015–2016 'migration crisis'.[1] Initially, Chancellor Angela Merkel appeared to espouse an 'open-arms policy'. She argued that Germany was able to absorb large numbers of asylum-seekers and migrants – a position famously summarised by her *Wir schaffen das* statement. However, this phrase would rapidly come to haunt the Chancellor, as her opponents, in particular from the far-right 'Alternative für Deutschland' (AfD, 'Alternative for Germany') party, seized upon this vague idea to criticise the results of the governmental policy.

As migration has captured the political agenda, academics have discussed the link between migration and security, which has sometimes been referred to as the 'migration-security' nexus (Bourbeau 2017a; Faist 2004; Karyotis 2003; Miller 2001;

Tirman 2004). Although some scholars have applied other approaches (see Bourbeau 2017a), a significant number of researchers have used some of the ideas developed by the Copenhagen School on securitisation (Buzan 1991; Buzan, Wæver, and Wilde 1998; Wæver 1993; Wæver 1995) in order to analyse how migration and security have been linked in various political contexts (Bigo 1998a, 1998b, 2001a, 2002; Bourbeau 2011, 2017b; Chebel d'Appollonia 2015; Guild 2003a, 2003b, 2003c, 2009; Huysmans 2000, 2006; Karyotis 2011, 2012; Lazaridis 2011; Lazaridis and Wadia 2015; Wæver 1993).

Despite some notable exceptions (Boswell 2007; Neal 2009), most scholars have contended that asylum and migration have been successfully securitised in Europe, that is, socially constructed as security issues. In an article published in 2010, Léonard (2010) argued that Frontex, the European agency supporting cooperation amongst EU Member States on the management of external borders (now known as the European Border and Coast Guard Agency), had significantly contributed to the securitisation of migration through its practices. As ten years have elapsed since the publication of this article and a major 'migration crisis' has affected Europe, it is worthwhile re-visiting the issue of the linkage between Frontex and the securitisation of migration. It is particularly important because Frontex, which had only started its operations in earnest in 2006, has significantly evolved since then. Also, as time has passed, it is now possible to gain a better appreciation of the activities of Frontex in a historical perspective.

In order to do so, this article draws upon a revised version of the Copenhagen School's securitisation framework. The following section presents this amended version of the securitisation framework, which highlights the importance of securitising practices and is underpinned by a conceptualisation of security as being located on a continuum. It is followed by an analysis of the evolution of the practices of Frontex. The article contrasts the practices of the Agency when faced with two different major 'migration crises' in 2005–2006 and 2015-2016, respectively. An analysis of the more recent practices of the Agency, during the 2015–2016 'migration crisis', shows that this 'crisis' has led to an intensification of the security practices of the Agency. This has contributed to a spiralling of the securitisation of migration in the EU.

A new securitisation framework

The core idea of the securitisation framework, which was originally developed by Ole Wæver and Barry Buzan, in cooperation with other colleagues of the so-called 'Copenhagen School', is that there are no objective security issues that exist 'out there' (Buzan, Wæver, and Wilde 1998). In contrast, there are only issues that are socially constructed as security threats through processes of 'securitisation'. Those can be defined as 'processes of constructing a shared understanding of what is to be considered and collectively responded to as a threat' (Buzan, Wæver, and Wilde 1998, 26). Buzan's and Wæver's conceptualisation of securitisation has a strong linguistic dimension, as they argue that security issues are socially constructed as such through 'speech acts' (Buzan, Wæver, and Wilde 1998, 26) (see also Wæver 1995, 54–55). According to Wæver (1995, 55), 'security is not of interest as a sign that refers to something more real; the utterance itself is the act. By saying it, something is done (as in betting, giving a promise, naming a ship)'. Moreover, the Copenhagen School claims that, by 'uttering security', the securitising actor 'moves a particular development into a specific area, and thereby claims a special right to use whatever means are necessary to block it' (Wæver 1995, 55). From that perspective, securitisation can be viewed as 'the staging of existential issues in politics to lift them above politics. In security discourse, an issue is dramatised and presented as an issue of supreme priority; thus, by labelling it as security, an agent claims a need for and a right to treat it by extraordinary means' (Buzan, Wæver, and Wilde 1998, 26). Moreover, the securitisation framework is underpinned by a 'traditional military-political understanding' of security (Buzan, Wæver, and Wilde 1998, 21), which equates security with survival (see also Williams 2003).

Over the years, the securitisation framework has attracted much praise, but has also been criticised from various perspectives (see Balzacq, Léonard, and Ruzicka 2016). Scholars have also put forward ideas to further develop or refine the framework in several respects. Two issues are of particular importance for the purpose of this article. The first is the idea that issues cannot only be constructed as security issues discursively, but also through practices. The second concerns the understanding of security underpinning the securitisation framework. These two issues are examined in turn in the remainder of this section.

With regard to the issue of discourses and practices, the securitisation framework as it was originally developed by the Copenhagen School put a significant emphasis on the social construction of threats through securitising 'speech acts'. In other words, it highlighted the importance of discourse for the social construction of security threats. However, Buzan, Wæver and their colleagues themselves already observed that some practices, such as those of the security services of a state, may take place without any public discourse to acknowledge or justify them (Buzan, Wæver, and Wilde 1998, 28). They also noted that securitisation may become institutionalised over time in cases of persistent or recurrent threats. In such instances, securitising speech acts become unnecessary in their view (Buzan, Wæver, and Wilde 1998, 27–28). Thus, although Buzan and Waver emphasised the discursive dimension of the social construction of security threats, they acknowledged themselves that there might be securitisation dynamics at play even in the absence of securitising speech acts.

This point was also made by Bigo (2000, 194), who argued that '[i]t is possible to securitise certain problems without speech or discourse and the military and the police have known that for a long time. The practical work, discipline and expertise are as important as all forms of discourse'. In other words, non-discursive acts, such as the development of public policies or the establishment of institutional bodies, may matter as much as – if not more than – discourse in socially constructing an issue as a security threat. Moreover, Bigo (1998b; 2001b) highlighted that there can be significant differences between official discourses and everyday practices. With regard to the specific issue of migration, he argued that

> [t]he securitization of immigration [...] emerges from the correlation between some successful speech acts of political leaders, the mobilization they create for and against some groups of people, and the specific field of security professionals [...]. It comes also from a range of administrative practices such as population profiling, risk assessment, statistical calculation, category creation, proactive preparation, and what may be termed a specific habitus of the "security professional" with its ethos of secrecy and concern for the management of fear or unease (Bigo 2002, 65–66).

Such ideas have been echoed by other scholars, including Huysmans (2004, 2006) who has emphasised the importance of examining security practices and their technological aspects. Likewise, Balzacq (2008, 75) has claimed that 'rather than investigating the construction of threats at the level of discourse, we should focus on the function and implications of policy instruments used to meet a public problem'.

Such ideas are particularly relevant to this article and its investigation of Frontex, given the increasing emphasis placed on technology in the development of border practices in Europe. Over the last few years, European governments have increasingly invested in sophisticated technological devices in order to strengthen border security, including radars and sensors, camera surveillance systems, unmanned aerial systems, and large-scale IT systems handling biometric data (Dijstelbloem and Meijer 2011; Gerstein 2018). Moreover, a focus on practices is more adequate in the case of a body like Frontex. Given its bureaucratic nature as a European agency, it is not prone to making official speeches in the same way as a President or a Prime Minister (Léonard and Kaunert 2019, 27).

Concerning the second issue, namely the understanding of security underpinning the securitisation framework, this article moves away from the Copenhagen School's narrow understanding of security – which is equated with survival and involves existential threats – to adopt a broader understanding of security. From that perspective, the ideas of survival and existential threats are not abandoned, but are placed at the end of a continuum. As advocated by Abrahamsen (2005, 59), security issues can be conceptualised as '[moving] on a continuum from normalcy to worrisome/troublesome to risk and existential threat – and conversely, from threat to risk and back to normalcy'. This enables researchers to analyse how some issues may be subjected to a process intensifying their security-ness, whilst still falling short of being presented and dealt with as existential security threats (Williams 2003, 521). From that viewpoint, existential threats, survival and arguably military practices can be seen as characterising the end point of this continuum, whereas the realm of security encompasses a broader part of the continuum than merely this end point. This conceptualisation is in line with the understanding of securitisation as a spiralling process, which is at the heart of this special issue and which refers to the idea that the intensity of a phenomenon can increase or decrease in a dramatic fashion and over a short period of time (see Bello 2022).

For these reasons, the securitisation framework used in this article draws upon the Copenhagen School's work, but alters it in two significant ways. First of all, it focuses on security practices, rather than discourse, and conceptualises security as a continuum, rather than equating it with survival. As a result, the subsequent empirical analysis focuses on the practices deployed by Frontex and examines the extent to and the ways in which those can be considered to be 'securitizing practices', that is, practices conveying the meaning that the issue they are addressing is a security issue. This article argues that there are two main types of such securitising practices. First of all, practices that are usually deployed to tackle issues that are widely seen as security issues, i.e. issues that were previously successfully securitised, such as a foreign armed attack or terrorism, can be seen as securitising practices. For example, the deployment of military troops or military equipment such as tanks for dealing with an issue conveys the message that this issue is a security threat that requires addressing, thereby socially constructing this issue as a security threat. Another type of securitising practices are cooperation practices with bodies or organisations that have traditionally been considered security bodies or organisations, such as those dealing with military or policing matters. The remainder of this article applies this analytical framework in order to analyse the role of Frontex in the securitisation of migration in the EU. It focuses on the practices of Frontex in the context of two 'migration crises' separated by a decade in order to highlight the evolution in the practices of the Agency.

The practices of Frontex in the 2005–2006 'migration crisis'

This section focuses on the first 'migration crisis' with which the EU as a whole – rather than some of its Member States – dealt, namely the 2005–2006 'crisis' at the Spanish external borders.

Although the Spanish authorities had at times seen large numbers of asylum-seekers and irregular migrants arrive since the 1990s, the events of 2005–2006 can be described as exceptional. Violent clashes between the border forces and migrants at the land borders between Morocco and the Spanish enclaves of Ceuta and Melilla left 14 dead in the space of a few days in September 2005 (Léonard and Kaunert 2019: 113). Whilst there had previously been deaths at the borders, never before had so many migrants died in such a short time period. Migration came back to the top of the political agenda a few months later, after large numbers of migrants and asylum-seekers began to leave West Africa by boat in order to reach the Canary Islands. These events were depicted as a 'migration crisis', which concerned not only Spain, but the entire EU.

This 2005–2006 'migration crisis' is also worth examining because it saw the 'baptism of fire' of the newly created European Agency for the Management of Operational Cooperation at the External Borders of the Member States (Frontex). This EU agency had been established by Council Regulation EC 2007/2004 of 26 October 2004 in order to coordinate operational cooperation amongst Member States with a view to enhancing security at the external borders of the EU Member States (Léonard 2009). Its founding regulation had given Frontex six main tasks, namely (1) coordinating operational cooperation between Member States regarding the management of external borders; (2) assisting Member States in the training of national border guards, including establishing common training standards; (3) conducting risk analyses; (4) following up on developments in research relating to the control and surveillance of external borders; (5) assisting Member States when increased technical and operational assistance at external borders was required; and (6) assisting Member States in organising joint return operations (see Léonard 2010).

The 'migration crisis' in Ceuta and Melilla did not lead to any immediate response from the EU, notably because the Spanish government did not request EU support. Nevertheless, the European Commission sent a 'technical mission on illegal immigration', which took place on 7–11 October 2005. Its main tasks were to evaluate the characteristics and the size of irregular migration flows from Africa through Morocco to the EU and to establish possible measures that would enhance the cooperation on irregular migration between the EU and Morocco. The mission report also noted that '[t]he technical mission did not seek to investigate the recent tragic incidents in Ceuta and Melilla nor did it aim to assess the ways that border management is carried out by Morocco or Spain' (European Commission 2005, 1). It is not surprising that the European

Commission would explicitly refrain from commenting on the conduct of border controls at the external borders of one of the Member States of the EU, as those are the responsibility of the Member States. The final mission report included several proposals for developing an EU response to irregular migration into the enclaves of Ceuta and Melilla, but those concerned broad, long-term solutions (European Commission 2005, 8–13).

In contrast, the EU played a more significant part in the response to the 'migration crisis' in the Canary Islands a few months later. This can notably be explained by the fact that the Spanish authorities requested EU assistance for dealing with the migration flows. At the end of May 2006, European Commissioner Franco Frattini declared that the Spanish government would receive operational assistance from the EU in order to address what he described as 'an urgent and difficult situation' (Brand 2006). This assistance took the form of a joint operation coordinated by the newly established Frontex agency, which was only becoming operational after it had been established by a Council Regulation in October 2004. The joint operation had a total budget of 3.5 million euros - 2.8 million of which were co-financed by Frontex – and comprised two 'modules', namely Hera I and Hera II.

Hera I began in July 2006 and entailed the deployment of national experts from various EU Member States, such as France, Germany, Italy, Portugal, the Netherlands, and the UK, as well as Norway, to support their Spanish colleagues in establishing the identity and the country of origin of the migrants who had arrived on the Canary Islands. This helped the Spanish government return some of these migrants to their country of origin. In other words, Hera I was a largely technical operation with a very specific purpose (Léonard and Kaunert 2019).

In contrast, Hera II was more ambitious and had a significantly broader scope. It was officially launched on 11 August 2006 for nine weeks. It was enthusiastically presented by EU Commissioner for Justice and Home Affairs Frattini as a 'truly historic moment in the history of the EU immigration policies and a very tangible expression of EU solidarity amongst Member States' (Migration News Sheet 2006 September, 4). In addition, he highlighted the 'humanitarian character' of the operation, which, in his words, aimed 'at saving lives at sea, as well as reducing illegal immigration and combating trafficking in human beings, a crime from which only traffickers benefit' (Migration News Sheet, 2006 September, 4).

However, Frattini's statement turned out to be rather removed from the reality on the ground. In practice, the operation was significantly delayed, since it had been initially discussed to deploy the surveillance vessels and planes in June. There were various reasons for the delay, including budgetary problems, a certain lack of interest in some EU Member States, as well as the willingness of the Spanish government to integrate the Senegalese and Mauritanian authorities into the operation, which led to further negotiations (Léonard and Kaunert 2019). Moreover, Hera II ended up having a more modest scope than what had been anticipated. At the end of May, various EU Member States had signalled their willingness to participate in the joint sea operation. In practice, only three eventually confirmed that they would contribute assets to the operation. Finland offered a plane, Italy contributed a coast guard patrol boat and a plane, whilst Portugal sent a corvette (Frontex, 2006). Nevertheless, two weeks after Hera II had officially started, only the Portuguese corvette was actually conducting surveillance operations, given that the Finnish and Italian assets had still not been deployed (Migration News Sheet 2006 October, 7).

These setbacks led the Spanish government to repeat its request for EU assistance at the informal meeting of the Justice and Home Affairs Council on 21 September 2006. However, it was opposed by several EU Member States. Some of those, such as Germany, Austria, France, the Netherlands, and Belgium, made it clear that they considered the Spanish government to have encouraged migration flows by holding a massive amnesty of irregular migrants in spring 2005. Eventually, all the assets that had been promised were deployed and patrolled the coastal areas of Senegal, Mauritania, Cape Verde and the Canary Islands. The Mauritanian and Senegalese authorities also took part in the joint sea operation with their own equipment and personnel on the basis of a bilateral agreement signed with the Spanish government (Léonard and Kaunert 2019). In its final press release regarding the operation, Frontex highlighted the humanitarian aspect of Hera II as it described its main aims as 'to detect vessels setting off towards the Canary Islands and to divert them back to their point of departure thus reducing the number of lives lost at sea'. It further noted that '[during] the course of the operation more than 3,500 migrants were stopped from this dangerous endeavour close to the African coast' (Léonard and Kaunert 2019, 126). Operation Hera II came to a close in December 2006.

It was followed by Operation HERA III, which was launched in February 2007, following a request of the Spanish authorities. Risk analysis by Frontex had also confirmed the continued importance of the southern sea borders as one of the main routes for irregular migrants into the EU. In line with its two predecessors, Operation Hera III had two main dimensions. First, joint patrols involving aerial and naval means took place along the West African coast in a bid to reduce migration flows. Those were conducted in cooperation with the Senegalese authorities and involved several EU Member States, including Spain, Italy, Luxembourg and France. Second, it aimed to assist Spanish authorities with interviewing irregular migrants after their arrival on the Canary Islands in order to establish their country of origin and their identity, as well as gathering intelligence on their journey, including the involvement of smugglers. Various Member States, including Germany, Italy, Luxembourg and Portugal, contributed experts for these purposes (Frontex, 2007).

Thus, the role played by Frontex in the 2005–2006 'migration crisis' had three main components. First of all, it carried out risk analysis, which confirmed the continuous importance of Spain as a gateway to the EU for irregular migrants and asylum-seekers coming from Africa. Moreover, Frontex provided the Spanish authorities with technical assistance for the specific task of establishing the identity and the country of origin of migrants who had landed on the Canary Islands, with a view to facilitating their return. Finally, the agency coordinated joint operations at sea involving the assets of various EU Member States. Such joint operations are arguably securitising practices, in the sense that their enactment suggests that migration flows to Europe represent a security threat that needs to be addressed. Traditionally, such coordinated action at sea involving various states has been organised to tackle issues that are largely perceived to constitute security threats, such as military attacks, piracy, or drug trafficking. Nevertheless, it is important to highlight the limited scope of the Hera joint sea operations in terms of their budget, the number of EU Member States involved, and the assets deployed.

The practices of Frontex in the 2015–2016 'migration crisis'

Another major 'migration crisis' unfolded in Europe a few years later. The 'crisis' that had affected Spain had been followed by a quieter period in the Mediterranean. This considerably changed in 2014, which saw a sharp increase in the number of people attempting to cross the Mediterranean in order to reach Europe, as well as the number of victims who lost their lives at sea. In 2015, the number of arrivals soared to over one million, whilst the tragic loss of lives at sea continued (European Parliament, 2016). In particular, in April 2015, a boat carrying about 700 migrants capsized 130 miles off the coast of the Italian island of Lampedusa, which caused the death of hundreds of migrants (BBC News 2015). It was not only the fast rise in the number of arrivals that was remarkable, but also the important shift in migratory routes into Europe away from the Western routes and the Central Mediterranean route towards the Eastern Mediterranean and the Western Balkan routes. This meant that Italy and Greece faced unprecedented numbers of arrivals on their shores as they became gateways to the EU for hundreds of thousands of asylum-seekers and migrants. According to the UNHCR (2015), more than three quarters of those arriving in Europe were fleeing from persecution and violence in Iraq, Syria or Afghanistan.

The sinking of the vessel on 19 April 2015 led to the organisation of a Special meeting of the European Council a few days later. A range of measures were announced at the end of the meeting, several of those concerning Frontex (European Council 2015). Overall, the role played by Frontex in the response to this crisis in the following months was to be significantly more important than the role it had played in the 2005–2006 'migration crisis' previously examined. It had three main dimensions: the coordination of joint operations, its participation in the so-called 'hotspots' and risk analysis.

Firstly, Frontex coordinated joint operations Triton and Poseidon, which supported Greece and Italy respectively. These two operations were already ongoing when it was decided to reinforce them at the April 2015 Special meeting of the European Council, notably by tripling their financial resources in 2015 and 2016 (European Council 2015). The main focus of these operations was border control and surveillance, although they also included search and rescue activities (see Cusumano 2019). In terms of their scope, they were significantly larger than the Hera operations previously analysed. For example, between January and August 2016, 667 Frontex officers were deployed, alongside 19 vessels, one aircraft and two helicopters as part of Operation Poseidon, whilst 523 Frontex officers, nine vessels, three aircraft and two helicopters participated in Operation Triton (European Commission 2016). What is also noteworthy in comparison to the previous narrow focus of the Hera operations is the range of security issues which Frontex tackled as part of these operations. As noted by the agency itself in the case of Triton,

> [the] operational focus of Triton [expanded] to include other forms of cross border crime. Apart from numerous arrests of people smugglers, the assets deployed by the agency increasingly [contributed] to the detection of drug smuggling, illegal fishing and maritime pollution (Frontex 2016).

In the course of Operation Triton, officers deployed by Frontex also assisted the Italian authorities in registering migrants and collected intelligence about the smuggling networks involved. This information was then passed on to the EU's Law Enforcement Agency (Europol) and the Italian authorities.

Another remarkable development in the context of these operations was the establishment of new practices of cooperation between Frontex and other actors dealing with 'harder' security issues, in particular the North-Atlantic Treaty Organisation (NATO), which is a military alliance. Frontex developed tactical and operational cooperation with NATO following the decision by NATO's Defence ministers to deploy Standing Maritime Group 2 (SNMG2) in the Aegean Sea in February 2016. This deployment aimed, in the own words of the alliance (North Atlantic Treaty Organisation 2016, 1), to 'support Greece and Turkey, as well as the European Union's border agency Frontex, in their efforts to tackle the refugee and migrant crisis'. NATO ships conducted reconnaissance, surveillance and monitoring in international waters, as well as in the territorial waters of Turkey and Greece. Thanks to liaison arrangements, including the deployment of Frontex liaison officers to the NATO operation, they were able to provide real-time information to Frontex and to the Greek and Turkish coastguards (North Atlantic Treaty Organisation 2016).

Secondly, Frontex played a key role in the 'hotspots', alongside other EU agencies, such as the European Asylum Support Office (EASO), Europol and the EU's Agency for Criminal Justice Cooperation (Eurojust). The 'hotspot' approach was proposed by the European Commission as part of the European Agenda on Migration, which was unveiled in May 2015. As it had actually been in preparation for a few months, it was not entirely prompted by the dramatic migration-related events of the previous months. However, because of the time of publication, there has been a tendency to view it as the EU's response to the 'migration crisis', which is not entirely correct. In its first part, the European Agenda on Migration identified priorities for immediate action, namely 'saving lives at sea', 'targeting criminal smuggling networks', 'relocation' for responding to the high numbers of arrivals, 'resettlement' for those in need of international protection, 'working in partnership with third countries to tackle migration upstream' and 'using the EU's tools to help frontline Member States' (European Commission 2015a). It is under that last heading that the European Commission indicated that it planned to develop a new 'hotspot approach. It described it as follows:

> the European Asylum Support Office, Frontex and Europol will work on the ground with frontline Member States to swiftly identify, register and fingerprint incoming migrants. The work of the agencies will be complementary to one another (European Commission 2015a, 6).

Frontex was also given the specific task of coordinating the return of those migrants found not to be in need of protection (European Commission 2015a, 6), whereas EASO was expected to support the efficient processing of asylum claims. As for Eurojust and Europol, they were tasked with helping the host Member States investigate and dismantle trafficking and smuggling networks. These 'hotspots' were expected to be established in some of the frontline Member States facing the arrival of large numbers of asylum-seekers and migrants. They were to be located at key arrival points in these countries with a view to managing the arrival of asylum-seekers and migrants in a more orderly manner, through a systematic and faster process of identification and registration.

In practice, the 'hotspot' approach was implemented in Greece and Italy, although other EU Member States could have also requested its implementation on their territory.

Five hotspots were established in Italy, namely in Messina, Taranto, Pozzallo, Trapani and Lampedusa, whilst five were set up in Greece on the islands of Leros, Kos, Chios, Samos and Lesvos. A report prepared for the European Parliament in 2016 observed that the '[rollout] of the hotspots proved initially sluggish, due in part to the need to build them from scratch and to remedy infrastructure shortcomings, but [...] gathered pace significantly [from] early 2016' (European Parliament, 2016, 8). In addition to fingerprinting officers and translators, Frontex sent Joint Screening Teams, which assisted the EU Member States in the identification and the registration of the migrants, including their need of international protection. Frontex also deployed Joint Debriefing Teams, which conducted 'interviews to collect information on the smuggling networks and the routes for the purpose of risk analysis and to feed criminal investigations' (Frontex, n.d.). The relevant intelligence from these debriefing interviews was then passed on to Europol with a view to supporting investigations (European Commission 2015b). The agency also assisted the Greek and Italian authorities with returning persons who do not have a right to remain in the EU, including asylum-seekers whose claim had not been accepted. Thus, Frontex considerably developed its cooperation with Europol in the 'hotspots' and its work contributed to the investigation and dismantling of smuggling networks.

Thirdly, Frontex produced a significant amount of risk analysis during the 2015–2016 'migration crisis'. Those included Western Balkans Annual Risk Analyses, Eastern European Borders Annual Risk Analyses, Annual Risk Analyses, Frontex Risk Analysis Network Quarterly Reports, Western Balkans Risk Analysis Network Quarterly Reports and Eastern European Borders Risk Analysis Network Quarterly Reports. A particularly interesting type of report was the annual Africa-Frontex Intelligence Community Joint Reports. The so-called 'Africa-Frontex Intelligence Community' (AFIC) was established in 2010 with the aim of constituting a framework enabling the sharing of knowledge and intelligence relating to border security between Frontex and African countries. With a focus on Western Africa, its African membership has steadily grown over the years. The AFIC Joint Reports indicate that participants in these meetings in 2015–2016 were not only discussing irregular migration, but also 'harder' security issues, such as terrorism (including al-Shabaab and Boko Haram) and organised crime (Frontex 2016, 2017).

Thus, one can see that the 2015–2016 'migration crisis' has led to an intensification of the security-ness of the practices of Frontex to a significant extent. This is particularly visible in the deployment of practices usually aimed at tackling widely accepted security threats, such as maritime joint operations that have become significantly more sophisticated than they were in the first years of Frontex's activities. Another remarkable development during that period is the development of Frontex's cooperation with bodies that have a stronger security profile, such as NATO – which is a military alliance – and Europol in the field of law enforcement. In that way, Frontex has assumed a key role in the collection and production of not only migration intelligence, but also other types of intelligence linked to 'harder' security threats, such as organised crime and terrorism. These qualitative changes in the security-ness of Frontex's practices are in line with the idea of the spiralling of the securitisation of migration, as developed by Bello (2022).

Conclusion

This article set out to investigate the evolving security practices of one of the key actors in the handling of asylum-seekers and migrants at the external borders of the EU Member States, the European Border and Coast Guard Agency, widely referred to as 'Frontex'. It did so by applying a revised version of the Copenhagen School's securitisation framework, which focuses on security practices and is underpinned by an understanding of security as belonging to a continuum, rather than being equated with survival and existential threats. The article has compared and contrasted the practices of Frontex in the context of two significant 'migration crises' in the Mediterranean, in 2005–2006 and 2015-2016, respectively. The analysis of the more recent practices of the Agency during the 2015–2016 'migration crisis' shows that this 'crisis' has led to an intensification of the security practices of the Agency, including the coordination of more sophisticated joint operations, the growing cooperation with security bodies, such as Europol and NATO, as well as the contribution to the collection and production of intelligence on various security issues. In the last few years, Frontex has therefore moved towards the end point of the security continuum, which is characterised by survival, existential threats, and militarisation. This has contributed to a spiralling of the securitisation of migration in the EU.

Note

1. In this article, the idea of 'migration crisis' is always presented in quotation marks to emphasise the socially constructed nature of such a 'crisis'.

Disclosure statement

No potential conflict of interest was reported by the author(s).

References

Abrahamsen, R. 2005. "Blair's Africa: The Politics of Securitization and Fear." *Alternatives: Global, Local, Political* 30 (1): 55–80.

Balzacq, T. 2008. "The Policy Tools of Securitization: Information Exchange, EU Foreign and Interior Policies." *JCMS: Journal of Common Market Studies* 46 (1): 75–100.

Balzacq, T., S. Léonard, and J. Ruzicka. 2016. ""Securitization" Revisited: Theory and Cases." *International Relations* 30 (4): 494–531.

BBC News. 2015. "Mediterranean Migrants: Hundreds Feared Dead After Boat capsizes", April 19, 2015.

Bello, V. 2022. "The Spiralling of the Securitisation of Migration in the EU: From the Management of a 'Crisis' to a Governance of Human Mobility?" *Journal of Ethnic and Migration Studies* 48 (6): 1327–1344. https://doi.org/10.1080/1369183X.2020.1851464.

Bigo, D. 1998a. "'Sécurité et Immigration: Vers une Gouvernementalité par L'inquiétude?'." *Cultures & Conflits* 31–32: 13–38.

Bigo, D. 1998b. "L'Europe de la sécurité intérieure: Penser autrement la sécurité." In *Entre Union et Nations. L'Etat en Europe*, edited by A. M. Le Gloannec, 55–90. Paris: Presses de Sciences Po.

Bigo, D. 2000. "When Two Become One: Internal and External Securitizations in Europe." In *International Relations Theory and the Politics of European Integration: Power, Security and Community*, edited by M. Kelstrup, and M. C. Williams, 171–204. London: Routledge.

Bigo, D. 2001a. "Migration and Security." In *Controlling a New Migration World*, edited by V. Guiraudon, and C. Joppke, 121–149. London: Routledge.

Bigo, D. 2001b. "The Möbius Ribbon of Internal and External Security(ies)." In *Identities, Borders, Orders: Rethinking International Relations Theory*, edited by M. Albert, D. Jacobson, and Y. Lapid, 91–116. Minneapolis, MN: University of Minnesota Press.

Bigo, D. 2002. "Security and Immigration: Toward a Critique of the Governmentality of Unease." *Alternatives: Global, Local, Political* 27 (Special Issue): 63–92.

Boswell, C. 2007. "Migration Control in Europe After 9/11: Explaining the Absence of Securitization." *JCMS: Journal of Common Market Studies* 45 (3): 589–610.

Bourbeau, P. 2011. *The Securitization of Migration: A Study of Movement and Order*. London: Routledge.

Bourbeau, P., ed. 2017a. *Handbook on Migration and Security*. Cheltenham: Edward Elgar.

Bourbeau, P. 2017b. "Migration, Exceptionalist Security Discourses, and Practices." In *Handbook on Migration and Security*, edited by P. Bourbeau, 105–124. Cheltenham: Edward Elgar.

Brand, C. 2006. "EU Force to Stem African migrants." *The Guardian*, May 24, 2006.

Buzan, B. 1991. *People, States and Fear: An Agenda for International Security Studies in the Post-Cold War Era*. 2nd edn. London: Harvester Wheatsheaf.

Buzan, B., O. Wæver, and de Jaap Wilde, eds. 1998. *Security: A New Framework for Analysis*. Boulder, CO: Lynne Rienner.

Chebel d'Appollonia, A. 2015. *Migrant Mobilization and Securitization in the US and Europe: How Does It Feel to Be a Threat?* Basingstoke: Palgrave Macmillan.

Cusumano, E. 2019. "Migrants Rescue as Organized Hypocrisy: EU Maritime Missions Offshore Libya Between Humanitarianism and Border Control." *Cooperation and Conflict* 54 (1): 3–24.

Dijstelbloem, H., and A. Meijer. 2011. *Migration and the New Technological Borders of Europe*. London: Palgrave Macmillan.

European Commission. 2005. *Visit to Ceuta and Melilla – Mission Report: Technical Mission to Morocco on Illegal Immigration, 7th October – 11 October 2005'*, MEMO/05/380, 19 October 2005. Brussels: European Commission.

European Commission. 2015a. *Communication from the Commission to the European Parliament, the Council, the European Economic and Social Committee and the Committee of the Regions: A European Agenda on Migration'*, COM(2015) 240 Final, 13 May 2015. Brussels: European Commission.

European Commission. 2015b. *'Explanatory Note on the "Hotspot" Approach'*. Brussels: European Commission.

European Commission. 2016. *'EU Operations in the Mediterranean Sea'*, Factsheet, 4 October 2016. Brussels: European Commission.

European Council. 2015. *'Special Meeting of the European Council, 23 April 2015: Statement'*, Press Release, 23 April 2015. Brussels: European Council.

European Parliament. 2016. *On the Frontline: The Hotspot Approach to Managing Migration*. Brussels: European Parliament (Policy Department for Citizen's Rights and Constitutional Affairs).

Faist, T. 2004. *'The Migration-Security Nexus. International Migration and Security Before and After 9/11'*, Willy Brandt Series of Working Papers in International Migration and Ethnic Relations 4/03. Malmö: Malmö University.

Frontex. 2006. *'Longest Frontex Coordinated Operation – HERA, the Canary Islands'*, 19 December 2006, Warsaw: Frontex.

Frontex. 2007. *'A Sequel of Operation Hera Just Starting'*, 15 February 2007, Warsaw: Frontex.

Frontex. 2016. *Africa-Frontex Intelligence Community Joint Report – 2015*. Warsaw: Frontex.

Frontex. 2017. *Africa-Frontex Intelligence Community Joint Report – 2016*. Warsaw: Frontex.

Frontex. n.d. *Situation at External Border*. Warsaw: Frontex. Accessed July 23, 2020. https://frontex.europa.eu/faq/situation-at-external-border/.

Gerstein, D. M., et al. 2018. *Managing International Borders: Balancing Security with the Licit Flow of People and Goods*. Santa Monica, CA: RAND.

Guild, E. 2003a. "International Terrorism and EU Immigration, Asylum and Borders Policy: The Unexpected Victims of 11 September 2001." *European Foreign Affairs Review* 8 (3): 331–346.

Guild, E. 2003b. "Immigration, Asylum, Borders and Terrorism: The Unexpected Victims of 11 September 2001." In *11 September 2001: War, Terror and Judgement,* edited by B. Gökay, and R. B. J. Walkers, 176–194. London: Frank Cass.

Guild, E. 2003c. "The Face of Securitas: Redefining the Relationship of Security and Foreigners in Europe." In *Law and Administration in Europe: Essays in Honour of Carol Harlow,* edited by P. Craig, and R. Rawlings, 139–153. Oxford: Oxford University Press.

Guild, E. 2009. *Security and Migration in the 21st Century.* Cambridge: Polity.

Huysmans, J. 2000. "The European Union and the Securitization of Migration." *JCMS: Journal of Common Market Studies* 38 (5): 751–777.

Huysmans, J. 2004. "A Foucaultian View on Spill-Over: Freedom and Security in the EU." *Journal of International Relations and Development* 7 (3): 294–318.

Huysmans, J. 2006. *The Politics of Insecurity: Fear, Migration and Asylum in the EU.* Abingdon: Routledge.

Karyotis, G. 2003. "European Migration Policy in the Aftermath of September 11: The Security-Migration Nexus." Paper Prepared for Presentation at the Second Workshop of the UACES Study Group 'The Evolving European Migration Law and Policy', Manchester, 11–12 April 2003.

Karyotis, G. 2011. "The Fallacy of Securitizing Migration: Elite Rationality and Unintended Consequences." In *Security, Insecurity and Migration in Europe,* edited by G. Lazaridis, 13–29. Farnham: Ashgate.

Karyotis, G. 2012. "Securitization of Migration in Greece: Process, Motives, and Implications." *International Political Sociology* 6 (4): 390–408.

Lazaridis, G. 2011. *Security, Insecurity and Migration in Europe.* Farnham: Ashgate.

Lazaridis, G., and K. Wadia, eds. 2015. *The Securitisation of Migration in the EU: Debates Since 9/11.* Basingstoke: Palgrave Macmillan.

Léonard, S. 2009. "The Creation of FRONTEX and the Politics of Institutionalisation in the EU External Borders Policy." *Journal of Contemporary European Research* 5 (3): 371–388.

Léonard, S. 2010. "EU Border Security and Migration Into the European Union: FRONTEX and Securitization Through Practices." *European Security* 19 (2): 231–254.

Léonard, S., and C. Kaunert. 2019. *Refugees, Security and the European Union.* Abingdon: Routledge.

Migration News Sheet. 2006, October. 'Director of FRONTEX shifts the blame for the late deployment of naval and aerial vessels on Spain', 7.

Migration News Sheet. 2006, September. 'First EU naval operation to combat illegal migration', 4.

Miller, M. 2001. "'A Durable Migration and Security Nexus: The Problem of the Islamic Periphery in Transatlantic Ties'." In *Migration, Globalization and Human Security,* edited by D. Graham and N. Poku, 92-108. London: Routledge.

Neal, A. W. 2009. "Securitization and Risk at the EU Border: The Origins of FRONTEX." *JCMS: Journal of Common Market Studies* 47 (2): 333–356.

North Atlantic Treaty Organisation. 2016. *'NATO's Deployment in the Aegean Sea', Fact Sheet, October 2016.* Brussels: NATO. Public Diplomacy Division – Press & Media Section.

Tirman, J. 2004. "The Migration-Security Nexus." *GSC (Global Security and Cooperation) Quarterly* 13. New York, NY: Social Science Research Council.

UNHCR. 2015. "2015: The Year of Europe's Refugee Crisis." December 8, 2015. Accessed July 22, 2020. https://www.unhcr.org/uk/news/stories/2015/12/56ec1ebde/2015-year-europes-refugee-crisis.html.

Wæver, O., et al. 1993. *Identity, Migration and the New Security Agenda in Europe.* London: Pinter.

Wæver, O. 1995. "Securitization and Desecuritization." In *On Security,* edited by R. D. Lipschutz, 46–86. New York, NY: Columbia University Press.

Williams, M. C. 2003. "Words, Images, Enemies: Securitization and International Politics." *International Studies Quarterly* 47 (4): 511–531.

EU border technologies and the co-production of security 'problems' and 'solutions'

Bruno Oliveira Martins and Maria Gabrielsen Jumbert

ABSTRACT
This article contributes to an understanding of how expert technological knowledge impacts the security-migration management nexus at the EU borders. It argues that recent migration flows augmented pre-existing dynamics of growing reliance upon technology in EU border management. These dynamics are assessed through a study of the way emerging technologies, in particular Unmanned Aerial Vehicles (UAV, commonly known as drones), and specific information and surveillance technologies installed on them, have become increasingly understood as crucial for the management of migration into the EU. The article synthesises securitisation theory with Science and Technology Studies to show, first, how the values reflected in border technologies often encapsulate a securitised understanding of the migrant, and second, how the migrants arriving in Europe have been characterised as both potential security threats and as individuals in need of rescue and protection. These frames trigger securitisation dynamics that portray the migration issue as amenable to state-of-the-art technology. In this logic, security 'problems' and security 'solutions' are co-produced within a complex multi-layered network of public and private actors.

Introduction

For more than two decades, since the Amsterdam Treaty, migration has been a dominant issue on the EU agenda. The management of the arrival of migrants into the EU territory has led to the creation of policy arenas dealing specifically with asylum seekers, regular and irregular economic migrants, and internal workers. These distinct policy areas have created differentiated legal and political spaces in which migrants are placed. These legal and political spaces, in turn, establish different policy regimes and encapsulate different understandings of 'the migrant'.

A crucial element in the differentiation of these policy spaces, and in the shaping of the EU's border management more broadly, is the level of available knowledge about 'the migrant'. 'We need to know more' is both a leitmotiv of border management and the idea that provides the structural logic behind surveillance. Yet, here we distinguish between two different levels of 'knowledge needs' in border management: a *top layer* referring to knowledge about the big trends of migration, about the movements towards or across the border, and having 'the group' as the referent object; and a *lower layer*, having 'the individual' as the focus of attention, concentrating on the knowledge about, and identification of, the individual migrant, i.e. their background, legal status, and personal history. The latter typically depends upon the verification and screening that occurs at border crossing points, carried out by authorities that verify individuals' identity and right to stay. This distinction is relevant insofar as it recognises that different referent objects originate different (real or fabricated) 'knowledge needs' and, concomitantly, require different technological solutions to address them. Whereas the 'knowledge needs' of the individual level lead to an employment of technologies such as body scans, biometrics or personal travel records (Bellanova and Duez 2016), the former, having 'the group' as the referent object, relies upon techniques of surveillance that include unmanned aerial vehicles (UAV, commonly known as drones) as an important instrument, in addition to radars, satellites and regular border patrolling information that feeds into systems and agencies such as the EU Border surveillance system (EUROSUR) (Jeandesboz 2016; Jumbert 2012, 2016) or Frontex (Csernatoni 2018) respectively.

This article focuses precisely on surveillance techniques aiming at addressing knowledge needs that have 'the group' as the referent object. In concrete, we investigate the way by which emerging technologies, such as drones, and specific information and surveillance technologies installed on them, have become increasingly understood as crucial for the management of migration into the EU. In this article, we are interested in understanding how, and with which consequences, expert technological knowledge shapes the security-migration management nexus at the EU borders.

Research design

For answering this research question, we conduct a case study based on a most-likely design. This design consists of an in-depth single case study of the way emerging technologies employed by drones have become increasingly portrayed as relevant in the management of migration into the EU. We synthesise securitisation theory with Science and Technology Studies (STS), drawing in concrete on the concept of 'security knowledges' (Vogel et al. 2017) with an understanding that conditions of ignorance can create a 'surplus of ambiguity' (Gusterson 2008) that some actors can benefit from. STS's approach to the relations between knowledge and security is multifaceted and opens up myriad opportunities to explore how society, security practices and security technologies are *co-produced*: through their work, people simultaneously arrange both the world and what we know about it (Miller 2017, 910; see also Jasanoff 2004).

In this sense, STS relates to the notion of '(in)securitization practices' (Bigo 2014), i.e. an understanding of securitisation as embedded in training, routine, skills, technological knowledge, and artefacts, rather than a product of a simple speech act. Here, the issue of (expert) technological knowledge is of paramount importance. From an STS perspective, we are interested in what Baird has called the production, circulation, and consumption of scarce forms of knowledge (Baird 2017). In the context of this special issue, this approach also allows an engagement with the idea of the spiral of the securitisation of migration (Bello 2017; Bello 2022), namely with its interest both in how practices and routines translate into perceptions of threats and in the role of non-state actors in framing border policies.

We have put in place a plurality of data generation techniques. Firstly, we generate data from official EU documents focusing on migration management, with a focus on the ones that highlight security concerns and/or refer to the 'need to know more'. Here we analyse public tenders issued by Frontex and the European Maritime Safety Agency (EMSA), press releases, communications, European Council conclusions, European Commission decisions, and general information provided on the webpages of official EU institutions and agencies. The second strategy is a participant observation, in the context of a meeting between Frontex, member states, and technology companies, occurred in late 2017. The third data generation technique relates to the authors' engagement in several EU-funded projects that conduct research on the technology – border management nexus, gathering government bodies, research institutions, and the tech industry. This circumstance enabled multiple participant observations across a long period of time, and this first-hand familiarity with EU-funded security and migration research allows us to better understand complex decision-making and agenda-setting processes that involve many actors beyond the EU officials. The information generated out of these sources was then cross-checked in seven semi-structured background informal interviews with EU officials (four), fundamental rights NGOs (one) and the industry (three), that took place between October 2017 and February 2018.

The article contributes to an expansion of the intersections between securitisation theory and STS, exploring the potential for cross-fertilisation between both bodies of literature. Additionally, the analysis of new empirical data through the article's theoretical lenses sheds new light into recent developments in EU border surveillance and on the growing importance of drones as a border surveillance technology.

Theoretical framework

From the late 1990s, securitisation theory has provided an important contribution to the debate between those who claim that threats are objective (i.e. what really constitutes a threat to international security) on the one hand, and those that maintain that security is subjective (what is perceived to be a threat) on the other (Van Munster 2012). Endorsing a process-oriented conception of security, securitisation has focused extensively on the field of migration. Balzacq et al refer that migration, particularly in Europe and the EU, is the issue to which securitisation theory has been applied most frequently (Balzacq, Léonard, and Ruzicka 2016, 508), from the exploratory works of Huysmans (1995, 2000) or Waever (1995) to more recent accounts (Bello 2017; Lazaridis and Wadia 2015). Over the last two decades, securitisation, as a theoretical proposition, has expanded widely and today its distinctiveness lies in its 'capacity to articulate a specific approach to security – influenced by the speech act – with an "analytics of government", which emphasizes practices and processes' (Balzacq, Léonard, and Ruzicka 2016, 494).

Yet, despite its immense use, securitisation has not generated consensus on 'what kind of theory – if any – ' it is (Balzacq and Guzzini 2015). For Hansen (2012), what unites the political theory dimension of securitisation and its applied literature is a concern with the normative-political potential of desecuritisation – an idea that we will resume later on.

Additionally, Vicky Squire points to the fact that, in securitisation studies in the field of migration, there is an 'entrenched divide' (2015, 20) between migration scholars and critical security studies scholars: while migration approaches tend to focus on institutionalist approaches, policy measures, and regulatory procedures, critical security studies perspectives look more into practices, routines, and other politico-sociological dynamics that emphasise context, perceptions and discourse.

This focus on security practices has been explored to study border management (Côté-Boucher, Infantino, and Salter 2014; Salter 2019) and it is adequate for exploring the processes by which technological knowledge impacts the security-migration management nexus at the EU borders. The idea here is that 'practices of control are routinely embedded in a practical sense that informs what controlling borders does and means' (Bigo 2014, 209), within the logic that 'technocratic and bureaucratic day-to-day practices, like population profiling, risk assessment and statistical calculation, communicated within specialist circles yield bigger influence on border securitization processes than political elites' capacity to speak security to large audiences' (Lemberg-Pedersen 2018; see also Léonard 2010). To use Bigo's words, for 'understanding practices of (in)securitization, actual work routines and the specific professional "dispositions" are therefore more important than any discourses actors may use to justify their activities' (Bigo 2014, 209).

Additionally, the migration-security nexus – in the context of European border management – cannot be examined without also taking into account the humanitarian discourse that surrounds the different efforts aimed at 'managing' the EU's external borders. As Aradau has shown, the discourses portraying migrants on their way to Europe as not only *a risk*, but also as being *at risk* are not mutually exclusive, but rather reinforcing each other in the efforts to govern migrants (Aradau 2004). This opens for a dynamic of care and control, where EU border management operations seek to legitimise their efforts as humanitarian, by stressing their search and rescue functions, all the while serving primarily to curb and control migration (Cusumano 2019; Pallister-Wilkins 2018; Tazzioli 2016).

In this article, we are interested in understanding the way expert technical knowledge influences EU border management. Within the realm of EU formal policy-making, expertise is often associated with the 'expert groups' established by the European Commission. These groups are formally defined as '(…) consultative bodies set up by the Commission or its departments for the purpose of providing them with advice and expertise (…) and which are foreseen to meet more than once', providing

> advice and expertise to the Commission and its departments in relation to: (a) the preparation of legislative proposals and policy initiatives; (b) the preparation of delegated acts; (c) the implementation of Union legislation, programmes and policies, as well as coordination and cooperation with Member States and stakeholders in that regard; (d) where necessary, the early preparation of implementing acts (…). (European Commission 2016)

Yet, in this article we engage with the literature that understands expertise and knowledge production beyond the formal setting of the Commission-regulated expert groups, referring to the professional knowledge ascribed to individual or collective professionals and recognised by a public authority with decision-making powers (Carmel 2017; Eriksen 2011; Gornitzka and Holst 2015; Maguire 2015; Huysmans in Salter 2019).

From a STS perspective, expert knowledge and the ways in which the 'production of knowledge is organized and regulated – and how this in turn creates areas of non-knowledge and ignorance – is a central question in any area of human activity' (Vogel et al. 2017, 980), and it provides valuable insights into the workings of specialised EU agencies in which expert knowledge is a dominant feature. For STS, the issue of expertise goes beyond knowing *who* has knowledge. In the words of Miller, it is

> also about how the making of knowledge is organized; who participates, in what ways, and at what points in the process; who has rights and responsibilities to speak authoritatively about knowledge; and the norms and rules for both making and applying knowledge to important societal decisions' (Miller 2017, 912)

In the context of EU border management, these insights from STS point to the prominence of both the tech industry and specialised EU agencies in the general architecture of border management. Emma Carmel has shown how practical knowledge in security research has 'enabled major European corporations to assert a privileged discursive and political position in the "linked ecologies" of formal scientific research, product development and EU policymaking' (Carmel 2017, 771). The research carried out here will provide new elements for evaluating who governs EU border management and assessing the consequences of over-reliance upon technological knowledge.

Finally, our reflections engage with Bello's notion of *spiral of securitization*, which claims that securitisation started with 'particular frames of interpreting our world' which latter, 'mixed with actual facts, politics, practices, narratives and techniques, have engendered a spiraling process that each of these factors has contributed to speeding' (Bello 2017, 62). This concept underlines the self-reinforcing logics that foster increasing levels of securitisation in particular domains. In the case of migration into the EU, this process has been observed in recent years and, indeed, relies upon a multiplicity of actors. These different actors that participate in the spiral of securitisation of migration are organised by Bello in binary categories: prejudiced/inclusive, violent/non-violent, public/private, and pursuing collective/individualistic interests (Bello 2017; Bello 2022). Our analysis will provide additional elements to understand how these self-reinforcing logics are created and how much they rely upon technological expertise.

Technology in EU border management

The process by which high levels of technology were increasingly seen as the most adequate solution to EU's border management challenges has been covered by the literature in recent years (Lehtonen and Aalto 2017; Rijpma 2017). This technologisation of EU border management goes back to the 2004 Hague Programme and received a decisive impetus with the 2011 Smart Borders Initiative, a crucial step in the discursive construction of a security-technology nexus in the field of border management. Responding to the European Council conclusions of June 2011 which called for work on 'Smart Borders' (European Council 2011), this initiative has triggered a number of developments that equated increasing security with technological solutions in the management of (documented and undocumented) movements across EU borders. Since then, the so-called Smart Borders package has been revised regularly and has acquired legislative form.

Most importantly, it helped framing migration as a security issue that can be addressed with better, more advanced, and 'smarter' technological solutions (Dijstelbloem and Meijer 2011).

These dynamics are certainly not new nor exclusive of the EU, as the pursuit of security has always triggered technological developments and used cutting-edge scientific knowledge. Authors looking into particular EU security/ised issues have problematised the role of private actors, expert bureaucrats, and novel forms of policy-making based on technocratic regulation where the governance of security escapes democratic control. Eriksen (2011) has called attention to how expert knowledge at the service of a comprehensive EU security strategy may not be democratically accountable, whereas other studies have raised similar concerns about several EU agencies, including security agencies.

This process happened in parallel with a growing securitisation of migration in Europe. Current security practices in EU's border management rely heavily upon knowledge that is technically so specialised that regular, elected policy-makers and their constituencies will be unable to understand it in all its outreach. Those security practices include the use of increasing robotisation, mounting use of biometrics, and state-of-the-art surveillance platforms, for example. Consequently, the governance of the migration-security field has increasingly been transferred to non-elected bodies such as Frontex, the EMSA, or the European Defence Agency (EDA), while a growing number of consortia involving the defence industries, research institutions and member states have become important actors in the production of knowledge and expertise that eventually contributes to shaping political decisions on this field (Martins and Küsters 2019).

In the context of EU's border management, the process by which increased security is associated with expanded technological devices is held together by 'multiple translations and enrolments through which the technical side of dataveillance – platforms, automated gates, matching systems, and so forth – has become associated with the processes of policymaking on border security and sustains the furtherance of mass dataveillance' (Jeandesboz 2016, 292). EU border security, with its complex assemblage of human actors and computorised systems, became what in STS can be called a 'dense socio-technical environment' (Bellanova and Duez 2016, 110).

From a STS perspective, the way specialised agencies mobilise knowledge, select technologies, adopt practices, and endorse 'technological solutions' is particularly relevant. As part of its research and innovation activities, Frontex, for example, studies the availability and readiness of technology for integrated border management. According to the agency's webpage describing its role in technology assessment, Frontex – in cooperation with Member States, industry and internal stakeholders – 'aims to identify technical solutions that could address operational needs, establish their readiness to be integrated and tested in a real operational scenario, and then make recommendations for introducing these solutions in the field' (Frontex 2019). To test potential solutions and assess their capabilities as well as identify future needs, Frontex organises demonstrations of technology, conducts technical feasibility studies and runs pilot projects at all types of border. Some of the agency's main activities and products in the area of technology assessment include tests and demonstrations of technologies for border control; examining emerging technologies and their readiness to respond to specific needs; identifying capability needs; facilitating working groups and workshops to exchange views; reporting on current practices for technology acquisition and deployment as well as presenting recommendations for EU-sponsored research (ibidem).

In the next section we explore these processes by looking at the specific case of drone technology and how it came to be portrait by Frontex, the EMSA, and the technology industries as a key system to reinforce surveillance at the border as part of an effort to increase security. While the social construction of drone technology as central for the management of EU border crisis has been highlighted in Jumbert (2016) and Csernatoni (2018), our contribution places these developments in the broader context of an increasing reliance upon technological knowledge for the definition of security 'solutions' to security 'problems'.

Issue framing: surveillance and drones as the solution for border challenges

Today, drones are an important part of many NGO and law enforcement activities in the Mediterranean. NGOs use drones as part of SAR operations, and law enforcement agencies of individual member states, as well as EU operations, have integrated surveillance drones in their missions. In March 2019 it was revealed that the EU was withdrawing its naval ships from its operation EUNAVFOR SOPHIA, conducted under the EU's Common Security and Defence Policy, in order to replace them by aerial surveillance conducted by aeroplanes and Predator drones provided by Italy (Der Spiegel 2019). Whereas SOPHIA was not a SAR mission, its ships were obliged under international law to provide support to migrants in distress (Howden, Fotiadis, and Loewenstein 2019).

In an interview for this article, a high-level Frontex official referred that as of February 2018 Frontex did not operate drones, and the same idea was voiced again publicly in August 2019 (Howden, Fotiadis, and Loewenstein 2019). Yet Frontex' official twitter account itself published a video in 22 June 2019 of a smuggling operation, with an ensuing *tweet* stating 'Frontex plane and drone kept observing the fishing trawler and the boat with migrants over several hours, alerting Italian and Maltese authorities' (Frontex twitter 2019a and 2019b). Frontex has been testing unmanned aircraft for border surveillance in Greece, Italy and Portugal since September 2018 (Frontex 2018), following procurement tenders initiated the year before. In an answer to a written question by a member of the European Parliament, the European Commission mentioned that the trial 'forms part of the assessment and evaluation of such platforms for border control purposes with a specific focus on their ability to deliver surveillance services in a regular, reliable, and cost-efficient way' (European Parliament 2018). As will be showed below, both Frontex and the EMSA have launched drone tenders to move towards integration of drones in their activities. Whether or not Frontex operates drones is less relevant a question for our inquiry; the agency plays an important part in the wider assemblage of EU actors that facilitate, promote and push forward the use of this technology for border management contexts.

The EU's increasing interest on drones as a surveillance platform necessary for border management has attracted some attention from the literature. Hayes, Jones, and Töpfer (2014) have showed how the enmeshment of the defence industries with key EU officials has decisively contributed to putting drone development and air traffic regulation in the agenda of the EU. The relations between the industry and EU agencies have contributed to a growing reliance upon technology for managing EU borders, especially in the Mediterranean (see also Csernatoni 2018). The fact that much of this technology is dual-use in nature (i.e, it can have both civilian and military application) creates new layers of complexity (Martins and Ahmad 2020): its dual-use character facilitates the militarisation of police, with clear manifestations in the case of border controls. Moreover, drone-based surveillance is a technology with military origin that was developed for conflict operational contexts. The visual images it generates used to be of enemies and combatents. Its use in a border management framework contributes to a portrayal and an understanding of the migrant as an alien, an intruder, an enemy.

Challenges related to border management, and especially border control activities at sea, are framed in a way where surveillance becomes the needed solution and drones the most adapted vehicle to carry out this surveillance (Jumbert 2012, 2016). Drones are portrayed as being the ultimate solution not just to spot unwanted migrants at sea (based on types of vessels and ports of departure and direction), but also to spot migrants in distress and to more efficiently bring search and rescue where needed (Jumbert 2016). Indeed, drone manufacturers have addressed not only member states and Frontex as their potential clients, but also humanitarian organisations – as seen with the search and rescue operation conducted by Médecins Sans Frontières (MSF) and the Migrant Offshore Aid Station (MOAS), organisations which in 2015 and 2016 were offered discount rates and two month free use of Schiebel CAMCOPTER* S-100 drones to help them in their efforts in the Mediterranean (MOAS 2015). Naturally, the use of drones by humanitarian NGOs raise a number of problematic questions connected to both the growing role of security industries in the maritime SAR enterprise and the possibility of sharing sensitive images and information with law enforcement authorities (see Cuttitta 2018; and also Marin 2016).

The challenges related to governing both the geographical space that constitutes Europe's southern borders and the subjects of surveillance – the so-called migratory flows – are framed to show, on the one hand, the difficulties to have a perfect oversight, and on the other, the need for more information in order to gain a better overview. Contrary to land borders, the external maritime borders of the EU are not a fixed line where border patrols can be set up, although land borders too face challenges related to the scope of the area to watch over. The Mediterranean sea is a vast area, with large stretches of international waters between Europe, Africa, and the Middle East, and it is geographically challenging to watch over (Jumbert 2012). Much of the policy discussion, jurisdiction and policy making over the last years has related to what EU member states or EU agencies can and cannot do in terms of border patrolling, surveillance, and border control at sea, in the sense of preventing the entry of unauthorised travellers. In this respect the landmark case of *Jamaa Hirsi and Others v. Italy* in 2012 led Italy to be condemned by the European Court of Human Rights for its practice of collective expulsion and breach of the obligation of non-refoulement, with the understanding that migrant vessels cannot be stopped at sea and brought back to North African shores (Papanicolopulu 2013).

While policy thinking and practice on this has continued to seek other ways to prevent the irregular migratory flows across the Mediterranean, the challenges have often been framed in terms of lack of sufficient information. This applies to the number of arrivals in Europe – to which border guards and Frontex respond that there is a need to know more about ports of departure, origins of the migrants, modus operandi of smugglers, shifting trends in migratory routes, etc. – or the shipwrecks and lives lost at sea – which have also often been followed by claims that a better overview or sharing of distress signals is needed. It is worth noting that the discourse on the 'need for more and better information' is prevalent both in the security and in the humanitarian sectors. Importantly, drones for maritime surveillance are currently a top priority in the recent sharp increase in EU's investiment in the development of defence technology. One of the pilot projects of the Preparatory Action for Defence Research – an action that paved the way for the current European Defence Fund – is the consortium OCEAN2020 (Open Cooperation for European mAritime awareNess). With 42 partners from 15 member states, and a budget of 35 million EUR, it has as a primary objective

> to demonstrate enhanced situational awareness in a maritime environment through the integration of legacy and new technologies for unmanned systems (…) by pulling together the technical specialists in the maritime domain covering the 'observing, orienting, deciding and acting' operational tasks. (OCEAN2020 2019)

An illustrative example of the framing of border management as a problem amenable to increased surveillance provided by drones is the drone tender opened by the EMSA in 2016 (EMSA 2016). This tender launched a pilot project aimed at creating operational and technical synergies between different Coast Guard functions at EU level particularly between EMSA, the European Fisheries Control Agency (EFCA), and Frontex. The tender was part of a broader reform and expansion of the EU's border agencies in the context of migration management adopted by the European Parliament and the Council in 2015, where the mandates of Frontex, the EFCA and EMSA were amended and a new cooperation article was introduced in their founding regulations, requiring them to work together in five areas: information sharing, surveillance and communication services, capacity building, risk analysis and capacity sharing (EMSA 2018a). The idea of increased integration and cooperation among EU agencies with a border management portfolio was further developed in Regulation 2016/1624, that established the principles for what was labelled 'European integrated border management' (European Parliament 2016). One of the 11 components of the European integrated border management is 'use of state-of-the-art technology including large-scale information systems' (European Parliament 2016, article 4, i).

Using the acronym Remotely Piloted Aerial Systems (RPAS), the EMSA announced the new agreement on drones mentioning that

> These new contracts (…) build on those already in place for marine pollution (oil spill) detection and ship gas emission monitoring. Through the RPAS portfolio available to member states and EU agencies, a wide range of coastguard functions can be supported including environment protection, maritime safety and security, fisheries control, border control, law enforcement and customs. (EMSA 2017)

Crucially, the EMSA's traditional mandate focused on maritime safety issues, such as oil spills or ship safety, and not on security and border management. But the understanding of migration as a 'problem' in search of a 'solution' enabled this extension of the mandate, that several EU member states were not convinced about (Stares 2016). In September

2018 the EMSA-contracted drones were used for the first time by Frontex to 'provide support to the Portuguese Guarda Nacional Republicana (Portuguese National Republican Guard), Air Force and Navy, as well as to the Eurosur National Coordination Centre' (EMSA 2018b). As highlighted by Nowak, 'the political consensus among EU governments to restrict migration reinforces the economic interests of the defence industry and vice versa, and the interest of national governments to attract high-tech investment adds to this' (Nowak 2019).

In addition to these recurring frames, the recourse to step up surveillance efforts, as a means to gather more information and *know more*, and doing so by investing in more sophisticated technologies, has the additional function of resorting to technical solutions to address a politically intricate and sensitive question, from legal, ethical and political points of view (Jumbert 2018). Arguing for more information, through new technology, may appear as the least controversial, and presented as most neutral, form of response, while at the same time serving the purpose of showing the capacity to take concrete action. Drones also come with the function, and promise, of providing this sought-after view from above, which can at the same time be more detailed than land-based radars or satellites (view from afar, with few details beyond direction/speed/type of vessel), and more flexible, wide-ranging, discreet, as well as cheaper, than manned border patrols (Jumbert 2012).

Language in the EU's socio-technical environment in border management

The reflections in this section, as well as the quotations, derive from three main sources: the authors' participation in EU-funded consortia dealing with technology development for border management, the seven interviews referred to in the methodology section, and one of the author's participant observation of a 2017 meeting between EU member states border authorities, industry representatives, and Frontex. These contexts provided both direct input to our reflections and background material that is included in the text after triangulation with official documents.

The discourse around the promises of drones in the EU border management context permeates official documents, industry presentations, and the broader 'border solution ecosystem', as the socio-technical environment in border management is often called. In these issue-framing processes, language and rhetoric are central for the formation of ideas about needs, problems, and solutions. When some of the companies present their drone portfolio, either in informal conversations or in formal settings, they refer that some of the vehicles have a 'combat proven-label', which is understood as something akin to a quality stamp. Yet, interestingly, this reference to the military domain is balanced with a highly euphemistic set of expressions that include calling 'bird' to the drones, labelling a group of drones as 'swarm of drones', or calling 'shield family' to a set of defensive technical infrastructures. At the same time, as explicitly put by a technology developer in an interview, drones – and robotics more generally – are now developed with the aim of possessing the five human senses: sight, hearing, touch, smell, and taste (see for example Simon 2018; SmarterWare 2019). These expressions attribute the technology an almost human character (Kaufmann 2016), and they often co-exist with a rhetoric and a language that de-humanises the migrant: the language employed to classify relevant people to monitor through the drone includes expressions such as 'object of interest' and 'intruder'.

Yet, as seen above, migrants crossing the borders into Europe are not only portrayed as a risk, but also as being at risk, i.e. a group in need of protection and care. This is most vividly reflected in the different NGOs' conducting search and rescue operations along the sea stretches where most ship-wrecks have occurred, between Libya and Italy and between Turkey and the Greek islands of Lesvos, Chios and Samos. The imperative to save vessels in distress at sea is however also very much present in the narratives of the developers of new security technologies. The idea that aerial surveillance may allow to better spot, and provide more efficient search and rescue, is an idea held high by both drone manufacturers, Frontex, and humanitarian organisations themselves (Jumbert 2016), despite its often problematic image. Using a humanitarian framing can serve as a powerful legitimating factor, not only when deployed by traditional humanitarian actors, but also efficiently so when used by more traditional security actors (Joachim and Schneiker 2012). It allows them to counter-balance their image: their solutions are not only about control, but also about care; two dynamics which, as seen above, contribute to reinforce each other. Indeed, this humanitarian rationale contributes to add another layer to the dynamic of securitisation, creating a double sense of 'emergency', where the best technological solutions, allowing the best possible overview and gathering of information, are in dire need.

It derives from these illustrations that issue-framing processes reinforce securitisation processes as well. In the words of a senior EU official interviewed in February 2018, the technology industries present practitioners 'with a puzzle that they (the industry) themselves then solve in front of our eyes'. In the case of drones, migration management is framed as a problem amenable to a technological solution: increased surveillance provided by drones. In other words, the contruction of migration as a security problem marked by scarce information is what makes drones the solution to it. As one representative of a defence industry company has mentioned in another interview, 'we will fly whatever solves your problem'. The challenges posed by sharply increased migrants flows to Europe therefore trigger securitisation dynamics that eventually seek for state-of-the-art technology, reinforcing the spiral of securitisation that Bello (2017) refers to.

Technological expertise, knowledge, and migration policy

How is technological knowledge produced, and how does it circulate and permeate policy-making within the migration-security nexus? Our theoretical section has pointed out to the fact that, within formal procedures, expertise in EU policy-making is often associated with the Commission-regulated Groups of Experts. Yet, as our empirical section has showed, the generation and circulation of expert knowledge also happens outside these rigid boundaries. Indeed, as highlighted by Emma Carmel, expert knowledge can be produced in

> networks of social relations among knowledge producers and knowledge brokers, organized around normative or paradigmatic differences, around member state commonalities; by money and its circulation to support particular policies or research; and by the fit of different kinds of knowledge with the temporal and political rhythms of policymaking. Thus, the knowledge generated in and through diverse practices of EU governance itself

constitutes ways of seeing, organizing and acting on the political space to be governed. (Carmel 2017, 778)

A key manifestation of expertise's role in security governance concerns the definition of 'what is risky and what a threat is, what should be dealt with as a security issue and what not' (Berling and Bueger 2015, 1). 'Expertise' also comes with a connotation of neutrality, elevated above politics. Yet our STS-based theoretical assumptions attach a political character to expertise as well. As we will show below, our empirical material contributes to challenge the 'notion of an apolitical sphere of science and expertise, while at the same time demonstrating how the politics of expertise shapes the authority and subjectivity of scientists and reconfigures the meanings and roles of scientific knowledge' (Rychnovska, Pasgaard, and Berling 2017, 327).

Border management technologies are particularly relevant to study through the lense of security experts and the roles they are assigned. As migration is a highly politicised field, and as the frequent application of the 'securitisation' framework suggests, it is also a field where elevating the discussion above the realm of politics is apparently particularly needed. Delegating important discussions to, and seeking advice from, expert groups on how to address given situations allows to take these discussions outside the political minefield. In practice, assigning security experts with the task of defining solutions also gives them the power to define of what the problem at stake is, in a logic that in STS is understood as co-production.

This role of security experts may be problematic for two reasons: first, the 'expert' view comes with a claim of truth and objective neutrality, that does not take into account how experts are selected, recruited, and how they make their assessments. This allows governments to rely on expert groups as a method in itself, assuming that the reference to the 'expertise' removes the need to justify what methods these experts rely on to make their claims. Second, this creates an opacity around how key assessments are made, which is problematic in terms of democratic access to key discussions in our societies. This lack of democratic control is expanded by the specific technical know-how that the security experts possess: technological knowledge of how drones or other surveillance technologies work and can work, in terms inaccessible to lay people, gives certain experts access to a conversation about the development of key security technologies while excluding the broader public (see Loukinas 2017). This is critical because most of the 'surveilled' migrants are people in particularly vulnerable situation. In a 2018 report addressing recent developments in IT systems employed by the EU in border management scenarios, the European Union Fundamental Rights Agency highlighted that

> "the weak position of the individuals whose data are stored in largescale IT systems creates many fundamental rights challenges. They range from respect of human dignity when taking fingerprints and challenges in correcting or deleting inaccurate or unlawfully stored data to the risk of unlawful use and sharing of personal data with third parties". (European Union Fundamental Rights Agency 2018, 9)

The elements provided in the previous section corroborate these claims and reinforce the notion that the dense socio-technical environment is populated by myriad actors that include not only official bodies but also private actors and formal and informal networks of experts. At the same time, the way that the EU has dealt with drone development in Europe for migration mangement purposes has contributed to reinforce the securitisation of migration. The treatment of migration-related technology development under the FP7 and Horizon 2020 security portfolios reinforces a double issue framing: firstly, it equates migration with security, reinforcing the securitisation of migration; and then, secondly, it presents securitised issues as amenable to technological solutions. This implies that EU security, as a field of EU governance, is thus

> represented in knowledge claims and expertise that appear to be detached from any particular social actors – policy solutions are reduced to problem-solving technological products. (…) Defence, security, border control and surveillance are unified as a single technological domain, generating increasingly dense webs of concepts which link economic innovation, market expansion, global economic competitiveness and 'European' security requirements, to shape governance practices. (Carmel 2017, 788)

This increasing importance of technology in EU border management has a number of additional ramifications. The first one relates to the growing centrality of expert knowledge in EU's security and migration agencies. Expert knowledge-based policy-making has systematically increased in the EU and became mainstream in virtually all the domains of the security agenda, understood here in its widest sense. This includes agencies on defence (EDA and EU Satellite Centre, SatCen), borders (Frontex and eu-LISA), health (European Centre for Disease Prevention and Control), and maritime security (EMSA), to name but a few actors.

The second consequence is the growing presence of hybrid rule in EU's migration management. Hurt and Lipschutz (2015) have argued that privatisation has counter-intuitively led to substantial growth in state/public power, rather than to its diminution. This is mostly manifested through hybrid rule, which refers to a set of practices that combine public and private resources to address one particular issue and to overcome political-ideological blocades (Martins and Küsters 2019). In the very critical definition of Hurt and Lipschutz applied to the security field,

> Hybrid rule results from a set of practices deployed by political elites that rely on the private sector to shield national security activities by expanding state power while constraining democratic accountability. This hybrid rule strategy seeks to safeguard the state's legitimacy through valorization of the market as a primary mechanism in pursuit of myriad political objectives. (Hurt and Lipschutz 2015, 2)

Thirdly, in areas whereas the technological expertise lies with private industries, and not within scientific communities exclusively, the issue of expertise inevitably crosses with interests. Expert groups emerging from the industry are then akin to interest groups, and their exchanges with policy makers are not necessarily in terms of provision of expert knowledge, but rather in terms closer to lobby and the pursue of economic self-interest. Indeed, Baird has shown that policy decisions concerning EU border management have been 'tailored to the preferences, identities, and frames of business actors' (Baird 2018, 118) through three different processes:

> Policy preferences are co-constituted by business actors through strategic communication, identities are constructed to gain political legitimacy through strategic legitimation, and social contexts are framed to fit business interests through practices of strategic contextualization (2017)

The interplays between the drone industry and key EU agencies emerging from our research have resulted in the framing process described above and illustrate the typology of interactions put forward by Baird.

Fourthly, a final aspect to consider here deals with the nature of the actors involved in the spiral of securitisation. Valeria Bello organises these actors according to a number of dichotomies: prejudiced/inclusive, violent/non-violent, public/private, and pursuing collective/individualistic interests. In the analysis conducted here, the main actors are EU agencies, EU institutions, the research consorcia, and the technology industries. They are non-violent but otherwise they fit all the above mentioned categories and fall outside pre-established binary categorisation. Indeed, the hybrid public-private consortia that conduct research on border security technologies involve the governments of the member states, third countries, research institutions, and the private sector. Precisely because of their hybrid nature, these partnerships are less visible and therefore less accountable (Leander 2015). These consortia are part of a broader market turn in EU governance (Mörth 2009) and, typically, are funded by the European Commission either directly via specific actions, or, in the majority of cases, indirectly through the EU framework programmes for research, such as the current Horizon 2020. In recent years, many of the hybrid consortia created by the EU under the security research programme in order to develop technology relate to the field of migration. Martins and Küsters show that, from Brussels' viewpoint, the hybrid consortia formed for the purpose of developing drones created value beyond their explicit purpose: they enmeshed the defence industries with public authorities (in the EU and in the member states), they fostered a common defence R&D community, they kept the European defence industry competitive, and they facilitated the emergence of a shared security and defence culture (Martins and Küsters 2019).

Conclusion

As part of a broader technologisation of border management in the EU, drones have consistently been framed as a 'solution' to a border management 'problem'. This 'problem', as presented by EU bodies and technology developers, is understood to be lack of information. According to this logic, a state-of-the-art aerial surveillance tool emerges as the inevitable solution. Surrounding this process is the idea that society, security practices and security technologies are *co-produced*: our understanding of societal issues, including migration or security, is strickly connected to the existing modes of imagining (technological) solutions. This corresponds to what Sheila Jasanoff call the co-production of science, technology and social order (Jasanoff 2004). Ordering knowledge impacts the ordering of society, and therefore understanding how the making of knowledge is organised, who participates, and who has rights and responsibilities to speak authoritatively about knowledge is crucial for understanding how solutions come to being. This article provides elements for understanding how and why security technologies came to be understood as crucial for solving EU's border problems and highlighted how the possession of technological expertise confers technology developers and other experts a discursive hegemony on border management and vests them with authority.

The security domain, for its reliance on state-of-the-art technology and for its socially sensitive nature, is an area where the challenges of expert-based knowledge are vastly amplified. As we showed here, technology and expertise at the border encapsulate a securitised understanding of the migrant and therefore reiterate securitisation processes that impact the way migration is understood. They engage many non-elected practitioners and a wide number of actors – public, private, and hybrid – across the policy formulation and implementation cycles. Many actors from the ideal types of non-state actors involved in the securitisation of migration presented by Bello (2017, 66) are found in the processes leading to drone usage for migration management purposes. These securitisation dynamics eventually seek for state-of-the-art technology, contributing the spiral of securitisation where security 'problems' and security 'solutions' are co-produced within a complex multi-layered network of actors whose activities are difficult to monitor and disentangle. Therefore, a de-securitisation of migration and a re-humanisation of the individual migrant require more transparency in decision-making processes and an acknowledgement of the co-production of security 'problems' and the corresponding security 'solutions'.

Disclosure statement

No potential conflict of interest was reported by the author(s).

Funding

This work was supported by Norges Forskningsråd [262565] and Horizon 2020 project Privacy, ethical, regulatory and social no-gate crossing point solutions acceptance (PERSONA), grant agreement ID: 787123.

References

Aradau, C. 2004. "The Perverse Politics of Four-Letter Words: Risk and Pity in the Securitisation of Human Trafficking." *Millenium: Journal of International Studies* 33 (2): 251–277.

Baird, T. 2017. "Knowledge of Practice: A Multi-Sited Event Ethnography of Border Security Fairs in Europe and North America." *Security Dialogue* 48 (3): 187–205.

Baird, T. 2018. "Interest Groups and Strategic Constructivism: Business Actors and Border Security Policies in the European Union." *Journal of Ethnic and Migration Studies* 44 (1): 118–136.

Balzacq, T., and S. Guzzini. 2015. "Introduction: What Kind of Theory – If Any – Is Securitization?" *International Relations* 29 (1): 97–102.

Balzacq, T., S. Léonard, and J. Ruzicka. 2016. "'Securitization' Revisited: Theory and Cases." *International Relations* 30 (4): 494–531.

Bellanova, R., and D. Duez. 2016. "The Making (Sense) of EUROSUR: How to Control the Sea Borders?." In *EU Borders and Shifting Internal Security – Technology, Externalization and Accountability*, edited by R. Bossong and H. Carrapico, 23–44. Heidelberg: Springer.

Bello, V. 2017. *International Migration and International Security. Why Prejudice is a Global Security Threat*. London: Routledge.

Bello, V. 2022. "The Spiralling of the Securitisation of Migration in the EU: From the Management of a 'Crisis' to a Governance of Human Mobility?" *Journal of Ethnic and Migration Studies* 48 (6): 1327–1344. https://doi.org/10.1080/1369183X.2020.1851464.

Berling, Trine Villumsen, and Christian Bueger, eds. 2015. *Security Expertise. Practices, Power, Responsibility*. London: Routledge.

Bigo, Didier. 2014. "The (in)securitization Practices of the Three Universes of EU Border Control: Military/Navy – Border Guards/Police – Database Analysts." *Security Dialogue* 45 (3): 209–225.

Carmel, E. 2017. "Re-interpreting Knowledge, Expertise and EU Governance: The Cases of Social Policy and Security Research Policy." *Comparative European Politics* 15 (5): 771–793.

Côté-Boucher, K, F Infantino, and M Salter. 2014. "Border Security as Practice: An Agenda for Research." *Security Dialogue* 45 (3): 195–208.

Csernatoni, R. 2018. "Constructing the EU's High-Tech Borders: FRONTEX and Dual-use Drones for Border Management." *European Security* 27 (2): 175–200.

Cusumano, E. 2019. "Straightjacketing Migrant Rescuers? The Code of Conduct on Maritime NGOs." *Mediterranean Politics* 24 (1): 106–114.

Cuttitta, P. 2018. "Repoliticization Through Search and Rescue? Humanitarian NGOs and Migration Management in the Central Mediterranean." *Geopolitics* 23 (3): 632–660.

Der Spiegel 2019. "Mit Drohnen sichten statt mit Schiffen retten" https://www.spiegel.de/politik/ausland/sophia-predator-drohnen-sollen-fluechtlinge-im-mittelmeer-finden-a-1259962.html.

Dijstelbloem, H., and A. Meijer. 2011. *Migration and the New Technological Borders of Europe*. Basingstoke: Palgrave Macmillan.

Eriksen, E. O. 2011. "Governance Between Expertise and Democracy: The Case of European Security." *Journal of European Public Policy* 18 (8): 1169–1189.

European Commission 2016. *Commission Decision of 30.5.2016 Establishing Horizontal Rules on the Creation and Operation of Commission Expert Groups*. Brussels, 30.5.2016, C(2016) 3301 final.

European Council. 2011. *European Council 23/24 June 2011 Conclusions*, Brussels, 24 June 2011 EUCO 23/11 CO EUR 14 concl 4.

European Maritime Safety Agency. 2016. *Contracts for Remotely Piloted Aircraft System (RPAS) Services in Support of the Execution of Coast Guard Functions*. http://www.statewatch.org/news/2016/oct/eu-emsa-2016-tender-specifications-rpas-security1.pdf.

European Maritime Safety Agency. 2017. "Quality Shipping, Safer Seas, Cleaner Oceans", *Newsletter* 144, March. http://www.emsa.europa.eu/news-a-press-centre/external-news/item/2973-newsletter-march-2017.html.

European Maritime Safety Agency. 2018a. *EMSA Programming Document 2019-2021*. http://www.emsa.europa.eu/news-a-press-centre/external-news/download/5493/3430/23.html.

European Maritime Safety Agency. 2018b. *EMSA Press Release: Remotely Piloted Aircraft Systems Enter Into Operation in Portugal for Border Surveillance*. http://www.emsa.europa.eu/news-a-press-centre/external-news/download/5378/3366/23.html.

European Parliament. 2016. *Regulation (EU) 2016/1624 of the European Parliament and of the Council of 14 September 2016 on the European Border and Coast Guard and amending Regulation (EU) 2016/399 of the European Parliament and of the Council and repealing Regulation (EC) No 863/2007 of the European Parliament and of the Council, Council Regulation (EC) No 2007/2004 and Council Decision 2005/267/EC*.

European Parliament. 2018. Answer given by Mr Avramopoulos on behalf of the European Commission Question reference: E-002403/2018, 13 September. http://www.europarl.europa.eu/doceo/document/E-8-2018-002403-ASW_EN.html.

European Union Fundamental Rights Agency. 2018. *Under Watchful Eyes – Biometrics, EU IT-Systems and Fundamental Rights*. Vienna: March. http://fra.europa.eu/en/publication/2018/biometrics-rights-protection.

Frontex 2018. "News Release: Frontex Begins Testing Unmanned Aircraft for Border surveillance", 27 September 2018. https://frontex.europa.eu/media-centre/news-release/frontex-begins-testing-unmanned-aircraft-for-border-surveillance-zSQ26A.

Frontex 2019. *Assessment of Technologies*. https://frontex.europa.eu/research/assessment-of-technologies/.

Frontex twitter. 2019a "A Frontex Plane and Drone Kept Observing the Fishing Trawler and the Boat with Migrants Over Several Hours, Alerting Italian and Maltese Authorities, as Well as @EUNAVFORMED_OHQ". https://twitter.com/Frontex/status/1142373175243804673

Frontex twitter. 2019b "Wait, Wait. Why is That Fishing Trawler Towing an Empty Wooden Boat at High Seas???". https://twitter.com/Frontex/status/1142373175243804673

Gornitzka, Å, and C. Holst. 2015. "The Expert-Executive Nexus in the EU: An Introduction." *Politics and Governance* 3 (1): 1–12.

Gusterson, H. 2008. "Nuclear Futures: Anticipatory Knowledge, Expert Judgement, and the Lack That Cannot be Filled." *Science and Public Policy* 35 (8): 551–560.

Hansen, L. 2012. "Reconstructing Desecuritisation: the Normative-Political in the Copenhagen School and Directions for how to Apply it." *Review of International Studies* 38 (3): 525–546.

Hayes, B., Jones, C. and Töpfer H. 2014. *Eurodrones.Inc*, London: Statewatch and Transnational Institute.

Howden, D, Fotiadis, A., and Loewenstein, A 2019. Once Migrants on Mediterranean Were Saved by Naval Patrols. Now They Have to Watch as Drones fly Over, *The Observer*, 4 August 2019. https://www.theguardian.com/world/2019/aug/04/drones-replace-patrol-ships-mediterranean-fears-more-migrant-deaths-eu.

Hurt, S, and R Lipschutz, eds. 2015. *Hybrid Rule and State Formation: Public-Private Power in the 21st Century*. Oxon: Routledge.

Huysmans, J. 1995. "Migrants as a Security Problem: Dangers of "Securitizing" Societal Issues." In *Migration and European Integration: The Dynamics of Inclusion and Exclusion*, edited by Robert Miles and Dietrich Thränhardt, 53–72. London: Pinter Publishers.

Huysmans, J. 2000. "The European Union and the Securitization of Migration." *JCMS: Journal of Common Market Studies* 38 (5): 751–777.

Jasanoff, S. 2004. *States of Knowledge: The co-Production of Science and Social Order*. London and New York: Routledge.

Jeandesboz, J. 2016. "Smartening Border Security in the European Union: An Associational Inquiry." *Security Dialogue* 47 (4): 292–309.

Joachim, J., and A. Schneiker. 2012. "New Humanitarians? Frame Appropriation Through Private Military and Security Companies." *Millennium: Journal of International Studies* 40 (2): 365–388.

Jumbert, M. G. 2012. "Controlling the Mediterranean Space Through Surveillance: The Politics and Discourse of Surveillance as an All-Encompassing Solution to EU Maritime Border Management Issues." *Espace Populations Sociétés* 2012 (3): 35–48.

Jumbert, M. G. 2016. "Creating the EU Drone: Control, Sorting and Search and Rescue at Sea." In *The Good Drone*, edited by Kristin Bergtora Sandvik and Maria Gabrielsen Jumbert, 89–108. London: Routledge.

Jumbert, M. G. 2018. "Control or Rescue at Sea? Aims and Limits of Border Surveillance Technologies in the Mediterranean Sea." *Disasters* 42 (4): 674–696.

Kaufmann, M. 2016. "Drone/Body: the Drone's Power to Sense and Construct Emergencies." In *The Good Drone*, edited by K. B. Sandvik and M. G. Jumbert, 168–194. London: Routledge.

Lazaridis, G., and K. Wadia2015. *The Securitization of Migration in the EU: Debates Since 9/11*. Basingstoke: Palgrave.

Leander, A.2015. "Seen and Unseen: Hybrid Rule in International Security." In *Hybrid Rule and State Formation: Public-Private Power in the 21st Century*, edited by S. Hurt and R. Lipschutz.

Lehtonen, P., and P. Aalto. 2017. "Smart and Secure Borders Through Automated Border Control Systems in the EU? The Views of Political Stakeholders in the Member States." *European Security* 26 (2): 207–225.

Lemberg-Pedersen, M. 2018. "Security, Industry and Migration in European Border Control." In *The Routledge Handbook of the Politics of Migration in Europe*, edited by A. Weinar, S. Bonjour, and L. Zhyznomirska. Oxon: Routledge.

Léonard, S. 2010. "EU Border Security and Migration Into the European Union: FRONTEX and Securitisation Through Practices." *European Security* 19 (2): 231–254.

Loukinas, P. 2017. "Surveillance and Drones at Greek Borderzones: Challenging Human Rights and Democracy." *Surveillance & Society* 15 (3/4): 439–446.

Maguire, M. 2015. "Migrants in the Realm of Experts: The Migration-Crime-Terrorist Nexus After 9/11." In *The Securitization of Migration in the EU: Debates Since 9/11*, edited by G. Lazaridis and K. Wadia, 62–87. Basingstoke: Palgrave.

Marin, L. 2016. "The Humanitarian Drone and the Borders: Unveiling the Rationales Underlying the Deployment of Drones in Border Surveillance." In *The Future of Drone Use*B. Custers, 115–132. The Hague: T.M.C. Asser Press.

Martins, B. O., and N. Ahmad. 2020. "The Security Politics of Innovation: Dual-use Technology in the EU's Security Research Programme." In *Emerging Security Technologies and EU Governance Actors, Practices and Processes*, edited by A. Calcara, R. Csernatoni, and C. Lavallée, 58–73. Routledge.

Martins, B. O., and C. Küsters. 2019. "Hidden Security: EU Public Research Funds and the Development of European Drones." *JCMS: Journal of Common Market Studies* 57 (2): 278–297.

Miller, C. A. 2017. "Engaging with Societal Challenges", In *The Handbook of Science and Technology Studies*, edited by U. Felt, et al, 4th ed., 909–913, Cambridge, MA: MIT Press.

MOAS. 2015. "MOAS Drones to Keep Flying Thanks to Generous Schiebel Donation." https://www.moas.eu/moas-drones-to-keep-flying-thanks-to-generous-schiebel-donation/.

Mörth, U. 2009. "The Market Turn in EU Governance: The Emergence of Public-Private Collaboration." *Governance* 22 (1): 99–120.

Nowak, J. 2019. "Drone Surveillance Operations in the Mediterranean: The Central Role of the Portuguese Economy and State in EU Border Control". *Border Criminologies*, 26 February. https://www.law.ox.ac.uk/research-subject-groups/centre-criminology/centreborder-criminologies/blog/2019/02/drone.

OCEAN2020 2019. OCEAN2020: About Us. https://ocean2020.eu/about-us/what-we-do/.

Pallister-Wilkins, P. 2018. "Hotspots and the Geographies of Humanitarianism." *Environment and Planning D: Society and Space* 0 (0): 1–18.

Papanicolopulu, I. 2013. "Hirsi Jamaa v. Italy. Application No. 27765/09." *American Journal of International Law* 107 (2): 417–423.

Rijpma, J. J. 2017. "Brave New Borders: The EU's Use of New Technologies for the Management of Migration and Asylum." In *New Technologies and EU Law*, edited by M. Cremona, 197–241. Oxford: Oxford University Press.

Rychnovska, D., M. Pasgaard, and T. V. Berling. 2017. "Science and Security Expertise: Authority, Knowledge, Subjectivity." *Geoforum; Journal of Physical, Human, and Regional Geosciences* 84: 327–331.

Salter, M. 2019. "Horizon Scan: Critical Security Studies for the Next 50 Years." *Security Dialogue* 50 (4S): 9–37.

Simon, M. 2018. "Give the Robots Electronic Tongues", *Wired*, 24 May. https://www.wired.com/story/give-the-robots-electronic-tongues/.

SmarterWare 2019. New Robots Can Sense Taste Beyond Human Capability, 17 May. http://smarterware.org/2019/05/new-robots-can-sense-taste-beyond-human-capability/.

Squire, V. 2015. "The Securitisation of Migration: An Absent Presence?." In *The Securitization of Migration in the EU: Debates Since 9/11*, edited by G. Lazaridis and K. Wadia, 19–36. Basingstoke: Palgrave.

Stares, J. 2016. "EU Plans Drone Fleet to Track migrants", *Politico.eu*, 6 April. https://www.politico.eu/article/european-union-fleet-of-drones-to-track-migrants-refugees/.

Tazzioli, M. 2016. "Eurosur, Humanitarian Visibility and (nearly) Real-Time Mapping in the Mediterranean." *ACME: An International Journal for Critical Geographies* 15 (3): 561–579.

Van Munster 2012. "Securitization". *Oxford Bibliographies*, Oxford: Oxford University Press. doi:10.1093/OBO/9780199743292-0091.

Vogel, K. M. et al. 2017. "Knowledge and Security", In *The Handbook of Science and Technology Studies*, edited by U. Felt, et al., 973–1001, 4th ed., Cambridge, MA: MIT Press.

Wæver, O. 1995. "Securitization and Desecuritization." In *On Security*, edited by R. D. Lipschutz, 46–87. New York: Columbia University Press.

Overcoming borders: the Europeanization of civil society activism in the 'refugee crisis'

Katharina Crepaz ⓘ

ABSTRACT
Civil society has become an active player in the public reception and handling of the 'refugee crisis', especially through the use of social media. People willing to engage are able to connect in a low-threshold, local, and interactive way, while also keeping connected to similar movements in other EU countries. This process of connection and collaboration can be regarded as an instance of 'bottom-up' Europeanization processes, in which national and subnational actors work together transnationally to reach a common goal. Social media as fora for exchange allow efficient communication, present a possibility to directly lobby the decision makers (e.g. local politicians), and provide an apt tool for the planning of collective actions. The internet offers de-securitising forces a forum for presenting alternative discourses on migration, contributing to de-securitisation processes by moving away from the predominant framing of migration as a threat. The present paper therefore aims to look at 'bottom-up' Europeanization and new possibilities for collaboration through the internet as a transnational, de-securitising open forum for discussion. A group of civil society pro-refugee activists in South Tyrol (Northern Italy) and their transnational activities will serve as a case study.

1. Introduction

Looking back on the media coverage of the so-called 'refugee crisis', the images of people welcoming refugees at train stations remain one of the most powerful portrayals of a general willingness to help. This euphoria has not been a lasting phenomenon, and public opinion has turned in the other direction, spiralling towards a construction of migration solely as a threat and a crisis – a securitisation process. However, as Bello argues in their introduction to this special issue,

> [...] it is equally true that there are forces that push the process towards an opposite direction. It is indeed possible that alternative actors, who do not hold a prejudicial narrative, with their resistance to securitization, enact discourses, techniques and practices, and induce policies, which are rather able to de-securitize this issue. (Bello 2022, 3)

Pro-refugee civil society actors can represent such a force capable of pushing the process in a different direction. They act against the predominant prejudicial narrative, by offering different views on both refugees themselves and the processes of flight and migration as a whole. Pro-refugee civil society groups can provide an important counter-point in a largely securitised public discourse on migration; although they may not be directly able to influence policies, they bring a different, humanitarian-based framing of migration into the discussion, and may contribute to public aware-ness-raising processes. Through internet and new media, these possibly de-securitising discourses can then be spread and action can be taken internationally.

The 'refugee crisis' constitutes an issue that needs to be addressed on the European level, as national solutions will surely fall short of a comprehensive approach. This is true for EU policy makers, but also for pro-refugee civil society organisations: transna-tional collaboration is needed, as both refugees and European host societies are faced with a similar set of problems across the continent. The EU level often fosters securitisa-tion processes through actors like FRONTEX (e.g. through a securitised language, refer-ring to refugees from Syria, Afghanistan and Iraq as *border-crossers*, Bello 2022, 24) and fails to find a common approach to the issue. On the other hand, 'Associations, volun-teers, spontaneous social movements, NGOs, along with border agencies and bodies, if holding a humanitarian and non-prejudicial approach, could all positively affect the situ-ation and contribute to stopping the social construction of migration as a threat' (Bello: 25). Pro-refugee civil society groups can thus act as a de-securitising force. They do so by constructing a different discourse on migration, moving from a crisis and threat-based view to a more normative and humanitarian action-based approach. By interacting through online media, their discourse is also open and easily accessible to people from diverse backgrounds, and fosters awareness-raising processes.

Civil society actors often consist of very heterogeneous people, coming from very different backgrounds, with sometimes opposing views, who are regardless united by a common aim; in the present case study, activists came from religious organisations, from left-wing social organisations or from the Green Party, and found common ground in the wish to aid refugees. The shared goal thus has to be strong enough to bridge other divides that might otherwise hinder working together. A look at common identity creation – often through adversarial construction – in civil society contexts will therefore constitute the starting point of the present paper. Identity formation is crucial for civil society groups. The heterogeneity of their members needs to be united through creating a common goal and a shared identity as people pursuing this goal. This is an important first step not only for civil society organisations, but for all processes of collective actor creation. While a common identity is vital both for civil society groups that are only active on the national level as well as for their transnational counterparts, actors operating on the European level also need to explore pathways for communication and collaboration. Europeanization is often viewed merely as a 'top-down' process, e.g. the European level of policy making exerting influence on nation-states (Vink and Gra-ziano 2007). However, Europeanization processes also consist of a strong 'bottom-up' side (Della Porta and Caiani 2009), which allows civil society and other actors to engage in transnational discourse and the planning of common action to influence different levels of decision-making. New information technologies and social media greatly facilitate the exchange of ideas, best practices or campaigning strategies on a day-to-day basis. They also constitute low-threshold 'ports of entry' for people who are interested in becoming active on a certain issue, but may hesitate to directly approach an NGO or other activist groups (Crepaz 2018). Social media interaction provides the opportunity to enter as a passive bystander, and to then either remain a silent supporter or actively engage in the discussion or in planning policy goals or other activities.

The present paper contributes to the analysis of the de-construction of migration as a security threat as outlined in the introduction to this special issue. It aims to investigate how and through which means pro-refugee civil society actors may act as a de-securitising force on a transnational and highly securitised topic like migration. The paper looks at transnational civil society cooperation by drawing on 'bottom-up' Europeanization theories, and investigates the role of social media as facilitators of cross-border collaboration. After the initial analysis of identity formation and 'transnationalization' in civil society, the concept of 'bottom-up' Europeanization (Della Porta and Caiani 2009) and its implications for civil society action in European contexts will be explained. A look at social media as participatory fora will serve as an additional frame of reference, and investigate to what extent new technologies have really influenced participation possibilities by introducing lower thresholds and diversifying interaction. Finally, findings from Europeanization and participation literature will be applied to an empirical example: a pro-refugee Facebook group and its transnational activities will serve as a case study. Data was collected through an analysis of in-group communication with a special focus on transnational interaction and activity; topics tackled in the group where evaluated according to thematic analysis (Braun and Clarke 2006). Group members were also asked to fill out an online questionnaire asking them about their personal background and about their motivation to become engaged in the group; unfortunately, turnout was relatively low (11 responses), but the questionnaire data can be used to complement the findings from the in-group interaction analysis.

2. Civil society and social movements as political actors: theoretical implications

What unites social movements and civil society collaboration is their structure: a network of different actors from diverse backgrounds loosely coordinated in a way that no single actor can claim to represent the movement as a whole (Della Porta 2015). In this regard, civil society collaboration could be viewed as the first state of an emerging, small-scale social movement. According to Rucht (2007), social movements need to fulfil two functions, namely appeal to potential allies and fight one or more opponents. He argues that

> it is time to abandon the simplified image of a two-party struggle between a (unified) movement and its (unified) opponent acting in some kind of a social vacuum. Unlike two individuals who may engage in personal struggles without spectators, social movements are internally differentiated actors operating within complex social settings that, in part, consist of public arenas. These settings are not just a kind of neutral background but include different kinds of actors with whom a social movement engages. (Rucht 2007, 197)

While it may be too far-fetched to look at transnational civil society collaborations as social movements, they do possess some of the characteristics of an emerging social movement, e.g. mobilisation for a common goal and against shared 'enemies'. Also, the diversity of actors described by Rucht for social movements is also one of the main defining aspects of civil society organisations; in the case of pro-refugee activism, people come from strongly religious as well as very left-wing backgrounds, connecting spectra that normally would not form an interest coalition. The common goal thus bridges usual societal divides, and becomes a strong unifying factor – one of the prerequisites mentioned for identity formation. In their analysis of the protesters engaging in the European Social Forum (ESF), Della Porta and Caiani (2009) stress the importance of a common set of values, in addition to the shared goal that brings the diverse actors in the network together. According to their survey at the first ESF, members come from very different backgrounds (e.g. Catholic Church, labour unions, Green Party, voluntary social workers), and all are 'deeply rooted in dense organizational networks' (Della Porta and Caiani 2009, 142). While a common goal therefore has a strong unifying power, shared values are also a necessary prerequisite of working together, even though they may stem from different motivations (e.g. from Christian beliefs or socialist discourses, both leading to humanitarian action). This corresponds to the data gathered in the Facebook group; its members come from very different contexts, but possess shared values and unite under a civil society action framework to achieve a common goal.

A strong common goal bridging potential other divides between members and shared adversaries are necessary to form a collective identity and create a collective type of action. As outlined above, civil society groups and social movements may consist of a very diverse spectrum of members; the same is also true for their opponents. 'Adversaries range from other social movements (i.e. countermovements) to interest groups, corporations, churches, political parties, and public administration to distinct political leaders' (Rucht 2007, 210). Countermovements are an interesting phenomenon when looking at pro-refugee activism: While anti-immigration civil society actors and protest movements have managed to draw relatively large crowds of supporters at the national level (e.g. the PEGIDA – *Patriotische Europäer gegen die Islamisierung des Abendlandes*/Patriotic Europeans Against the Islamization of the Occident – and their marches in Dresden and other German cities), their attempts to expand to a transnational dimension have largely not been very successful. PEGIDA aimed at organising marches in other European countries, but failed to generate the large turnouts achieved in Germany. As Berntzen and Weisskircher (2016, 564) argue,

> [...] PEGIDA has met resistance. In general, their activists have been massively outnumbered by counter-protesters, always consisting of left-winged antifascists, sometimes of broader groups within society.

PEGIDA has therefore not only failed to expand internationally and to rally its international supporters, but it has even acted as an adversarial mobilising force for pro-refugee actors. Pro-refugee civil society collaboration could therefore represent an important player in counteracting the social construction of migration as a threat, and in decelerating securitisation processes (Bello 2017, 69).

Jackie Smith (2007, 318) defines transnational civil society collaboration as an aspect of 'sociocultural globalization, or the transnational interaction among individuals and groups that generate the ideologies, identities, and cultures that transcend national boundaries'. While arguably some of the ideologies and identities where already there as the cause for coming together and taking action, Smith's definition highlights the concept of identity – and civil society identity in particular – as something that is in a state of flux, and that changes and responds to a variety of outside influences.

Transcending national boundaries and an expansion of one's field of action towards different levels of policy-making in a European multi-level structure are also at the core of 'bottom-up' Europeanization, to be looked at in more detail in the next section.

3. 'Bottom-up' Europeanization

Traditional Europeanization research focuses largely on 'top-down' developments, e.g. how decisions made on the European level affect the national and subnational levels (e.g. Vink & Graziano 2007; Schimmelfennig and Sedelmeier 2005). Europeanization 'top-down' is concerned with the implementation of the *acquis communautaire*, but also with further impact of European decision-making on the national and subnational levels. It looks at the EU and its member-states as a multi-level governance system, and analyses the processes through which common policy measures, but also norms and values find their way to the different levels and actors involved.

However, this 'top-down' framework of analysis cannot account for all political processes and activities influenced by the European level as a forum for decision-making, collaboration and exchange of ideas. Therefore, traditional definitions of Europeanization have recently been supplied with a 'bottom-up' side, focusing on the role of subnational entities like regions as well as on non-state actors like civil society organisations. Developments impacting the creation of transnational advocacy networks and fostering a common European public sphere for discourse can also be categorised as 'bottom-up' Europeanization. Della Porta and Caiani (2009) look at how Europeanization occurs through social movements. They describe 'bottom-up' Europeanization as a process of 'Europeanization of and by civil society' (Della Porta and Caiani 2009, 25). Taking on a constructivist approach, they see Europe as an emerging polity and 'bottom-up' Europeanization as a tool to counter the often-quoted democratic deficit by providing additional democratic legitimation. Civil society is regarded as a self-organised citizenry encompassing both grass-roots movements and formalised NGOs; through a process of 'Europeanization by externalization' – 'raising' an issue to the European level – stronger pressure can be exerted on national policy makers. Collective actors of the domestic public sphere (such as e.g. pro-refugee activists) can foster Europeanization processes, by 'organizing at the European level, making demands on European institutions, or framing their demands within a European discourse' (Della Porta and Caiani 2009, 35). Looking at the transnational collaboration of pro-refugee NGOs, all points mentioned by Della Porta & Caiani become visible: a Europeanization process of pro-refugee civil society is taking place, and it is being carried out by members of civil society organisations, speaking out against migration being constructed as a threat and promoting a humanitarian counter model to the migration-crime-terrorist nexus (Bello 2017, 58). A 'bottom-up' Europeanization framework is thus the most appropriate lens for looking at pro-refugee civil society collaboration: the issue of migration itself is European, migration policy cannot be confined to nation-states, and pro-refugee activists strongly root and frame their demands within a European discourse, e.g. counteracting the notion of a 'fortress Europe'. This become especially evident for pro-refugee activists operating in cross-border contexts, such as the members of Facebook group in the case study to be analysed in the next section of this paper. Pro-refugee activists meet in a European context, rendered more important by their frame of operation in a border region. Their demands are explicitly also aimed at the European level of decision-making, e.g. the signature collection for a more just and humane Common European Asylum System carried out during the transnational migrant strike, explained in more detail below. While their actions have so far not been successful in changing European policies, they have contributed to public awareness-raising, to offering a humanitarian and non-threat-focused discourse on migration and thus to a de-securitisation process.

The 'refugee crisis' constitutes an issue that affects all of Europe, and European trans-national exchange could allow for the exchange of best practices, but also help to put more pressure on states whose policies on the matter are considered to counter European solidarity. Pro-refugee civil society actors organise at the European level, and use it as a forum to connect, collaborate, plan future strategies or simply as a platform for discourse – Europeanization can be seen as an ongoing process, rather than an outcome of policy developments (Radaelli and Exadaktylos 2012). Demands and objectives are framed as goals to be commonly reached on the European level; national policies also still play a role, but they constitute more of a background for the common 'we' acting on the European public sphere. Looking at Europeanization as a two-way process encompassing both 'top-down' and 'bottom-up' developments (Crepaz 2016), one may argue that the 'top-down' process of creating a Common European Asylum System has in turn sparked a 'bottom-up' development of NGOs and other pro-refugee civil society actors redirecting their activities towards the European level. Similarly, the securitisation process taking place at the Council level (Bello 2017, 68) has triggered a de-securitising and mainly humanitarian focused development at the pro-refugee civil society level.

Pro-refugee civil society organisations acting as carriers of 'bottom-up' Europeanization could also be described as transnational advocacy networks, that is 'networks of activists distinguishable largely by the centrality of principled ideas or values in motivating their formation' (Keck and Sikkink 1998, 1). Diverse actors such as international and domestic NGOs, foundations, the media, trade unions, consumer unions, parts of inter-governmental organisations and parts of the executive and/or parliamentary branches of government may be present in advocacy networks; although it is unlikely that one network encompasses all of the above-mentioned types of actors. This diversification is also visible in pro-refugee activists, many of whom have not been politically active before, and who come from very different backgrounds – in the Facebook group analysed for my case-study, political parties, churches, clerical organisations and trade unions were featured among the members' socialisation towards activism. Bohman (2007) sees transnational advocacy networks as a sign of the shift from one nation-state *demos* to multiple European *demoi*, underlining the notion of a European *demoicracy* in which different *demoi* may be aligned according to different issue areas. According to Della Porta and Caiani (2009), a Europeanised civil society may also target different levels of decision-making, depending on which level has immediate decision-making power or which seems the most accessible. In pro-refugee activists, this becomes visible especially with actions aimed at raising awareness and mobilising at the regional level, which has a European dimension both due to its cross-border nature as well as due to institutionalised collaboration in form of the European Region 'Tyrol – South Tyrol – Trentino'. Material and cultural resources as well as domestic political traditions will also play a role in the formulation of policy goals and in shaping the day-to-day action of transnational collaboration (Della Porta and Caiani 2009).

4. Social media as participatory fora for civil society interaction?

The internet and particularly Web 2.0 developments like social media have widely been hailed as promising new spaces for participatory involvement (e.g. Campante, Durante, and Sobbrio 2017; Gil de Zúniga, Puig-I-Abril, and Rojas 2009), or even connected to ideas of implementing a deliberative democracy led by Habermasian ideals (Dahlberg 2001). While the initial enthusiasm has been somewhat dampened by studies showing that it is still largely resourceful, educated elites who participate in online political discourse (e.g Metje 2005; Waldschmidt 2009), the internet and social media remain powerful tools facilitating international communication. Transnational collaboration has become less resource-intensive, and thus more open to different spectra of society. In order to connect with an activist advocating for a similar cause, civil society actors no longer need to travel the world; an online contact is enough to initiate a potential future collaboration. Communication is thus at the core of network and social movement formation:

> For society at large, the key source of the social production of meaning is the process of socialized communication. Socialized communication exists in the public realm beyond interpersonal communication. The ongoing transformation of communication technology in the digital age extends the reach of communication media to all domains of social life in a network that is at the same time global and local, generic and customized in an ever-changing pattern. (Castells 2015, 6)

It is possible to engage in political communication in both local and global settings by using new technology: the range of action and potential extension of an activist network are no longer limited to immediate surroundings, and technology may also constitute an easier mode of entry into the activist sphere for members in geographic proximity to each other. Sandoval Almazan and Gil-Garcia (2014, 368) describe this development as 'cyberactivism 2.0': 'Cyberactivism 2.0 allows regular participation without time or place restrictions and increases the different levels of participation and engagement, allowing an individual to support the protest with a simple link to the others'. They develop a circular model explaining how online activism may serve as a precursor to activism in the physical world, counteracting the notion that movements or actions started online may remain pure paper tigers of the digital sphere. Their model starts from a triggering event (e.g. in the present paper's case the 'refugee crisis' as a whole, instances of migration-threat framing, or incidents of refugee suffering experienced in personal contexts), which leads to a media response. The media response happens much faster in social than in traditional media, and possesses a participatory character; information costs are low. The mass response to a certain event creates viral organisation, and leads to online community building – through ideas of collaboration, a shared identity emerges. Organisation must be horizontal and decentralised (e.g. free access and no official leadership). The ideas and plans for collaboration made through social media are then translated to a physical response, leading to concrete common actions (Sandoval Almazan and Gil-Garcia 2014, 369–370). However, viral organisation is not always translated into a physical response; some of the activists collaborating online may not wish to or have the possibility to engage in physical responses or concrete actions. Online community-building represents a value for participatory processes in itself, as it creates a sphere for deliberation and awareness-raising. In the case of pro-refugee activism, this could then lead to de-securitisation processes through establishing different discourses on migration. In order for a physical response to ensue, there must be activists with personal resources and mobilising potential bringing concrete action. In the case of pro-refugee groups, such actions may at first be 'hands on', e.g. the collection of food and clothing for refugees, while political protests follow later on.

Social media thus serve a variety of purposes in civil society collaboration: they constitute a forum for discourse and interaction, an arena for identity construction, a space for planning responses in the physical world and a low-threshold possibility for participation, especially for members who may not have been politically active before or want to inform themselves about an issue before actively getting involved. Siedschlag's (2003) concept of 'digital democracy' also presents the creation of new channels for citizen-to-citizen interaction as one of the possibilities for civil society participation brought along by social media and web 2.0. The issue of whether or not social media may encourage those who were not active before to participate is a highly debated question; studies point towards a 'reinforcement' (Metje 2005) of participation from people who were already active. However, social media can serve as a low-threshold 'port of entry' for citizens whose interest in civil society activism on a certain topic has been raised, and who may take the first steps towards active participation by adhering to a Facebook group or another type of social media forum. Expectations for entering participants are low, and while many remain 'watchers' not actively engaging in activism, other members then follow-up by taking part in discourse and participating in activities in the physical world (Crepaz 2018). Online communities can contribute to de-securitisation processes by providing a forum for discourse going beyond the securitised framing of migration as an 'emergency' or a 'crisis'. They offer fora for interaction between group-members that are already real-life activists and those who are interested in different discourses but not yet active themselves, serve as a planning board for political engagement and as a platform for transnational interaction not bound by local or national public spheres. As outlined by Bello in the introduction to this special issue (Bello 2022, 23), 'Civil society associations, NGOs and other spontaneous social movements, for instances solidarity movements and volunteers, which are clearly inclusive towards migration, contribute to decelerating the spiralling of the securitization of migration'; the next section of this paper will therefore look at a Facebook group and its online and offline activities as a case study for pro-refugee civil society organisations as actors fostering de-securitisation processes. While pro-refugee organisations may not have enough resources and political leverage to stop European securitisation processes or induce higher level policy changes, they are able to offer alternative humanitarian-focused cognitions, cooperate transnationally and raise awareness for refugee issues on the local and regional political level.

5. Dynamics of initiatives on social media: group *Solidarität mit Flüchtlingen / solidarità con i profughi* (solidarity with refugees)

In their introduction to this special issue, Bello (2022, 25) highlight that

[a]ssociations, volunteers, spontaneous social movements, NGOs, along with border agencies and bodies, if holding a humanitarian and non-prejudicial approach, could all

positively affect the situation and contribute to stopping the social construction of migration as a threat.

Through an analysis of a Facebook group operating across-borders, I will now provide empirical data on how transnational civil society collaboration through the use of social media takes place, and how it may help to change a securitised migration discourse.

The group, called *Solidarität mit Flüchtlingen / Solidarità con I profughi* (Solidarity with Refugees), was chosen because of its geographical positioning in one of the most important border regions for migratory movements in Europe (the Brennero/Brenner border between Italy and Austria), its transnational character as a meeting place for activists from different countries, and its combination of online awareness raising and discussion with hands-on offline engagement. The group was founded by activists from the Northern Italian province of Bozen/Bolzano. South Tyrol, as the area is also known, is Italy's northernmost region on the border to Austria, rendering it one of the places most directly impacted by migratory routes leading North to Austria and further on to Germany. Regional cross-border cooperation in the area is fostered by the European Region 'Tyrol – South Tyrol – Trentino'. As part of the Schengen Agreement, the Austrian-Italian border controls at Brenner/Brennero were abolished in 1997, but the reinstallment of border protection measures on behalf of Austria has been a frequent point for discussion over the last two years. Although no such measures have been implemented so far, the possible re-erection of a nation-state border also holds high symbolic value: South Tyrol was part of the Austro-Hungarian Empire until 1918, and is inhabited by a German-speaking minority population (constituting the majority at the regional level). Re-installing old borders thus not only counters the spirit of European Integration, but also endangers the re-unification of a historical regional unit cooperating closely politically and economically.

As of June 2020, the group has 2,698 members. Group interaction largely takes place in German, reflecting the linguistic proportionality of the region; however, the principle is that everyone may post in German/Italian (or English if necessary) and will usually be responded to in that same language. The group description quite simply states that its aim is to 'provide help to those being dragged off trains at Bozen and Brenner with small things liked food and drinks' (Solidarität mit Flüchtlingen/Solidarità con i Profughi, author's translation), and that everyone wishing to get engaged or donate is welcome to do so but should read the pinned guideline post beforehand. A second paragraph mentions the necessity of work for building a future, and encourages those who may have potential job offers (gardening work, tourism, agriculture, internships, etc.) to get in touch with the organisation *Binario1* (Track 1) – a civil society organisation which developed from the informal gathering of activists in the Facebook group. The group thus offers an alternative framing of refugees on two levels: refugees are not primarily a security threat, but people in need; refugees do not have to or want to remain passive recipients of aid, but strive for work to provide for their own living. These notions counteract predominant media views, and offer a non-securitised humanitarian and empowerment-driven discourse on refugees, which contributes to de-securitisation efforts.

The origins of the group can be traced back to 2014, when the first refugees were being sent back to Italy from Austria, as they had first entered the EU in Italy, and Italy was thus responsible for their asylum procedure (according to the Dublin III Agreement). People were often left 'stranded' at the Brenner/Brennero border, without access to information on what was happening to them, without interpreters and without food or adequate clothing: the border is located at 1370 m of altitude, and cold and wintery conditions can be a challenge. Pro-refugee civil society actors, among them the *Alexander Langer Foundation*, decided that a monitoring team should be installed at the border, being present at the train stations to provide information, legal counselling and humanitarian help. Transnational pro-refugee civil society collaboration was essential from the beginning, as the activists were operating in a border context. According to Monika Weissensteiner, who was part of the monitoring team, networks with actors working on refugee issues on national and European levels were built (Weissensteiner 2015, 23). This meant that the above-mentioned re-framing of refugees and the following de-securitisation discourses were also taking place in a transnational manner right from the beginning; de-securitisation processes were embedded in a European context and took place in a multi-level and multi-actor way.

Pro-refugee civil society mobilisation started when an early winter hit the border in October 2014, creating an emergency situation due to cold and snow. While official measures mainly consisted of border monitoring, exerting a securitising force, civil society acted as humanitarian-oriented, de-securitising counterpart. Pro-refugee activists were present at the border; according to Lorenzo Zamponi (2018, 107) they 'expressed precise political claims and demands from the beginning', thus going beyond mere humanitarian aid and starting a de-securitisation discourse aimed at different levels of government. The actions taken by the group were aimed at helping people at the border, but they always also included a political framework and a set of demands to policy makers in order to improve the situation. The activists' engagement contributed to raise awareness for the issue, and to shed a different light on refugees at least in the local news media, by also highlighting the dangers they were exposed to when trying to cross the border, and the lack of official measures to counteract this precarious situation. Clothing collections were started, and citizens volunteered to donate food and warm clothes at the border. During this time, the Facebook group was initiated as a means to facilitate communication and to allow interested activists to come together and get involved. The group was first called *Winterhilfe für Flüchtlinge* (winter help for refugees), and then renamed to *Solidarität mit Flüchtlingen / Solidaritá con i profughi* (Solidarity with Refugees), as it became clear that it would continue to exist beyond the winter emergency. First instances of transnational pro-refugee civil society collaboration emerged shortly afterwards, when activists from South Tyrol and neighbouring Tyrol in Austria organised a common demonstration for the Global Migrants Action Day in December 2014. One of the frequent points for discussion was the need for a European approach to the topic, and how to go about pressuring the responsible bodies to seek that kind of solution. On 1st March 2015 activists from Italy, Austria, Germany and Switzerland met at the Brenner/Brennero border for transnational mobilisation in the context of the *Tag des Transnationalen MigrantInnen-Streiks* (day of transnational migrant strike), an event that brought considerable media attention to non-securitised discussions about migration. The South Tyrolean activists additionally collected signatures for a different EU Asylum System, a measure aimed at local, national and EU policy-makers (Weissensteiner 2015, 27–28). These activities underline the character of pro-refugee civil society as a de-securitising force; the activists did not only provide help in terms of clothing etc. at the border, but added an explicitly political and de-securitisation-oriented dimension to their actions. Through a 'bottom-up' Europeanization processes, they collaborated with organisations from neighbouring countries and framed migration as a European topic, but without the often predominant 'crisis' rhetoric. Instead, a humanitarian-focused discourse was proposed, in the real-life action taken at the border as well as in discussions in the Facebook group.

Monika Weissensteiner recalls that the connection and mobilisation of people through Facebook was very fast. They connected and coordinated their activities through the group and via social messaging services such as WhatsApp, and also put political pressure on local authorities who were often hesitant to act on the matter (Weissensteiner 2015, 29). In the case of the Facebook group, the transition from online activism to physical world engagement therefore took place quickly and efficiently. This denotes that social media can indeed serve as participatory fora and exert mobilising power that does not remain confined to the virtual realm. The solidarity movement started on Facebook then also took on a more institutionalised form by creating the volunteer organisation *Binario1-Gleis1* (track 1), as the railway station's tracks constituted their first area of action. They continue their engagement through the Facebook group, which has also proven to be a useful tool for organising local awareness raising events (Weissensteiner 2015, 30). By doing so, the activists provide de-securitisation processes through the offering of alternative discourses on migration both online and offline, thus considerably extending the range of people they can potentially reach with their actions.

The group's members come from heterogeneous linguistic and political backgrounds, and many have not been active in other civil society organisations before. In explaining their motives for becoming active, the European level is also frequently invoked (Crepaz 2018) – a common approach to the problem therefore also requires a connected transnational pro-refugee civil society. In the daily dynamics of the Facebook group, people come in to discuss concrete action, but also share personal stories or media coverage of refugee issues. Pro-refugee activists from Germany or Austria engaging with refugees who face being sent back to Italy also address the group for collaboration purposes, or for more basic tasks like the translation of documents issued by Italian authorities. Although its origins are in a measure designed to provide immediate help – during the early winter of October 2014 – the group has evolved into a stronger organisational structure leading to a volunteer organisation. It has become a widely recognised forum for information, discussion and a point of first entry for people wishing to get engaged in pro-refugee activism. The group and the pro-refugee organisation created afterwards have therefore gone beyond a tool for organising hands-on aid and become an active force in promoting de-securitisation processes through action, information and non-securitised discourse offers both on – and offline.

6. Conclusions

The present paper has aimed to look at transnational pro-refugee civil society collaboration and de-securitisation processes in the context of social media and 'bottom-up' Europeanization exerted by civil society. It focused in particular on the Facebook group

Solidarität mit Flüchtlingen / Solidaritá con i profughi and its activities. Like most activist action, the group was started by a triggering event – the early winter and the precarious situation of refugees at the Brenner/Brennero border in October 2014. Used first as a tool for immediate response to a crisis situation, the group remained active and left its initial restricted purpose ('winter help') for a broader approach to civil society engagement. It provided activists with a low-threshold, quickly responding means for communication, and also became a forum for discussion for like-minded people. It thus constituted the public sphere needed for identity formation, and constructed itself as a counter model to the prevalent migration-security nexus. The group and its members were therefore important actors in the de-securitisation of migration discourses, at least in the local and regional context of the Brenner/Brennero border, where their online presence became a recognised source for information and their real-life actions received considerable local media coverage.

Due to its placement in a border-region, a transnational component was inherent to the group's work from the beginning. The first instances of collaboration with activists from neighbouring countries soon followed, and led to awareness raising events and action days that were organised together. The European level as the main arena for lobbying was also addressed, and common efforts were made to point out alternative solutions to the current Asylum System, viewed as unjust and inefficient. While the Council and nation-state governments fostered the securitisation of migration by mainly framing it as a security threat, the activists promoted a humanitarian approach exerting de-securitising power. They did not only provide hands-on help, but also raised awareness for discourses looking at migration not only from a 'crisis' or 'emergency' perspective.

The group formed at the regional level, but quickly also directed its activities towards transnational collaboration and especially towards European pro-refugee civil society interaction for measures aimed at the EU-level – an instance of a 'bottom-up' Europeanization process, triggered by transnational civil society collaboration. The internet and especially the Facebook group as a participatory forum provided a means for connection and interaction, and facilitated the definition of shared goals and the planning of shared action. The often-postulated limits of online participation (e.g. failure to translate activism to the 'real' world, lack of truly 'new' participation possibilities as only those who were already active before get engaged) cannot be observed in this case. Physical world activism followed almost immediately – although not for all members of the group – as did transnational collaboration efforts and appeals to policy makers at various levels of government (regional, national, European). Also, many group members stated that they had not been active in other civil society contexts before (Crepaz 2018); this hints at the potential of online activism to act as a low-threshold 'port of entry' for people wishing to get involved, but who may prefer to slowly transition from bystanders to activists. Such behaviour may be frowned upon when physically entering an activist gathering, but is acceptable in the world of social media. Although not all group participants will become active volunteers, even passive ('reading') group participation could lead to increased knowledge, awareness raising processes, a more differentiated use of terminology and a different, de-securitised framing of migration in public discourse. By offering a forum for different views moving away from migration as a 'crisis', discussion about migration can become more layered and the spiralling of the securitisation of migration can be slowed down or even counteracted by a de-securitisation process.

Disclosure statement

No potential conflict of interest was reported by the author(s).

ORCID

Katharina Crepaz ⓘ http://orcid.org/0000-0003-1033-0823

References

Bello, Valeria. 2017. *International Migration and International Security: Why Prejudice is a Global Security Threat*. London: Routledge.

Bello, V. 2022. "The Spiralling of the Securitisation of Migration in the EU: From the Management of a 'Crisis' to a Governance of Human Mobility?" *Journal of Ethnic and Migration Studies* 48 (6): 1327–1344. https://doi.org/10.1080/1369183X.2020.1851464.

Berntzen, Lars Erik, and Manès Weisskircher. 2016. "Anti-Islamic PEGIDA Beyond Germany: Explaining Differences in Mobilisation." *Journal of Intercultural Studies* 37 (6): 556–573.

Bohman, James. 2007. *Democracy Across Borders: From Demos to Demoi*. Cambridge: MIT Press.

Braun, Virginia, and Victoria Clarke. 2006. "Using Thematic Analysis in Psychology." *Qualitative Research in Psychology*. 77–101.

Campante, Filipe, Ruben Durante, and Francesco Sobbrio. 2017. "Politics 2.0: The Multifaceted Effect of Broadband Internet on Political Participation." *Journal of the European Economic Association* 16 (4): 1094–1136.

Castells, Manuel. 2015. *Networks of Outrage and Hope: Social Movements in the Internet Age*. Cambridge: Polity Press.

Crepaz, Katharina. 2016. *The Impact of Europeanization on Minority Communities*. Wiesbaden: Springer VS.

Crepaz, Katharina. 2018. "A 'Common Commitment': Civil Society and European Solidarity in the Refugee Crisis." In *A European Crisis: Perspectives on Refugees in Europe*, edited by Nevena Nancheva and Timofey Agarin, 29–49. Hannover: Ibidem.

Dahlberg, Lincoln. 2001. "The Internet and Democratic Discourse: Exploring The Prospects of Online Deliberative Forums Extending the Public Sphere." *Information, Communication and Society* 4 (4): 615–633.

Della Porta, Donatella. 2015. *Social Movements in Times of Austerity*. Cambridge: Polity Press.

Della Porta, Donatella, and Manuela Caiani. 2009. *Social Movements and Europeanization*. Oxford: University Press.

Gil de Zúniga, Homero, Eulàlia Puig-I-Abril, and Hernando Rojas. 2009. "Weblogs, Traditional Sources Online and Political Participation: an Assessment of how the Internet is Changing the Political Environment." *New Media & Society* 11 (4): 553–574.

Keck, Margaret E., and Kathryn Sikkink. 1998. *Activists Beyond Borders: Advocacy Networks in International Politics*. Ithaca, London: Cornell University Press.

Metje, Christian. 2005. *Internet und Politik – Die Auswirkungen des Onlinemediums auf die Demokratie*. Berlin: Logos.

Radaelli, Claudio M., and Theofanis Exadaktylos. 2012. "Lessons Learned: Beyond Causality." In *Research Design in European Studies: Establishing Causality in Europeanization*, edited by Claudio M. Radaelli and Theofanis Exadaktylos, 255–264. Houndmills, New York: Palgrave Macmillan.

Rucht, Dieter. 2007. "Movement Allies, Adversaries and Third Parties." In *The Blackwell Companion to Social Movements*, edited by David Snow, A. Soule, A. Sarah, and Hanspeter Kriesi, 196–216. Malden: Blackwell Publishing.

Sandoval Almazan, Rodrigo, and Ramon J Gil-Garcia. 2014. "Towards Cyberactivism 2.0? Understanding the use of Social Media and Other Information Technologies for Political Activism and Social Movements." *Government Information Quarterly* 31 (2014): 365–378.

Schimmelfennig, Frank, and Ulrich Sedelmeier. 2005. *The Europeanization of Central and Eastern Europe.* Ithaca, London: Cornell University Press.

Siedschlag, Alexander. 2003. "Politologische Annäherung an die Digitale Demokratie - Ein Kommentar zum Forschungsstand." In *Wie das Internet die Politik Verändert - Einsatzmöglichkeiten und Auswirkungen,* edited by Arne Rogg, 9–17. Opladen: Leske + Budrich.

Smith, Jackie. 2007. "Transnational Processes and Movements." In *The Blackwell Companion to Social Movements,* edited by David Snow, A. Soule, A. Sarah, and Hanspeter Kriesi, 312–335. Malden: Blackwell Publishing.

Solidarität mit Flüchtlingen / Solidarità con i Profughi. Facebook Group. Accessed June 25, 2020 . https://www.facebook.com/groups/1534046566840868/.

Vink, Maarten P., and Paolo Graziano. 2007. "Challenges of a New Research Agenda." In *Europeanization - New Research Agendas,* edited by Paolo Graziano and Maarten P Vink, 3–20. London: Palgrave Macmillan.

Waldschmidt, Anne. 2009. "Politische Partizipation von Menschen mit Behinderungen und Benachteiligungen." In *Lebensgestaltung bei Behinderungen im Erwachsenenalter und Alter.* Basiswissen Sonderpädagogik 5, edited by R. Stein, 118–152. Baltmannsweiler: Schneider.

Weissensteiner, Monika. 2015. "Die Brenner-Grenze: Bewegungen, die Bewegen." In *Gaismair-Jahrbuch 2016: Zwischentöne,* edited by Horst Schreiber, Monika Jarosch, Lisa Gensluckner, Martin Haselwanter, and Elisabeth Hussl, 22–32. Innsbruck: Studien Verlag.

Zamponi, Lorenzo. 2018. "From Border to Border: Refugee Solidarity Activism in Italy Across Space, Time, and Practices." In *Solidarity Mobilizations in the 'Refugee Crisis' - Contentious Moves,* edited by Donatella Della Porta, 99–124. London: Palgrave Macmillan.

The role of non-state actors' cognitions in the spiralling of the securitisation of migration: prejudice, narratives and Italian CAS reception centres

Valeria Bello

ABSTRACT

Today's management of migration is strongly dependent on the role of reception centres. Despite their crucial role, scholars of the securitisation of migration have overlooked at how they affect the process. In the light shed by this special issue, the present contribution analyses non-state actors' cognitions and narratives in the management of reception centres, so as to explain their performative roles in securitising or de-securitising human mobility as a threat. Its findings prove that, when reception centres' managers hold prejudicial cognitions, they develop negative practices that produce hostile and stereotyped narratives. A multi-method comparative case study, including covert ethnography, field observation and in-depth interviews, shows that, differently from speech-acts, narratives do not need to be accepted by the audience to exercise their effects. The audience is impressed from the narratives, which in a performative act, make people feel and perceive what the narration stages [Alexander, J. 2004. 'Cultural Pragmatics: Social Performance between Ritual and Strategy.' *Sociological Theory* 22 (4): 527–573; Lyotard, J. F. 1979. *La condition postmoderne: rapport sur le savior. English Translation "The Postmodern Condition: A Report on Knowledge"*. Manchester University Press]. Akin accountings contribute to spiralling the process, by self-fulfilling and reinforcing the securitisation of migration.

Introduction

Today's management of migration is often strongly dependent on the activity of a variety of non-state actors, particularly when it comes to border controls or to first reception of migrants (Bello 2017a; Bloom 2014): from border guards to businessmen, NGOs and civil society, along with UN agencies and churches, they all play a crucial role at different stages of migratory journeys. Matters of life and death often depend on their very intervention. Although there have been interesting analyses of FRONTEX's activity (Neal 2009; Léonard 2010), most works on the topic have limited their study to the role of either states or institutions in which states play a predominant part (Huysmans 2006; Squire 2015; Karamanidou 2015). A few others have instead considered both the process of the securitisation of migration and the consequences it entails for some non-state actors' activities – such as xenophobic movements and detention centres (Lazaridis and Wadia 2015), or civil society's activism (Squire 2011), and NGOs' rescue operations (Cusumano 2019a).

Among non-state actors, reception centres are crucial for the research to take into account, as they affect both migrants' and receiving populations' lives. They often performatively establish the relations between newcomers and the local communities, and, thereafter, perceptions of migration more widely in receiving countries (Bello 2017a). Many times, issues related to specific reception centres are at the core of electoral campaigns and political decisions, and they become reasons to further subordinate migrants' positions in a country (Dine, Montagna, and Ruggiero 2014). A notorious case is Italy. Matteo Salvini, leader of the party The League (La Lega), when he was in power as Ministry of Interior between early 2018 and the summer of 2019, put in place policies criminalising migrants and making their integration in the country extremely arduous, mainly through some crucial changes to the system of reception. Namely, the two Salvini's security decrees have decisively diminished the role of those integration centres that were included in the System of Protection for Asylum-seekers and Refugees (SPRAR) (Decreto Legge, 04/10/2018 n° 113, Gazzetta Ufficiale 04/10/2018) by significantly reducing their funds. The two security decrees instead increased the budget for both extraordinary reception centres (CAS), which do not offer any type of integration programmes to newly arrived migrants, and centres of expulsions (CPR), which entail prison-like conditions for migrants, and thus establish a migration-crime nexus. Salvini's security decrees benefitted in particular extraordinary reception centres (CAS), which had often been both at the core of harsh political debates and in the media focus for some presumed negative impact on local communities. CAS reception centres consequently represent a crucial case of analysis to contribute to understanding how the spiralling of the securitisation of migration (Bello 2017a, 2022) has taken place in the country.

Despite the relevance of reception centres, if we exclude two works on migrants detention centres (Ceccorulli and Labanca 2014; Wadia 2015), scholars of the securitisation of migration have overlooked at how they affect the process of securitisation. A similar research gap is worth exploring and the current study contributes to filling it by analysing the consequences of prejudicial cognitions in reception centres. The introduction to this special issue has indeed classified non-state actors' cognitions as useful to explain their performative roles in securitising or de-securitising human mobility as a threat (Bello 2022). In such a light, the present work provides some reflections and findings on the repercussions that specific cognitions shown in reception centres, produce in the spiralling of the securitisation of migration. In particular, it identifies in prejudicial cognitions what allows some reception centres to contribute to the upward spiralling of the securitisation of migration, thus supporting one of the arguments of the theoretical framework of this special issue (Bello 2022). When reception centres' managers hold prejudicial cognitions, they develop negative practices that produce hostile and stereotyped narratives and allow a self-reinforcing spiralling of the securitisation of migration. Differently from speech-acts, narratives in fact do not need to be accepted by the audience to exercise their effects. The audience is impressed from the narratives, which in a performative act, make people feel and perceive what the narration stages (Alexander 2004; Lyotard 1979).

The actors reproducing the narratives act as 'impression managers' before the audience (Goffman 1959; Braun, Schindler, and Wille 2019). Reception centres managed through prejudicial cognitions reproduce securitising narratives and consequently further increase prejudice within countries. This work claims that prejudice engenders, through practices and narratives, a spiralling self-reinforcing progression of the securitisation of migration.

In order to prove that prejudicial cognitions enact practices and narratives whose outcomes are key elements for an understanding of the role of non-state actors in the spiralling of the securitisation of migration, this study presents the results of a comparative case study of migrant reception centres in Italy. The analysis was based on a fieldwork conducted between 2014 and 2017, which included covert ethnography, participatory observation, and unstructured and semi-structured interviews. The findings confirm that prejudice has actually played a crucial role not only in increasing the perceptions of migrants as threats, but also in creating dynamics that both self-fulfil its predicaments and spiral the process of securitisation.

Prejudice and non-state actors in the spiralling of the securitisation of migration

Prejudicial narratives in the spiralling of the securitisation of migration

It is evident that there is a general tendency to associate migrants with crimes, terrorism and, more generally, insecurity, and when not directly depicted as criminals, they can be referred to as catalysts of organised crime and a harbinger of corruption, thus implying any way the construction of a migration-security nexus (Huysmans 2007). Nevertheless, it is equally clear that there also exist some non-state actors that, instead, help desecuritise migration, and namely some UN agencies, NGOs and some civil society associations (Bello 2017a; Crepaz 2020; Della Porta 2018; Squire 2011). However, especially the latter category is generic enough to allow in its inclusion very different types of citizens' spontaneous or less spontaneous movements. For example, the transnational movement 'Defend Europe', which rented a boat to operate a surveillance of the activities of those NGOs rescuing migrants in danger at sea, shows how civil society organisations are not automatically and always playing similar roles. Their impact depends on a variety of factors (Castelli Gattinara 2018; Cusumano 2019b; Schneiker 2019). While the positive role of civil society has already been depicted in some studies (Crepaz 2020; Della Porta 2018; Squire 2011), there is a lack of analysis of the consequences that prejudicial cognitions can entail for non-state actors' role in the securitisation of migration.

Prejudice has in the past been identified as a negative attitude towards others, and in particular towards immigrants (Pettigrew 1980). More specifically to this theoretical framework, prejudice is understood here as a faulty cognition or, to put it more simply, a misleading mind-set, or frame of interpreting the world, according to which the presence of others would in more or less serious ways always compromise what is a desirable life in a place (Bello 2017a). The assumption and generic affirmation that migrants, without distinctions, pose a threat to national, or individual or collective security is *per se* prejudicial towards individuals. Due to its implicit characteristics, the phenomenon of the securitisation of migration is an intrinsically prejudicial process.

As part of the literature has identified (Bello 2017a; Huysmans 2000; Karamanidou 2015; Sasse 2005), both national and regional regulatory frameworks can entail, among their consequences, the formation of negative perceptions of migration. For instance, an important element that has been recognised as a source of perceptions of migrants as threats lies in the increasing linkages connecting migration and minority policies to security and rights (Sasse 2005). However, practices can also engender prejudice. An example among such practices is the focus placed on the procedure of the asylum request after the 'threat to the border' has been staged: the EU establishes that those asylum-seekers who cannot prove their status of 'refugees' within 18 months will be expulsed (European Parliament 2015). Those persons, who have travelled without proper documentations and do not immediately state that they wish to request asylum, are sent to readmission (or expulsion) centres, in prison-like conditions, and then 'returned' to their countries. The fact that there is given no other option than the readmission centre in prison-like conditions to the persons who have committed the administrative offence (or civic violation) of travelling without proper documentation perpetuates a rhetoric that criminalise an administrative or civic violation, which only happens in the case of migration. Similar practices and criminalising rhetoric amplify the narratives of both an existential threat at the border and the nexus between migration and crime (Bello 2017a). Such a rhetoric finds its perfect loci in those reception centres that relegate migrants to a separate place in the world, where they stay until their status is 'checked and verified'. The audience of such narrative – the society of the country at large – assists, as in a public ceremony, about migrants and migration mostly through the news reporting threats at the borders and their 'temporarily trapped' presence in these reception centres. No other performance is offered of migration: the life of migrants and their contribution to society is not portrayed at any other stage. The consequent perception is that migrants – and the entire phenomenon of migration – mainly exist at the borders and within these centres, and they solely use the resources of states and do not contribute to its welfare (Bello 2017a). Narratives further spreading from perceptions of this kind can engender other prejudicial ideas, in a self-fulfilling dynamic that spirals over time.

Until now, the analyses of the securitisation of migration have focused upon speech-acts, which need the acceptance of an audience (Buzan 1991; Waever 1996; Balzacq 2010). However, when the process entails narratives, such as, for instance, stories passed orally, in personal networks, the audience has very limited alternatives to accepting the messages. The very act of uttering stories that started to be told under the form of a personal knowledge or experience of the first narrator and then recounted across networks, in the function of its performativity, cannot be challenged as different from the truth (Goffman 1959; Lyotard 1979). As Lyotard clarifies: 'True knowledge, in this perspective, is always indirect knowledge; it is composed of reported statements that are incorporated into the metanarrative of a subject that guarantees their legitimacy' (Lyotard 1979, 35). One needs to add to such a consideration that narratives can be openly rejected by some, but they do not to need to be accepted by all the others to exercise their effects. They convince of their intrinsic truth all those interlocutors who do not share an alternative version of the story, a counternarrative which needs to be immediately and openly proposed in order to reject the securitising narrative of the performative act of utterance.

The main difference between a speech-act and a narrative is that, while for the first the audience has to 'accept' the message, for the second (the narrative) the audience 'is impressed' from it and, if the actor is successful, *feels* what the matter at stake is (Alexander 2004). The narrative is a performative act in itself and the actors that contribute to it are 'impression managers' before an audience (Goffman 1959; Braun, Schindler, and Wille 2019). In a postmodern understanding, the narratives represent 'true knowledge' that cannot be challenged by the audience (Lyotard 1979), but needs to be 'resisted' with alternative narratives.

Along these lines, societies sometimes witness but more often *feel* the arrival, detention and removal of migrants. Recent research has shown that, while the presence of long-term migrants is connected to an increase of positive attitudes towards newcomers even in times of economic crisis, the appearance of short-term migrants and return migration will be associated with a rise in prejudice because it solely highlights the flows of migrants arriving and leaving these countries (Bello 2017b). Therefore, some consequences of administrative practices in accepting or rejecting migrants' asylum requests and in the management of reception centres are key reasons for the development of perceptions of migrants as threats and the reproduction of stereotyped narratives. These practices derive from both regional and national policies (Huysmans 2000, 2007; Squire 2015) but more importantly translate into narratives of migration and consequent perceptions that create more prejudice towards newcomers (Karamanidou 2015) and, more precisely, towards those perceived as 'outsiders' because of a variety of visible elements that allow specific biological, cultural or ethnopolitical forms of racism and discrimination (Bello 2017a).

The role of non-state actors in the securitisation

The literature on the securitisation of migration (Balzacq 2010; Bigo 2002; Buzan 1991; Caviedes 2015; Huysmans 2006; Léonard and Kaunert 2010; Waever 1996) has already clarified the reasons for looking specifically at the role of non-state actors. In particular, Buzan (1991) and the Copenhagen School were amongst the first to emphasise both the importance of different actors and sectors in the securitisation of migration, and the role of the audience in the acceptance of those speech-acts that transform a socio-economic, political or cultural issue into an existential threat (Buzan 1991; Waever 1996). Bigo instead focused on a crucial category of non-state actors in the securitisation, and namely those security professionals who intervene in 'the management of the unease' (Bigo 2002). Huysmans examined the creation of insecure communities through policies and techniques as the referent objects within the process (Huysmans 2006). Balzacq (2010) has then placed specific attention to the role of the audience that received the information and admitted it as true for a successful securitisation. In Balzacq's collection, Léonard and Kaunert addressed the lack of a necessary 'conceptualisation of the relationship between the securitising actors and the audience' (Léonard and Kaunert 2010, 57). More recently, Caviedes (2015) has tested the role of narratives as a result of securitising policies by part of an array of actors in different countries with a comparative perspective and has found that, from 2008 through 2012, these have been consistent only when related to the threat at the borders. However, Cavidies has not considered the consequences of the narratives, but only their content and consistency.

From all these works, it emerges that the securitisation of migration is also linked to some non-state actors' activities in the management of migration, and in particular: (1) policies, discourse, practices and techniques, which public and private non-state actors use; (2) the symbols and narratives, which emerge from their management of migration, particularly when the focus is on the threat at the borders; and (3) the consequent perceptions that the audience form out of these situations, which constitute the new forces that help spiral the process of securitisation. Of all these elements of connection, there is a lack of analysis of the practices of non-state actors and the consequent narratives and perceptions that the audience form out of them.

The role of non-state actors in framing migration

Waever et al. (1993) were among the first to highlight that the concerns that migration seems to provoke in the domain of societal insecurity would have been key in the stability of Europe in the future. Waever (1996) himself illustrated some further consequences. Identity dynamics are twisted with security issues in Europe to a point that, if not resolved, will threaten the stability of this region of the world and possibly the whole globe. Among these identity dynamics, there are we-identities that *move* the reactions of non-state actors. On the one hand, non-state actors include civil society (Feischmidt, Pries, and Cantat 2019; Lazaridis and Wadia 2015) and private actors (Bloom 2014; Moreno and Price 2017), such as the corporations of security professionals or even sometime extremely violent paramilitaries, such as in the case of the Balkans (Zavirsek 2017). On the other hand, there are a variety of non-state actors, such as national and European border controls agencies and migration centres, whose roles have not been studied enough in the framework of the securitisation of migration – if one excludes those existing works on Frontex (Neal 2009; Léonard 2010) and border surveillance system (Jumbert 2012; Martins and Küsters 2019; Martins and Jumbert 2020). The 'generalised diplomat' that Waever identifies can operate in different directions: the securitisation or its deconstruction. In such a light, it is key today to understand the roles of non-state actors at different stages in the process of securitisation (Waever 1996, 126).

The introduction to this special issue has illustrated that for certain types of non-state actors (see Bello 2022: Table 1), in particular those holding collective interests, it is possible to anticipate their role in the spiralling as their cognitions are predictable. Instead, the role of non-state actors holding individualist interests is more difficult to anticipate, because they do not need to publicly clarify their activity to an audience. Their role in either securitising or de-securitising migration needs further studies to be identified. In particular, it is not possible to establish a priori if individualist non-state actors are prejudiced or inclusive towards migrants and migration. Such a theoretical question makes them a perfect case study to empirically contemplate the role of cognitions in the securitisation of migration and whether they eventually lead to a spiralling process. This work claims that, among key non-state actors in the management of human mobility, reception centres holding a prejudicial cognition would engender a variety of practices that produce prejudicial narratives and further negative perceptions of migrants. New stereotyped narratives will be recounted by all those interlocutors who do not hold already opposite cognitions and related alternative and resisting narratives, indispensable to reject the prejudicial ones. All the 'neutral' interlocutors would therefore be impressed from the first impression manager they encounter and could eventually recount the same narratives to other interlocutors and bring into existence more stereotyped ideas of migrants. In such a performative function of narratives, it is possible to understand why prejudice can create a self-reinforcing dynamic within the spiralling of the securitisation of migration. This study has focused on reception centres, whose analysis could confirm the role of non-state actors' cognitions and their ensuing narratives in either constructing or deconstructing human mobility as a threat.

Methodology of a comparative case study of reception centres in Italy

Methodology and methods

In order to understand if prejudice could be confirmed as a key cognition in identifying non-state actors' practices and narratives in the securitisation of migration, this work has relied on a comparative case study methodology on the role of migrants reception centres in the southern part of Italy, and namely in Campania, one of the main areas where migrants are hosted upon arrival.

Reception centres are among those non-state actors that could either be prejudiced, and as a result enact an upward spiralling of the securitisation of migration, or be inclusive and thus decelerate the securitising forces. The role of Italian reception centres, usually managed by non-state actors with individualist interests (Bello 2022), cannot be *a priori* defined as prejudiced or inclusive and, as such, if increasing or decreasing the securitisation of migration. Therefore, the identification of two examples of very similar reception centres that only differ by their cognitions makes possible to delve into the repercussions of their management, in order to consider whether prejudicial cognitions contribute or not to spiralling the securitisation of migration. This analysis constitutes a comparative study that employs *most similar cases* strategy (George and Bennet 2005). Because both the context and all other characteristics are analogous, in case they differ in the outcomes, it will be confirmed that the only distinctive element (an inclusive *vs* a prejudiced cognition) is the main reason that triggers practices and narratives spiralling the securitisation of migration.

As this study attempts to establish links between causes and observed outcomes, it has employed the analytical method of process-tracing and a multi-method approach of data gathering. 'Process-tracing might be used to test whether the residual differences between two similar cases were causal or spurious in producing a difference in these cases' outcomes' (George and Bennet 2005, 6–7). Process-tracing is a method that contributes to causal inference in multi-method research (Checkel and Bennet 2012). In particular, it is useful to generate causal-process observations (CPOs), and to validate hypotheses in qualitative research, and particularly in multi-method research. Following Checkel and Bennet's (2012) suggestion, the process-tracing has been particularly useful to control the effects of possible confounding variables and make sure that these did not influence the impact of the independent variable.

In this work, process-tracing is used in an interpretivist perspective, which is most appropriate for an understanding of this case study.

In an interpretivist perspective, process tracing allows the researcher to look for the ways in which this link manifests itself and the context in which it happens. The focus is not only on what happened, but also on how it happened. It becomes possible to use process tracing to examine the reasons that actors give for their actions and behaviour and to investigate the relations between beliefs and behaviour. (Vennesson 2008, 233)

The multi-method data gathering for the comparative case study has involved covert ethnography of two reception centres in 2016 and 2017, participatory observation of the field from 2014 to 2017, which includes the two small towns in which the reception centres are located, and nine in-depth interviews in the summer of 2017 for the process-tracing techniques. These in-depth interviews have included seven semi-structured interviews with managers of reception centres, and two unstructured interviews with managers of reception centres. Also, during the participatory observation of the field, a variety of unstructured interviews with citizens, managers and migrants were conducted in the two small towns.

Ethical issues

For ethical issues and concerns that emerged from a consultation held with an advisory board, the choice for this study was directed towards a covert ethnography of reception centres to mainly guarantee both the researcher's and the respondents' safety and at the same time providing accurate findings on the subject of study.[1] In order to not break the trust between the researcher and the participants in the study, when dealing with the information revealed during the covert field work, interviewees have been asked if they would repeat those affirmations in public occasions and have always confirmed their replies. Such a strategy allowed to adjust the personal level of involvement and remedy the research concealment in ways that were similarly used and suggested by other researchers (Lewis and Ritchie 2003; Li 2008).

The context and cases selection

The territory of Campania, in the Southern part of Italy, was selected for this field study, for the reason that it is the region hosting most migrants in 'extraordinary reception centres' (Centri di Accoglienza Straordinaria – CAS) once migrants leave the first hotspots in which they are brought after being rescued at sea. The Italian system of reception had, until the recent changes brought about on 4 October 2018 by Salvini's First Security Decree,[2] three stages:

1) Upon arrival, the hotspots (CPSA: Cento di Prima Accoglienza e Soccorso): migrants are identified and, supposedly, in a few hours relocated.[3] Sometimes, this relocation can take much longer, up to one or two weeks, depending on several factors that are the consequence of considerations by part of both the prefect (*Prefetto*), who is an administrative official of the state in charge of decision-making for the relocation upon arrival, and the managers of reception centres. It was alluded in one unstructured interview that this delay in the process of relocation could be the consequence of bribes and corruption in that particular area. For instance, five persons, including one member of the staff of the Office of the Prefect (*Prefettura*), one member of the

staff of the Ministry of Justice and a policeman, together with two managers of reception centres, were arrested in June 2018 for corruption, fraud and revelation of secrets of public acts related to the management of immigration relocation, as an Italian national newspaper reports (Il Mattino 21 June 2018; Bello 2021, forthcoming).

2) First reception of migrants: CDA (Centri di Accoglienza – Reception Centres), CARA (Centri di Accoglienza per Richiedenti Asilo – Reception Centres for Asylum Seekers) and CAS (Extraordinary Reception Centres). Normally, those who would immediately express the intention to request asylum would be located in CARA centres and all the others to CDA. However, due to the high number of arrivals that exceed room in these centres, CAS extraordinary reception centres were created in order to remedy this 'exceptional situation'. However, CAS have now become the norm rather than the exception (Bello 2021, forthcoming), and most migrants were hosted here after their relocation from the hotspot, as an Italian Parliamentary Commission on Migrants Reception has verified.[4] These CAS reception centres are managed by businessmen or other for-profit associations, which have responded to public tenders to reorient a no-longer-profitable business in the care sector or in accommodating services into a migrant reception centre.

3) Second reception: System of protection for asylum-seekers and refugees (SPRAR): These centres were initially conceived by UNHCR Italian Office together with the association of Italian municipalities (ANCI)[5] to provide refugees and asylum-seekers with specific language and professional trainings, along with psychological assistance and support for their mental health, and with a view to make refugees' integration in the country possible. These centres actually strive to mend the main element of criticism in refugee's integration system across the EU, which, as identified in the literature on refugees, lied in their post-traumatic stress disorder (Lindert and von Ehrenstein 2018). With the creation of SPRAR centres, UNHCR Italian Office, along with the association of Italian municipalities (ANCI) aimed to make sure that these persons could eventually integrate more positively after their traumatic experience. These centres' activities, based on the experience that the care service had developed across decades in Italy, seemed to actually constitute a very good practice and framework model in the integration of refugees. Their very existence is currently threatened by the 2018 'Security Decree' signed by the then Ministry of Interior, Matteo Salvini, which has entailed the dismantling of CARA reception centres, an important reduction of the SPRAR's system of integration, and the normalisation of the CAS extraordinary reception centres[6] (Bello 2021, forthcoming). Such a fact *per se* provides a hint of how the securitisation of migration has spiralled in Italy, as The League party had at first included integration policies for refugees with the Bossi-Fini law, and has instead abandoned the logic of integration more recently, through an executive decision of the then Ministry of Interior, Matteo Salvini.

For the majority of migrants who arrive in Italy are hosted in CAS, these were the centres selected for the case study. The selection of the two reception centres fell on two CAS centres managed by non-state actors, in this special issue categorised as non-state actors with individualist interest (Bello 2022). The two CAS centres are referred here as centre A and centre B. They are perfectly comparable in all aspects: they can host between 10 and 20 migrants each, and they both consist of a small independent house at the limits of the territory of two small towns in the same valley. The two small towns are 15 min away from each other and of similar dimensions (around 10,000 people). They share the same geographical, socio-cultural and economic context. The participatory observation in the two towns was used to take into account changes in populations' feelings towards migrants.

The covert ethnography and the two unstructured interviews concerned on the practices (management and activities of the two reception centres, their relations with local police and with the local populations), the related narratives reproduced in the town and the consequences in local perceptions. The covert ethnography was the only method of investigation that allowed to both access the sites and observe the actual dynamics happening in the two centres and their relations with police and with local populations, and ensuring at the same time safety of all the subjects involved in the research. These centres do not normally grant access to researchers and, whereas they do, the visits happen in particular days, and both migrants and employees of these centres are usually instructed on what to reply, instructions with which they will comply, otherwise they could suffer consequences. The seven semi-structured interviews held with key informants were intended to crosscheck *a posteriori* for spurious connections and control for eventual confounding variables as requested by the process-tracing method of analysis.

Findings of a comparative case study of reception centres in Italy

The field observation of the two centres made clear that one centre (centre A) is managed by a small business made of consultants and managers, already active in the past in providing social services to specific vulnerable groups in the area; the other centre (centre B) is managed by a private businessman who converted one of his properties into a CAS centre. Both these centres can thus be identified as non-state actor with individualist interests.

Cognitions

Upon covert ethnography, then confirmed in the in-depth interviews in 2017, it became clear that the managers of centre A started its activities being already quite positive towards migrants and strongly aware of the eventual prejudice that local populations can hold against migrants, for which they often intervene in defence of migrants when they are victims of discriminatory attitudes or narratives. The businessman that runs centre B, instead, is strongly prejudiced towards them, and views them as 'uncivilised' and ungrateful people. It is thus possible to affirm that centre A holds inclusive cognitions of migrants; while, centre B presents important prejudicial cognitions related to migrants, which, thanks to the information gathered through the covert ethnography,[7] could be more specifically considered as cognitions consisting of 'ethnopolitical and biological types of racism' (Bello 2017a; Fanon 1967) and particularly towards Sub-Saharan persons, which, in the manager's own words, were compared to 'savages' and 'wild animals'. The two centres, therefore, represent two most similar cases that only differ for the independent variable: the prejudiced cognition, which is present only in one of the two centres, centre B. It is, therefore, possible to compare these two centres to consider the outcomes in terms of securitisation of their management styles and consequent narratives.

Practices: management styles

The two centres presented akin characteristics in terms of the number of migrants hosted but, as a consequence of the different cognitions, the management style of the two centres significantly varies. Centre A leaves migrants to autonomously organise their daily life in the centre, but provides a lot of support in external activities and intently collaborates with the local police and receive their support in dealing with administrative issues, always acting as intermediaries between the local police and the migrants. Centre B is much stricter when it comes to situations internal to the centre, but disengages from migrants' activities outside the centre and with their relations with both the police and the local population. Centre A regards local police as a strong ally in their activity and report to have learnt with surprise the kind and patient work that local police do with migrants. Centre B has very few exchanges with local police, and views them as controllers. The seven semi-structured interviews checked that these managements styles' differences were also observed in other reception centres holding inclusive cognitions. Such a fact confirmed that the connection was not spurious and that the management style does not constitute a confounding variable that depends on other factors but a direct outcome of specific cognitions.

Outcomes of different cognitions and their management styles

The participatory observation showed that both the local population of centre A town and centre B town are prejudiced towards migrants; many persons present racist attitudes either based on ethnopolitical forms of racism – based on elements of ethnicities and related civilisational ideas – or biological forms of racism – based on physical elements.[8] However, while centre A's managers recognised in the unstructured interview that, thanks to personal contacts, neighbours became increasingly positive towards their guests, in the town of centre B, instead, most neighbours do not have any contacts with the persons hosted in these centres, with the exception of those interactions happening when migrants beg for money in the street, in the proximity of supermarkets and malls.

The observations emerged in the participatory observation of the field in town B were also confirmed in the unstructured interview with the manager of centre B during the covert ethnography. According to the man, local population would make sure not to stay too close to 'them', as, in his own words, 'they are dangerous and dirty savages'. These interactions have often increased negative attitudes in the local population. Despite the stereotypes, a few people still interact with them positively, and when the manager of centre B was asked why some persons have personal exchanges with them, he considered that such a circumstance might be a consequence of Christian elements of charity. According to this man, therefore, there is never the possibility that local people could interact with these migrants as they would do with any other person. Said cognition has actually framed the way he has managed the centre and has had further consequences, particularly in terms of violent behaviours and tensions in the centre.

In reception centre A, migrants have never had problems with local police and have never been involved in crimes or accidents, except in one very isolated situation that was occasioned by one migrant who stole money from one of the managers of the centre. The incident, however, did not engender stereotypes for all migrants. Instead, the migrants hosted in centre B have more often been involved in accidents and disturbs. They seem to be more hostile towards other migrants and fight for getting the best spots where to beg for money. Police has had to intervene in several occasions.

Such contrast is evidently the outcome of the divergent cognitions and management styles of the manager of Centre B. Because of the very negative and prejudiced behaviour that he shows towards his guests, then they are subjects to a variety of verbal abuses and dehumanised treatments. Obscene language and degrading manners increase tensions in centre B, and they very often aggravate some of the aggressive behaviours that those migrants who suffer of post-traumatic stress disorder actually present (Lindert and von Ehrenstein 2018). In CAS centres, differently from what happens in SPRARs, migrants receive no regular help or support by specialised psychological medical staff. They can request it and then, as per extraordinary measures, they will be assigned a psychologist if a CAS manager asks for it. In centre A, the manager has asked on some occasions the help of a psychologist. In centre B, the manager has never asked the support of a specialist at any time.

Some examples of these dehumanised treatments in centre B were: constant verbal abuse, the denial of the need of medical attention for pregnant women or for other guests who had health issues, and the scarceness of food provided to pregnant women or other guests. These examples were reported by a local citizen who found some of these migrants in very bad health conditions in the street one night and consequently drove them to a doctor's clinic.[9]

As a consequence of these increased tensions in centre B, guests often have issues with each other, but such conflicts cannot be solved within the centre, due to the strict management style of the manager of centre B, who supervises all activities in the centre and threatens to send migrants away and report to the police if they have altercations within the centre. An intimidation alike substantially represents a way to menace them to jeopardise their visas requests, because visa are always denied in case either migrants flee centres or are reported to police and thus expulsed from centres. Therefore, migrants who are hosted in centre B discuss all those issues that arise among them outside the reception centre. Because of the prejudiced managements styles, important tensions actually arise in centre B, which often entail true fights among guests, with the development of aggressive behaviours and violence.

The narratives

For such plethora of reasons, the local population of the town where centre B is located often sees most of these migrants as aggressive and dangerous. Narratives of migrants fighting, robbing and being more generally dangerous start to circulate in the town. Even those persons who have never had contacts with migrants sooner or later are told of 'these negros who fight, rob and do not want to work but only beg in the streets'. Narratives clearly socially construct migrants as threats in local population's views in the town. Only those who are already very politically active for the creation of inclusive policies resist these narratives in centre B town.

Migrants suffered of post-traumatic stress disorders and sometimes showed aggressive attitudes also in centre A, and at times important tensions arose in centre A as well. However, the different cognitions and consequent management style reproduced in the centre allowed these tensions to be resolved in more or less peaceful ways, depending on occasions, but always within the centre, and with the mediation of centre A's managers. As previously mentioned, the tender terms of CAS' management do not include the provision of psychological or medical staff who could help those in need within the centre. Therefore, in centre A, the managers did all the possible in order to provide support with reasonable talks and mediation. However, in some cases, centre A's managers have requested to hospitalise some of their guests so as to provide them with medical and professional help. In any case, these situations have never entailed issues or tensions outside the centre or with the local population of the town where centre A is located. Migrants have always solved all their personal issues within the centre. Their contacts with the local population were absolutely normal. Some pregnant women after the labour have, for example, received gifts for their babies by part of neighbours, as this is the local tradition in such occasions.[10] Narratives concerning migrants are mostly about unfolding of family life, or personal stories, and much less stereotyped. Some of these migrants have actually found work in town and stayed when they got their visas. These facts show that migrants' relations with the local population in the town where centre A is located and narratives about migrants are completely discordant from those developing in the town of centre B.

Conclusions: the spiralling of the securitisation of migration seen through the activities of reception centres

The findings of the comparative case study corroborate that only in the case of the individualist non-state actor holding prejudicial cognitions (reception centre B), violence among migrants has increased and has both produced practices and reproduced stereotyped narratives that have entailed negative relations between migrants and local population, socially constructing migrants as a threat. The results confirm that prejudice increases the spiralling of the securitisation of migration. The comparative case study has shown that, at all effects, prejudice can represent a decisive element in explaining the role of non-state actors in the securitisation of migration, while a non-state actor holding inclusive cognition, such as centre A, will not play a role in securitising migration; at least not in ways that could be highlighted through this case study.

In particular, the use of a comparative case study with process-tracing and multi-method approach has been appropriate to understand that actors holding prejudicial cognitions eventually intervening in the activity of reception centres entail a mismanagement of these places, for a variety of reasons. Firstly, it worsens migrants' capacity to cope with post-traumatic stress disorder. Secondly, it engenders aggressive behaviours that negatively affect relations both among migrants, and between them and local populations. Thirdly, it exacerbates tensions ultimately leading to conflicts and violence that request the intervention of the local police. Finally, it produces stereotyped narratives among the local populations, which can hardly be taken as different from the truth, because they are recounted on the basis of a personal experience or story that has started to circulate within personal networks. A finding of this kind also demonstrates that narratives, differently from speech-acts, do not need to be accepted to establish a securitisation of migration but, as Lyotard puts it (1979), share the quintessence of 'true knowledge', composed of stories included into the narrative of a subject granting them legitimacy. The aforementioned stereotyped characterisations are also likely to affect other newcomers, by both self-reinforcing prejudices and increasing those perceptions and social constructions of migrants as security threats.

To conclude, this study confirms that prejudicial cognitions and consequent narratives spiral the securitisation of migration, with an escalation of social and inter-group conflicts. More studies in this direction would help cover the gap about the role of diverse non-state actors, the influence of narratives in the management of migration, and possible measures to foster positive dynamics rather than negative ones. One of these measures would be to ensure that all persons who participate either in the governance of human mobility or in tenders from public authorities to deal with the management of migration, prove that they do not hold prejudicial cognitions.[11] Such a simple policy could help achieve that securitisation dynamics do not spiral over time.

Notes

1. The persons interviewed in 2017 gave their informed consent to the study and all personal details have been removed and the interviews data were stored in anonymised files. The information revealed from the persons who have been involved by the research has been reported in the most accurate account and have been used in a way that does not break the trust between the researcher and the participants in the study.
2. Decreto Legge, 04/10/2018 n° 113, Gazzetta Ufficiale 04/10/2018.
3. Interview number 2 with a manager of a CAS, August 2017.
4. See Camera dei Deputati- Parlmento Italiano: 'Commissione parlamentare di inchiesta sul sistema di accoglienza, di identificazione ed espulsione, nonché sulle condizioni di trattenimento dei migranti e sulle risorse pubbliche impegnate'. Available online at http://www.camera.it/leg17/1281?shadow_organo_parlamentare=2649&shadow_organo=102&natura=M (last accessed 14 November 2018).
5. SPRAR centres were made official by Italian Law 30 July 2002 on 'Changes to immigration and refugee policies'. http://www.camera.it/parlam/leggi/02189l.htm
6. Decreto Legge, 04/10/2018 n° 113, Gazzetta Ufficiale 04/10/2018.
7. Covert Ethnography Notes, 16 April 2017. 'Visit to the centre on Easter Day'.
8. Persons who present an ethnopolitical form of racism believe that people of different ethnicities are less civilized and less useful to the society. While persons who present a biological form of racism, consider that individuals who present different physical features, namely in this case skin colour, are inferior to other human beings. Both forms of racism can arrive to the point of dehumanizing persons who present these characteristics (Bello 2017a).
9. Participatory observation notes, 13 July 2016.
10. In-depth interview with the managers of centre A, 23 August 2017.
11. There are several social psychology studies explaining how to evaluate if a person is prejudiced even when the prejudicial attitudes are not openly expressed or when there are attempts to conceal these faulty cognitions. Measures of implicit prejudice are based on associations between race-related stimuli and word valence (Arkes and Tetlock 2004).

Disclosure statement

No potential conflict of interest was reported by the author(s).

References

Alexander, J. 2004. "Cultural Pragmatics: Social Performance between Ritual and Strategy." *Sociological Theory* 22 (4): 527–573.
Arkes, H. R., and P. E. Tetlock. 2004. "TARGET ARTICLE: Attributions of Implicit Prejudice, or 'Would Jesse Jackson "Fail" the Implicit Association Test?'." *Psychological Inquiry* 15 (4): 257–278.
Balzacq, T. 2010. *Securitization Theory. How Security Problems Emerge and Dissolve.* London: Routledge.
Bello, V. 2017a. *International Migration and International Security. Why Prejudice Is a Global Security Threat.* London and New York: Routledge.
Bello, V. 2017b. "Interculturalism as a New Framework to Reduce Prejudice in Times of Crisis in European Countries." *International Migration* 55 (2): 23–38.
Bello, V. 2022. "The Spiralling of the Securitisation of Migration in the EU: From the Management of a 'Crisis' to a Governance of Human Mobility?"*Journal of Ethnic and Migration Studies* 48 (6): 1327–1344. https://doi.org/10.1080/1369183X.2020.1851464.
Bello, V. 2021, forthcoming. "Normalizing the Exception: Prejudice and Discriminations in Detention and Extraordinary Reception Centres in Italy." In "Shiftin Borders", Special Issue edited by S. Panebianco, and B. Tallis. *International Politics.*
Bigo, D. 2002. "Security and Immigration: Toward a Critique of the Governmentality of Unease." *Alternatives: Global, Local, Political* 27 (1): 63–92.
Bloom, T. 2014. "The Business of Migration Control: Delegating Migration Control Functions to Private Actors." *Global Policy* 6 (2): 151–157.
Braun, Benjamin, Sebastian Schindler, and Tobias Wille. 2019. "Rethinking agency in International Relations: performativity, performances and actor-networks." *Journal of International Relations and Development* 22 (4): 787–807. https://doi.org/10.1057/s41268-018-0147-z.
Buzan, B. 1991. *People, States and Fear: An Agenda for International Security Studies in the Post-Cold War Era.* 2nd ed., 2007. Colchester: ECPR Press.
Castelli Gattinara, P. 2018. "Europeans, Shut the Borders! Anti-refugees Mobilization in France and Italy." In *Solidarity Mobilization in the "Refugees Crisis": Contentious Moves*Della Porta, 271–298. Basingstoke and New York: Palgrave Macmillan.
Caviedes, A. 2015. "An Emerging 'European' News Portrayal of Immigration?" *Journal of Ethnic and Migration Studies* 41 (6): 897–917.
Ceccorulli, M., and N. Labanca. 2014. *The EU, Migration and the Politics of Administrative Detention.* London: Routledge.
Checkel, J. T., and A. Bennet. 2012. *Process Tracing. From Metaphor to Analytic Tool. Simons Papers in Security and Development.* Vancouver, Canada: Simon Fraser University.
Crepaz, K. 2020. "Overcoming Borders: The Europeanization of Civil Society Activism in the 'Refugee Crisis'." In the Special Issue edited by V. Bello and S. Léonard. *Journal of Ethnic and Migration Studies.*
Cusumano, E. 2019a. "Straightjacketing Migrant Rescuers? The Code of Conduct on Maritime NGOs." *Mediterranean Politics* 24 (1): 106–114.
Cusumano, E. 2019b. "Humanitarians at sea: Selective Emulation Across Migrant Rescue NGOs in the Mediterranean Sea." *Contemporary Security Policy* 40 (2): 239–262.
Della Porta, D., ed. 2018. *Solidarity Mobilization in the 'Refugees Crisis': Contentious Moves.* Basingstoke and New York: Palgrave Macmillan.
Dine, M., N. Montagna, and V. Ruggiero. 2014. "Thinking Lampedusa: Border Construction, the Spectacle of Bare Life and the Productivity of Migrants." *Ethnic and Racil Studies* 38 (3): 430–445.

European Parliament. 2015. "Migrants in the Mediterranean: Protecting Human Rights. Directorate General for External Policies." *Policy Department Study*. Accessed September 11, 2017. http://www.europarl.europa.eu/RegData/etudes/STUD/2015/535005/EXPO_STU (2015)535005_EN.pdf.

Fanon, F. 1967. *Black Skin, White Masks*. New York: Grove Press.

Feischmidt, Margit, Ludger Pries, and Celine Cantat. 2019. *Refugee Protection and Civil Society*. Basingstoke and New York: Palgrave Macmillan.

George, A. L., and A. Bennet. 2005. *Case Studies and Theory Development in the Social Sciences*. Cambridge, MA: MIT Press.

Goffman, E. 1959. *The Presentation of Self in Everyday Life*. Garden City: Doubleday.

Huysmans, J. 2000. "The EU and the Securitization of Migration." *Journal of Common Market Study* 38 (5): 751–777.

Huysmans, J. 2006. *The Politics of Insecurity: Fear, Migration and Asylum in the EU*. London and New York: Routledge.

Il Mattino. 2018. "Lucravano siu migrant: 5 ordinanze eseguite a Benevento". Il Mattino. 21 June 2018. Accessed November 14, 2018. https://www.ilmattino.it/benevento/truffa_ai_danni_dello_stato_5_ordinanze_eseguite_a_benevento-3810036.html.

Jumbert, M. G. 2012. "Controlling the Mediterranean Space through Surveillance: The Politics and Discourse of Surveillance as an All-Encompassing Solution to EU Maritime Border Management Issues." *Espace Populations Sociétés* 2012 (3): 35–48.

Karamanidou, L. 2015. "The Securitisation of European Migration Policies: Perceptions of Threat and Management of Risk." In *The Securitisation of Migration in the EU: Debates since 9/11*, edited by G. Lazaridis, and K. Wadia, 37–60. Basingstoke and New York: Palgrave Macmillan.

Lazaridis, G., and K. Wadia. 2015. *The Securitisation of Migration in the EU: Debates since 9/11*. Basingstoke and New York: Palgrave Macmillan.

Léonard, S. 2010. "EU Border Security and Migration into the European Union: FRONTEX and Securitization Through Practices." *European Security* 19 (2): 231–254.

Léonard, S., and C. Kaunert. 2010. "Reconceptualizing the Audience in Securitization Theory." In *Securitization Theory. How Security Problems Emerge and Dissolve*, edited by T. Balzacq, 57–76. London: Routledge.

Lewis, J., and J. Ritchie. 2003. *Qualitative Research Practice*. London: Sage.

Li, J. 2008. "Ethical Challenges in Participant Observation: A Reflection on Ethnographic Fieldwork." *The Qualitative Report* 13 (1): Article 8. Accessed November 14, 2018. https://nsuworks.nova.edu/cgi/viewcontent.cgi?article=1608&context=tqr.

Lindert, J., and O. von Ehrenstein. 2018. "Anxiety, Depression and Post-traumatic Stress Disorder among Refugees – A Systematic Review." *European Journal of Public Health* 28 (Suppl_1): 141–142.

Lyotard, J. F. 1979. *La condition postmoderne: rapport sur le savior. English Translation "The Postmodern Condition: A Report on Knowledge"*. Manchester: Manchester University Press.

Martins, B. O., and M. G. Jumbert. 2020. "EU Border Technologies and the Co-Production of Security 'Problems' and 'Solutions'." In the Special Issue edited by V. Bello, and S. Léonard. *Journal of Ethnic and Migration Studies*.

Martins, B. O., and C. Küsters. 2019. "Hidden Security: EU Public Research Funds and the Development of European Drones." *Journal of Common Market Studies* 57 (2): 278–297.

Moreno, K., and B. E. Price. 2017. "The Social and Political Impact of the New (Private) National Security: Private Actors in the Securitization of Immigration in the U.S. Post 9/11." *Crime, Law and Social Change* 67 (3): 353–376.

Neal, A. W. 2009. "Securitization and Risk at the EU Border: The Origins of FRONTEX." *Journal of Common Market Study* 47 (2): 333–356.

Pettigrew, T. 1980. "Prejudice." In *The Harvard Encyclopaedia of American Ethnic Groups*, edited by S. Themstrom, A. Orlov, and O. Handlin, 820–829. Cambridge, MA: The Belknap Press.

Sasse, G. 2005. "Securitization or Securing Rights? Exploring the Conceptual Foundations of Policies Towards Minorities and Migrants in Europe." *Journal of Common Market Study* 43 (4): 673–693.

Schneiker, A. 2019. "The New Defenders of Human Rights? How Radical Right-Wing NGOs are Using the Human Rights Discourse to Promote their Ideas." *Global Society* 33 (2): 149–162.

Squire, V. 2011. "From Community Cohesion to Mobile Solidarities: The City of Sanctuary Network and the Strangers into Citizens Campaign." *Political Studies* 59 (2): 290–307.

Squire, Vicki. 2011. "From Community Cohesion to Mobile Solidarities: The *City of Sanctuary* Network and the *Strangers into Citizens* Campaign." *Political Studies* 59 (2): 290–307. https://doi.org/10.1111/j.1467-9248.2010.00865.x.

Squire, V. 2015. "The Securitisation of Migration: An Absent Presence?" In *The Securitisation of Migration in the EU: Debates since 9/11*, edited by G. Lazaridis, and K. Wadia, 19–36. Basingstoke and New York: Palgrave Macmillan.

Vennesson, P. 2008. "Case Study and Process Tracing: Theories and Practices." In *Approaches and Methodologies in the Social Sciences. A Pluralist Perspective*, edited by D. Della Porta and M. Keating, 223–239. Cambridge: Cambridge University Press.

Wadia, K. 2015 Regimes of Insecurity: Women and Immigration Detention in France and Britain." In *The securitisation of migration in the EU: Debates since 9*, edited by G. Lazaridis and K. Wadia, 91–118. Basingstoke and New York: Palgrave Macmillan.

Waever, O. 1996. "European Security Identities." *Journal of Common Market Studies* 34 (1): 105–130.

Waever, O., B. Buzan, M. Kelstrup, and P. Lemaitre. 1993. *Identity, Migration and the New Security Agenda in Europe*. New York: St Martin's Press.

Zavirsek, D. 2017. "The Humanitarian Crisis of Migration Versus the Crisis of Humanitarianism: Current Dimensions and Challenges for Social Work Practice." *The International Journal of Social Work Education* 36 (3): 231–244.

Index

Note: Figures are indicated by *italics*. Endnotes are indicated by the page number followed by 'n' and the endnote number e.g., 20n1 refers to endnote 1 on page 20.

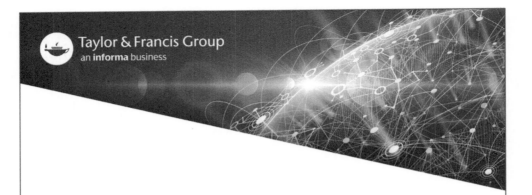